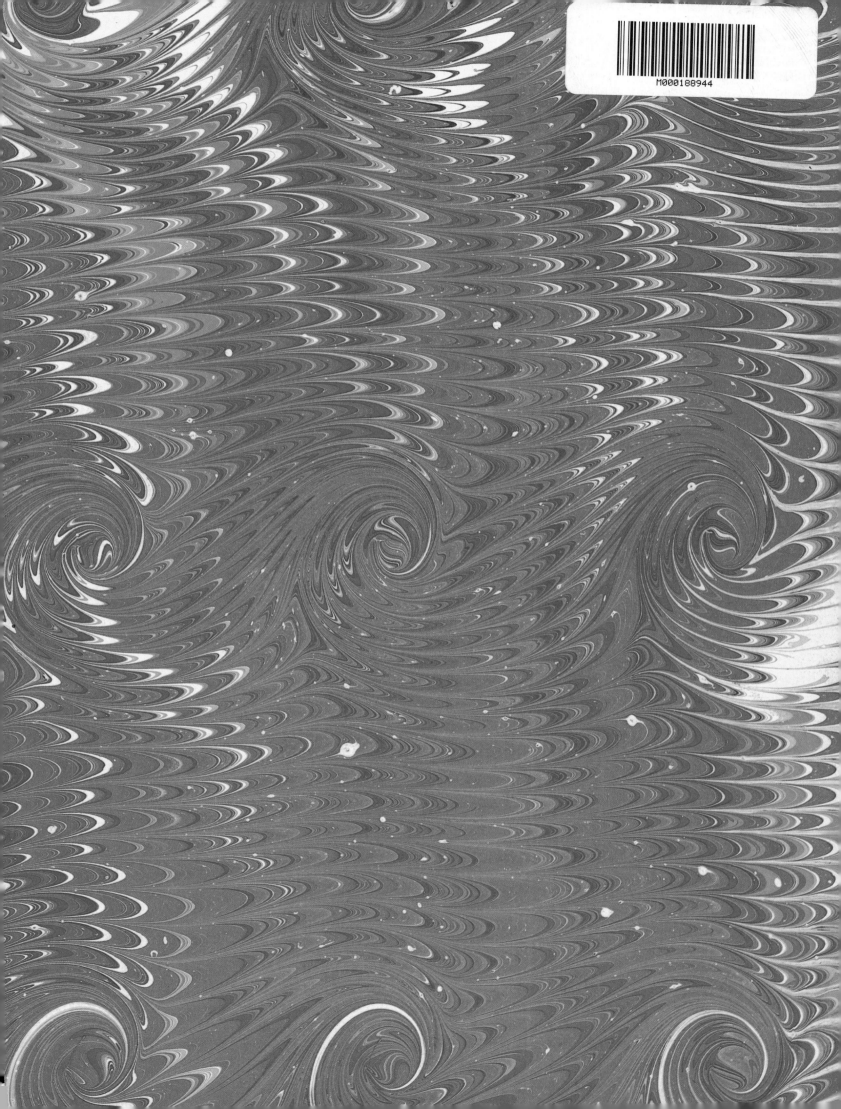

Perfume, Cologne and Scent Bottles

Jacquelyne Y. Jones North   Photography—Duane A. Young

Schiffer Publishing Ltd

West Chester, Pennsylvania 19380

This book is dedicated to:
Mel Mitchell
Gene Galloway
Janis Helmer
Pauline De Morcia
Mary and James Zavada
Wilhelmina Bruton
and
Our Families
Also to:
Madeleine France
Laurens Tartasky
and
Ken Leach

Duane Young, the photographer of this book, is a freelance professional commercial and portrait photographer. He is a member of the National Professional Photographers, Southwest Professional Photographers, the Texas Professional Photographers, and the Dallas Professional Photographers. He has a studio in Dallas and also runs his own custom color, and black and white lab. To contact him in Dallas, call information for Photographic Assets Inc.

Duane is the brother of the author and is married. His wife's name is "Quata" and they have two children, a son Duane Anson, and daughter Lacy. Duane enjoys traveling and challenging assignments in photography.

Revised edition with updated Price Guide

Copyright 1986 © by Jacquelyne North.
Library of Congress Catalog Number: 86-61205.

Designed by Ellen J. (Sue) Taylor
Printed in the United States of America.
ISBN: 0-88740-072-8

Published by Schiffer Publishing, Ltd.
1469 Morstein Road
West Chester, Pennsylania 19380
Please write for a free catalog
This book may be purchased from the publisher.
Please include $2.00 postage.
Try your bookstore first.

Front Cover:
Double dove "L'Air du Temps" bottle made for Nina Ricci by Lalique. U.S. introduction 1946 (4-1/4").

Table of Contents

Acknowledgments

ACKNOWLEDGMENTS

To all those who were involved in the making of this book, I owe profound thanks: Rose Tree Inn Antiques, Tombstone, Arizona; Rita Heeney, Bella Vista, Arkansas; Antiques Books Collectibles, Fayetteville, Arkansas; Antique Locator Service, Greenwood, Arkansas; Bayhill Antiques, Hot Springs, Arkansas; Martha's Antiques & Dolls, Mena, Arkansas; The Ackerman's Antiques, Baldwin Park, California; Penny G's, Inc., Greeley, Colorado; Jeri Schwartz, Stanford, Connecticut; Attic Antiques, Inc., Indian Rocks, Florida; The Kraus, Winter Park, Florida; Melvyn and Jennifer Traub, Chicago, Illinois; Farm House Antiques, Galesburg, Illinois; Chita's Curio Closet, Fort Wayne, Indiana; J & R House of Antiques, Des Moines, Iowa; Don Williams Antiques, Ottumwa, Iowa; Hinrichs Antiques, Spencer, Iowa; Valley Antiques, West Des Moines, Iowa, Silver Matching Service, Arkansas City, Kansas; Antique Mary, Manhattan, Kansas; Old Mill Antiques, South Hutchinson, Kansas; B & B Antiques & Auction, Mrs. B's Antiques, and Don E. Tilton, Topeka, Kansas; Ernest Hicks Antiques, and Imes Antiques, Wichita, Kansas; Marjorie Madey Antiques, Baton Rouge, Louisiana; Shaffer Gallery, South Lancaster, Maine; Blythe Spirit, Brookline, Massachusetts; T.J. Holmes Inc., Chartley, Massachusetts; Big "D" Antiques, Grand Rapids, Michigan; Blanche Hearsch, Romeo, Michigan; Ann M. Fury, Excelsior, Minnesota; Gale Studio, Minnesota; Bronze Lady Antiques, Minneapolis, Minnesota; Markell's Antiques, Clayton, Missouri; Linda's Loft, Fair Grove, Missouri; "STUFF", Gladstone, Missouri; Silver Flute Antiques, Springfield, Missouri; Bee's Antiques, and D & J Antiques, St. Joseph, Missouri; Empire Galleries, and Hirschfeld Galleries, St. Louis, Missouri; Century Antiques, Bellevue, Nebraska; Bobbie Jones, and Linsons Antiques, Lincoln, Nebraska; Penny Lane, Tecumseh, Nebraska; Angie Ricciardi Antiques, Bellmawr, New Jersey; Lander Co. Inc., Engelwood Cliffs, New Jersey; Corning Museum of Glass, Corning, New York; The Antique Shoppe, Hamburg, New York; Catherine Barré, Philippe Dehais, Tom DeRosa, Robert Du Grenier, David Kratz, Irving W. Rice & Co. Inc., Saint Gobain Desjonquères, Nancy Sandone, and Verreries Brosse, New York, New York; Bettiques, Rochester, New York; Jill Pence, Oklahoma City, Oklahoma; Beal's Auction Service, Shawnee, Oklahoma; Gloria Barbour, Oklahoma; Marie's Antiques, Tulsa, Oklahoma; Britannia Antiques, Embassy Row, and Donna Fischer, Austin, Texas; Chapin's Antiques, Commerce, Texas; Kathleen Allen, The Associates, Kara Leann Brown, Wilhelmina Bruton, Convey To Yesterday, George Corley, Crown Linens & Antiques, Pauline De Morcia, Emmy Gagnon, Granny B., Granny Had It, Duddly L. Hargrove, Janis Helmer, Jan-Lyn Collectibles, Ernestine Jones, Justin Jones, Eva Judge, Diane Kaufmann, Jan Knowles, Alaine Landers, L'Image, Lee C. Maltzman, Tim Mason and Mike Hulme, Memory Lane Antiques, Trudy Miller Antiques, Arlene Mooney, Thomas North, The Partnership, Amy and Jason Polland, Kathy Ratcliffe, Rosemary Antiques, K. Ross Productions, The Roxy, Gail Sargent, Jean Sorrells, Stone Balloon Antiques, Aileen Thomas Gallery, Marcia Wade, Whitmeyer Antiques, Gloria Young, and Quata Young, Dallas Texas; Harmony Hill Antiques, El Paso, Texas; Monti's, Euless, Texas; The Den of Antiquity, and Mary and James Zavada, Fort Worth, Texas; Unique, Houston, Texas, Uniques Etc., Jefferson, Texas; The Silver Spoon Antiques, Longview, Texas; Pack Rat Antiques, Luling, Texas; Vista Antiques & Collectables, Rio Vista, Texas; Warman Antiques, Wichita Falls, Texas; Bennington Museum, Bennington, Vermont; Ken Forster, Alexandria, Virginia; Cocktails and Laughter Antiques, Arlington, Virginia; Huntington Galleries, and Robert Rowe, Huntington, West Virginia; The London Gallery, and The Victoria and Albert Museum, London, England.

With a special Thank You to:
Carl Johnson,
Charles Wheatly,
Bawcon's Antiques,
Jack Webb, and
6th Floor Government Publications Desk Dallas Public Library

A Short History of Scent and Scent Bottles

All through the civilized eras of mankind a fundamental factor in the luxury and pleasure of perfume has been the beauty or novelty of its holder. Various materials such as alabaster, enamel, terra cotta, metals, semi-precious stones, porcelain, wood and recently plastic have been used in the production of scent bottles and containers, however the most favored of all has been glass. Every society, culture, and age, each historic art or decorative style movement has extended its influence over the design of scent bottles made during its reign.

"Through Smoke" is the literal meaning of the word perfume in Latin and indicates that the oldest perfumes were probably incense, which was burned. In the old testament of the Bible, God gave unto the prophet Moses specific directions for mixing myrrh and other ingredients to burn upon the altar of Jahwah. In the new testament, among the gifts that the wise men brought to the infant Jesus were precious frankincense and myrrh. Incense and perfume are mentioned many other times in the Bible, especially in the Song of Solomon.

The oldest surviving examples of perfume containers that have been found by archaeologists are Egyptian terra cotta, onyx, or alabaster heads dated about the 6th century B.C. Myrrh, spikenard, cinnamon, aloes, olibanum, sandelwood, and frankincense were all known to the ancient rulers of Egypt and used in profusion for embalming, personal enchancement, religious and funerary ceremonies. During the highest glory of the Dynasty, the citizens were admonished by priests to perfume themselves every Friday as a religious rite, and during the seasonal festivals incense and aromatic woods were burnt at the temples and in the streets. Every day at sunrise, mid-day, and sunset incense was sacrificed by acolytes at Heliopolis to the sun god Ra.

The Egyptians were true masters of the art of self adornment. Different colored eye paints were mixed and applied according to the season of the year. Rouge was skillfully put to use on cheeks and lips. The ruling class also stained its finger and toe nails reddish-yellow with henna juice. Many of the cosmetic containers were of carved alabaster in the form of ducks or fish.

The Egyptian reputation throughout the ancient world for blending and inventing new perfume combinations was unsurpassed. The Greek essayist Plutarch (46-120 A.D.) praised the Egyptian compounded perfume Kypi, which was supposed to "lull to sleep, allay anxieties, and brighten the dream." The recipe he gives for it includes honey, wine, cypress, raisins, myrrh, aspalathus, seselis, stoenanthus, saffon, dock, juniper, cardamom, and aromatic reed.

The 18th Dynasty (1500 B.C.) saw the first use of glass bottles as containers for perfumes, oils, and cosmetics. These were made by first attaching a sand core to a rod made of metal. The sand core was then dipped into molten glass or had a softened bar of glass wrapped around it. The exterior was smoothed by reheating and rolling the bottle on a level surface. The resulting bottles were brightly colored in opaque shades, usually a dark or light blue, to imitate semi-precious stones and decorated with zig-zag or wavy glass threads of contrasting color. The majority of the bottles were only about 4 inches tall and marketed for the nobility and very wealthy.

1. Mould blown Roman Empire head perfume flask. Circa 1st century A.D. Photo courtesy Corning Museum of Glass.

2. Scent flask made of colorless, non-lead glass, blown, enameled, and cut. Europe, probably France. Circa 1690-1700. (11.4 cm). Photo courtesy Corning Museum of Glass.

3. Small moulded scent bottle in the form of a Negro's head. Facon de Venise. Circa 17th century. (2''). Photo courtesy Corning Museum of Glass.

The ancient Greeks believed that perfume had inherent medicinal properties. White violet was recommended to smooth an upset stomach, vine-leaf was said to overcome headaches, and essence of quince was recommended to the dyspeptic. The Greek philosopher Apollonius of Tyana believed that perfume should be worn on the wrist to ward off illness.

Greek women were ingenious in their use of perfume. They applied a different scent to each part of their body: for the head, marjoram; for the face and chest, palm oils; for the legs, ground ivy; and for the arms, mint. After a time, men also became enthusiasts, and Solon (about 600 B.C.) the Athenian statesman, promulgated a law forbidding the sale of fragrant oils to the men of Athens.

The Greeks stored their perfumes in containers made of onyx, alabaster, and terra cotta in shapes such as the globular aryballos and the tubular alabastron which were widely imitated in the Mediterranean area. Some of the most beautiful of these were adorned with a frieze of dancing figures or warriors in black against a tan ground. Perfume bottles have also been found ingeniously formed to represent animals or women's heads in terra cotta.

Perfume also played an important role in the lives of the Romans who used them for personal enhancement, religious rites, and as aphrodisiacs. Nobles annointed themselves regularly three times a day with costly unguents and at feasts; guests, pages, tables, and draperies were all drenched with scents. Both Caligula and Nero spent enormous fortunes for perfumes. At the funeral of his wife Poppea, Emperor Nero (37-68 A.D.), last of the Caesars, was supposed to have used more perfume and incense than could be produced during one whole year in Arabia. Essence of Rose was Rome's favorite perfume, as it was later to be the favorite of the Tudors of England.

The discovery made about the 1st century A.D. in Syria of blowing glass into two or three piece moulds greatly facilitated the manufacture of bottles to contain perfume. The colors were confined chiefly to transparent browns, greens, and purples, although bottles of mosaic glass and imitation stone were produced for the wealthy. The range of designs made were quite remarkable considering that the objects were merely everyday containers for scents, salves, and oils. Some bottles were many-sided and some were moulded with designs such as shells, mythological figures, grapes, and human heads, a fashion which was revived in the 19th century.

With the fall of the Roman Empire, the art of glassmaking suffered an enormous setback, surviving mainly in the eastern Mediterranean cities under Byzantine rule and in the Near East for export and local markets. After the 7th century wheel-cut perfume bottles of glass, frequently ornamented with geometric motifs, were available in the Islamic market.

Mohammed, in his description of Paradise, tells of black-eyed houris who are to welcome the male heavenly newcomers with the sprinkling of fragrant liquids and the waving of gauzy scarfs. Legend also has it that two famous mosques, Zobaide at Tauris and the mosque at Kara Amid, were made of mortar mixed with large quantities of musk so that when the sun shone brightly upon them the buildings would become hazy with perfumes. Among the most prized perfumes in Arabia were lily, orange-flower, sweet basil, lotus, musk, and civet. Civet, a glandular discharge of the civet cat, was used to perfume a man's beard and moustache.

The Venetians from the thirteenth century produced small glass bottles for containing costly scents. Very few examples have survived, those that have imitate semi-precious stones, such as chalcedony and aventurine. In the 16th century, simple, yet elegant scent bottles were made of clear cristallo glass then embellished with bright blue glass threads trailed around the feet, handles, and rims.

Perfume did not come into regular use in Europe until near the end of the 15th century, although it was imported in London by the Guild of Pepperers beginning in 1179 and France's earliest perfume makers were in Paris by 1190. The French were eventually to become the world's masters in the art of perfumery. Scent making became a prolific business. As a result beautiful bottles in glass, gold, silver, and enamel, ornamented in the fashionable style of the period became popular.

Perfume containers became part of the inventory of glass manufacturers in France, Silesia, Bohemia, Italy, and England in the 16th and 17th centuries. In England the manufacture of glass scent bottles, was well established by 1630. In the 17th century, the glassblowers of Murano made their finest scent flacons in flamboyant styled coloured glass with millefiori or latticinio decoration. In Germany scent bottles were made of milchglas, an opaque-white glass. These were frequently adorned with figures or flowers in colored enamels. The French during the 17th century produced splendid flacons, often in fancy shapes, in colored or opaline glass.

During the 16th century perfumed gloves made from special skins, impregnated with civet, musk, or ambergris were imported into France from Italy and Spain. This custom made its way to England about 1550. Queen Elizabeth was so fond of the fashion she even had perfumed Spanish leather shoes and cloaks made for her.

It was during the 18th century that the scent container was elevated to the status of an object of art. During this time there developed a close liaison between perfumers such as Lubin and Houbigant and such fashionable craftsmen as jewelers, goldsmiths, silversmiths, and porcelain makers in the manufacturing of vessels worthy of the precious liquid. Perfumes were still a luxury during this time and only the nobles and well-to-do could afford the expense.

During the reign of Louis XV of France (1715-74), who raised the standard of self-gratification to an all time high and bankrupted his country in the process, it was customary for the court to be supplied daily with a different scent for spraying clothes, accessories, and ornamental objects. The costly perfumes were delivered in small bottles of richly colored glass mounted in gold and silver. Madame de Pompadour, Louis' mistress, who set fashion at the extravagant court, had bills amounting to some hundreds of thousands of francs yearly for perfumes and cosmetics.

From about 1750 onward porcelain was used more and more in the manufacture of perfume containers. The leading European porcelain house at Sevres, owned by Louis XV, made porcelain perfume bottles ornamented with enamel plaques of Rococo flowers and scenes. In Germany the Meissen factory, near Dresden, produced scent flacons in a similar romantic style. Among the inventory listed by the English Chelsea factory in 1754 were smellng bottles. Chelsea made porcelain perfume containers in many forms which would have been impossible to produce in glass. These chic, sophisticated adult toys were modeled as humans, animals or bouquets of flowers whose heads or tops opened to reveal the inner stopper. The earliest examples of Chelsea scent bottles provided a container for decorative facial patches in the hollow base. In later examples the bottle stoppers were often disguised as flowers, bunches of fruit, or perching birds. Derby, in England, also manufactured a large number of early porcelain scent flacons garnished with birds or flowers against a dark background. Wedgwood produced many attractive scent bottles in jasper-ware and black basalt. These were flattened oval shaped bottles ornamented with tiny cameo portraits or classical figures.

From the mid-18th century enamelled copper scent bottles were made in Battersea, Bilston, and Wednesbury, England for the middle classes in imitation of the costly gold and jeweled articles which the Swiss and French produced for the very wealthy. The best of the Wednesbury scent bottles were decorated by Margaret and William Beilby. The Bilston enamellers included such artists as Dovey Hawksford and the Homer brothers. The decoration on Staffordshire enamel scent bottles is predominately flowers and landscapes, but occasionally portrait miniatures are found. The best of the English enamels are characterized by fine soldering and jointing of the copper plates and meticulous enameling. Manufactured until the late 19th century, the finest examples were produced in the first thirty years, then quality dwindled rapidly.

In England the production of colored lead glass scent bottles is usually associated with Bristol. Made between 1760 and 1825, blue was the predominant color followed by opaque white, green, amethyst, and very rarely dark red. The colors were created by the addition of various metal

4. Scent flask of mould blown, transparent blue glass made in France, probably Orleans, glassworks of Bernard Perrot. Circa late 17th century. (9.2 cm). Photo courtesy Corning Museum of Glass.

5. Black amethyst glass mould blown bottle in the form of two shells, with opaque white foot. Circa late 17th, early 18th century. (3"). Photo courtesy Corning Museum of Glass.

6. German porcelain scent bottle, made at the Royal Saxon Porcelain Works in Meissen, decorated with wreaths and flowers. Circa 1790. (5'').

7. Scent bottle of colorless, free-blown, lead glass with three colorless and crimped ribbons on surface was made in the U.S. by an unknown manufacturer. "Seahorse" bottle is colorless with opaque white and blue threading, applied colorless rigaree. U.S. or England. Circa 1800. (6.5 cm and 6 cm). Photo courtesy Huntington Galleries; Gift of Dr. and Mrs. B.H. Willet.

9. Scent bottle of cobalt blue, wheel-cut, blown lead glass, cut in central almond shape diamond design, fans, cross-hatching, shoulders and sides are notch cut. Ireland. Circa 1810. (6.1 cm). Photo courtesy Huntington Galleries; Gift of Dr. and Mrs. B.H. Willet.

8. Sapphire blue, 17-rib, mould-blown scent bottle, label reads "Pungent Smelling Bottle Prepared And Sold By Geo. Brinkley Druggist". U.S., attributed to Henry William Stiegel Glassworks, Manheim, Pennsylvania. Circa 1764-1774. (3-1/8"). Photo courtesy Huntington Galleries; Gift of Mr. and Mrs. Ronald Drucker.

oxides, such as cobalt for blue. Scent bottles in clear glass were also made, often exquisitely cut and engraved. Decoration is unusually simple for the era, although the earlier pieces were frequently embellished with elaborate gilding, diamond-faceting, enamelling, and gold repoussé tops. James Gile (1713-80) was one of the finest decorators of Bristol glass scent bottles. His motifs varied from elegant classical designs of flowers, urns, and pheasants to chinoiseries on both white and colored glass. Occasionally superb miniature sets of four bottles about two inches high fitted in open-work gilt metal cases were made, also pairs of bottles with protective shagreen cases.

Perfume and scent bottles were among the earliest items produced by American colonial glasshouses. Henry William Stiegel opened a glassworks in Pennsylvania in the last half of the 18th century. This glass factory fashioned moulded scent bottles, which are now famous, in great quantities. The amethyst colored bottles were made from a single gather of glass which gives them a delicate, fragile appearance. None of the bottles executed by Stiegel bears any discernible factory mark.

John F. Amelung of Germany established a glassworks called New Bremen in Maryland also late in the 18th century. Among the many types of glass in his repertoire, scent bottles were included. They followed the lead set by Stiegel and created bottles blown in various shades of blue or amethyst. Both New Bremen and Stiegel faced overwhelming and fatal competition from fashionable Anglo-Irish export ware.

Some unusual, oddly-shaped scent bottles of the early 19th century are the so-called "sea-horse" bottles. The base of the bottle was curled into a spiral shape giving the appearance of a sea-horse tail. They were first free-blown, then tooled into shape. Most have lattice-like or twisted stripes and are festooned with hand-applied crimped decoration. The bottles measure from two to four inches long and have two or three colors combined. The colors used were blue, green, amber, purple, opaque white and clear. Instead of a matching glass stopper, small corks or metal caps were used to seal the opening. The majority of these bottles were made in England and New England.

10. Deep purple blue, blown, lead glass scent bottle with cut, enameled, and gilded decoration. England, attributed to Bristol. Circa 1770. (7.5 cm). Photo courtesy Corning Museum of Glass.

12. Scent bottle of opaque, blown glass, possibly enameled by the Beilbys. England, possibly Newcastle-on-Tyne. Circa 1782. (7.3 cm). Photo courtesy Corning Museum of Glass.

11. Perfume sprinkler or dropper shaped like a bird, probably Egyptian. Circa 7th-10th century A.D. Photo courtesy Corning Museum of Glass.

Diamond cut scent bottles, especially in clear crystal, were all the rage in the British Isles during the very late 18th and early 19th centuries. Before circa 1790 the composition of the glass being made was suitable only for shallow relief cutting, since then deep cutting became immensely popular, especially during the Regency period. From about 1820-1830, diamond cut bottles were being produced in amber colored glass and in a rarer pink color.

Among the most beautiful and collectible of the early 19th century scent bottles were those created by Apsley Pellatt in England. His company executed both intaglio cut portrait and cameo encrustation bottles. Pellatt patented, in 1819, a method of making profile portrait medallions from a special porcelain. These were known as sulphides, and wouldn't break or crack when brought into contact with molten glass. Most of the scent bottles inset with the sulphides were further enhanced with resplendent diamond cutting. The Pellatt bottles were almost always marked Pellatt & Co. Patentees on the bottom.

Cologne, perfume diluted with alcohol, was introduced to the U.S. around 1830. Since more cologne must be used to achieve the same effect as perfume, cologne bottles were usually larger than those manufactured for perfumes.

In the United States the Boston and Sandwich Glass Co. manufactured lovely heavy flint glass cologne bottles from the 1840's to the 1870's. These bottles were almost always hexagonal in shape and came in a wide variety of colors, including green, clear, opaque white, canary, and opaque blue. Cologne bottles were also produced by their rivals in Pittsburgh, the Midwest, and by the New England Glass Co. in Massachusetts. Most of the bottles were free-blown, mould-blown, or less frequently pressed in simple moulds. They were further enhanced with simple engraving, cutting, or gilding.

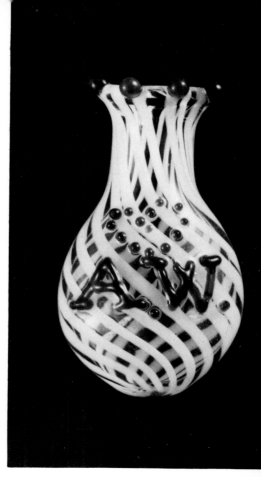

14. Colorless, striped with opaque white, lead glass miniature scent bottle, blown with applied decoration. England, attributed to Bristol. Circa 1820. (3.0 cm). Photo courtesy Corning Museum of Glass.

13. Scent bottle of marbled glass with adventurine inclusions and four portrait canes, "Pio Nono", Garibaldi, Cavour, and Pope Sixtus IV. Italy, Venice, attributed to Franchini. Circa 1845-1855. (5.3 cm). Photo courtesy Corning Museum of Glass.

15. Enameled, milk glass perfume bottle in the shape of a clenched hand. Southern Germany. Circa 18th century. (10.4 cm L.). Photo courtesy Corning Museum of Glass.

16. Cut glass scent bottle with strawberry diamonds flanked by plain and serrated ribs. Pittsburgh, Pennsylvania. Circa 1815-1840. Photo courtesy Huntington Galleries; Gift of Mr. and Mrs. Ronald Drucker.

17. Two stiegel-type, rib mould-blown lead glass scent bottles. Probably Pennsylvania. Circa 1764-1820. (8.3 cm, 8.5 cm). Photo courtesy Huntington Galleries; Gift of Dr. and Mrs. B.H. Willet.

18. Aqua blue scent bottle, blown in a two part mould, beaded border, seven-petal flower and stem on one side and a pinnate leaf design on the other. Pittsburgh, Pennsylvania, most likely blown by Edward Ensell, or his son, of the firm Ensell, Wendt and Co. Circa 1810-1820. (2-3/4''). Photo courtesy Huntington Galleries; Gift of Mr. and Mrs. Ronald Drucker.

20. Cased, opaque white scent bottle with clear outer layer, mould-blown lead glass, sheared lip, open pontil mark. U.S., unknown manufacturer. Circa 1800-1840. (7.7 cm). Photo courtesy Huntington Galleries; Gift of Dr. and Mrs. B.H. Willet.

19. Colorless, hand-blown glass scent bottle made in the midwestern U.S. by an unknown manufacturer. Circa 1850-1870. (13.2 cm). Photo courtesy Huntington Galleries; Gift of Collins and Mayo Collieries, Inc.

21. Small Bristol glass scent bottle with simple cut and gilt design. Circa 1820. (3'').

23. Pear-shaped mould-blown amber glass perfume flask decorated with Fleur-de-lys in high relief. French (Orleans). Circa late 17th century. Photo courtesy Victoria and Albert Museum.

22. Agate double scent bottle in the form of a boy holding a lamb. The neck and base mounts are gold. The inscription "Je vous l'offre" is enamelled around the boy's neck. The figure was possibly carved by an Italian and mounted in England. Circa mid 1760's (89 mm). Photo courtesy Victoria and Albert Museum.

24. Silvergilt scent flask. German. Circa 17th century. Photo courtesy Victoria and Albert Museum.

25. A pine cone shaped scent flask mounted in enamelled gold. Spanish. Circa 17th century. From the treasury of the virgin of the pillar, Saragossa. Photo courtesy Victoria and Albert Museum.

26. Shell-shaped scent flask of silver gilt decorated with niello. Spanish. Circa 17th century. Photo courtesy Victoria and Albert Museum.

27. Silver gilt scent flask with enamelled decoration. Spanish. Circa early 17th century. Photo courtesy Victoria and Albert Museum.

28. Silver gilt scent bottle engraved with lucretia, a cherub, and foliage. English. Circa late 17th century. Photo courtesy Victoria and Albert Museum.

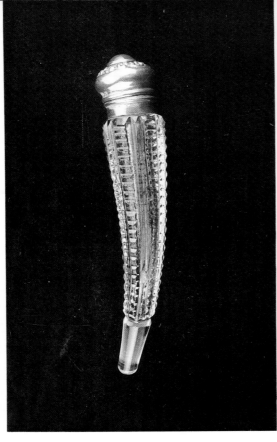

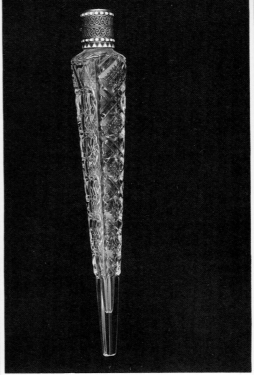

3. Long cone-shaped glass lay-down dresser bottle with enameled brass hinged top. (7-3/4'').

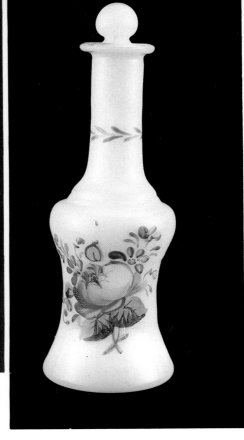

1. Small cut glass chatelaine bottle with jade set in gold washed top. Made in England. Circa 2nd half 19th century. (4'').

5. Hand-blown dresser bottle in Bristol glass. Circa 1885. (5-1/2'').

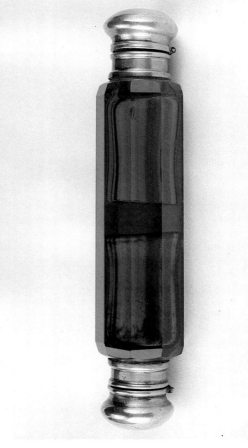

2. Small cut glass glove or purse bottle with silver screw-on top. Made in England. Circa 2nd half 19th century. (3'').

4. Free-blown tulip bottle in Bristol glass with hand enameled decoration, probably French. Circa 1890. (10-3/8'').

6. Victorian double scent bottle in cobalt glass with brass fittings. Made in England. Circa 2nd half 19th century. (5-1/4'').

Chapter 2

The Victorian Period to World War One

The Victorian period brought with it an explosion of exotic and varied styles, forms, and colors in perfume bottles. The great strides in chemistry and physics in this era made possible new ways of decorating glass and led to better control over the composition of the metal and, consequently, of its finished appearance. These discoveries gave rise to novel designs and led to departures from traditional methods of manufacture. When we consider the glass of such well-known figures as Tiffany, Gallé, Daum, De Vez, and others of the same movement, we have notable results which would have been impossible at an earlier time.

During the Victorian and Edwardian periods, colognes and perfumes were most often purchased by the middle and lower classes from the local drugstore. The druggist bought scents such as rose, patchouli, lavender, and carnation in bulk quantities and then repackaged them into smaller home-use containers. Druggists frequently preferred the inexpensive mould-blown, engraved, or cut styles available from a company such as Whitall, Tatum, & Co. of Millville, N.J. who were specialists in this type of bottle. Alternatively, the plainer bottle from the drugstore was usually taken home and the contents decanted into something more fashionable like the cameo or cut glass colognes. These bottles were chosen by the mistress of the house as permanent adjuncts to her dressing table and were reused indefinitely until discarded for something more stylish.

Cologne bottles with a blossom shaped receptacle as the top of its stopper are called "Tulip" or "Candlestick" bottles. Europe is the likely origin for the majority of these bottles during the last quarter of the 19th century. The bottles are very tall and hold up to a pint or more of cologne. A portion of the fragrant contents of the bottle were poured into the stopper receptacle to offset the bad odours which were common in the early days of poor or non-existent plumbing. Most of the examples seen at antique shops and shows are handblown frosted or Bristol glass with delicate, feminine enameled designs and a ruffle edged stopper.

An immensely popular type of bottle invented during the Victorian period was the English double scent bottle. The double bottle was usually made by fusing two mass produced bottles together. One bottle would hold smelling salts and the other perfume. The vogue for double scent bottles started during the 1850's and continued until the turn of the century. The most common colors to be found are clear, red, blue, and green. The rarest colors are purple, amber, and vaseline. A wide range of metal mounts were used from an inexpensive gilded brass alloy to gold and silver.

Small Victorian bottles with a chain and ring attached were created to be worn on a broach, from a neck chain, or to hang from a chatelaine. Chatelaines were worn on the waist-belt or sash with small, handy items such as scissors, thimble, keys, etc. attached to it by fine chains. This custom survived until World War I. Small cone-shaped bottles without chains were designed for a purse or glove if they were four inches or shorter. Longer bottles in this shape were usually placed on the dressing table.

England, during the Victorian era, produced an enormous variety of decorative glass perfume bottles in predominently derivative techniques and styles. Among the most successful companies was the firm of Thomas Webb and Sons of Stourbridge who produced fine art glass perfume

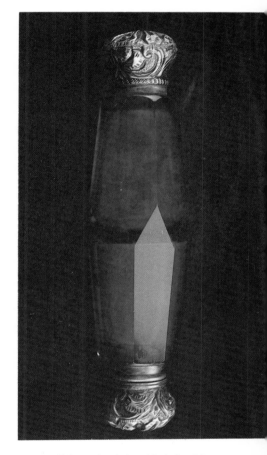

7. English, red, eight-sided double scent bottle with silver-plated fittings. Circa 2nd half of 19th century. (5-1/2").

8. English pinchback perfume pin with stopper attached by beaded chain. Circa 1900. (1-3/4").

9. Fine French green opaline chatelaine bottle with original ring and chain. Circa 1870. (2-1/2").

11. Round cobalt blue chatelaine bottle with sterling silver top. Circa 2nd half 19th century. (1-3/4").

12. English chatelaine bottle engraved on both sides with "R.B. Cooper Patent London" on top. Circa 1900. (2-1/2").

10. Ruby flashed over clear glass acid engraved purse bottle. Circa 1905. (2-1/2").

containers beginning in 1837. They created fine examples in cameo glass, enameled ware, and pieces with applied glass ornaments. The butterfly was a favorite motif with which they have become associated. Another glass company in Stourbridge who created beautiful art glass perfume bottles was Stevens and Williams. They manufactured glass for nearly a century beginning in the 1830's. Only some English bottles bear the maker's name, but all English silver or gold fittings are hallmarked if they are above a certain weight. From these hallmarks it may be possible to date scent bottles by consulting a book on English silver.

In France, from 1845 on, Baccarat produced lovely scent bottles with a heavy millefiori base. The famous Baccarat Glass Co., near Luneville, started production in 1765. They also created scent bottles in many other types of glass and styles including amberina, opaline, and cut crystal. In nearby Belgium, the Val St. Lambert Cristalleries, since its inception at the turn of the 19th century, has fashioned perfume flacons of high quality glass, especially in crystal and cameo.

Beginning in the early 19th century, the most fertile source of new ideas and new fashion in glass was Bohemia. Bohemian glassmakers created a virtual flood of choice glass products that were exported to other countries. Rich, deep colors such as blue, ruby, and deep green were used for flashing over clear glass through which a design was cut or etched. Between 1830 and 1917 Bohemian glass manufacturers were responsible for some very special perfume flacons in etched ruby, cut, flashed, and engraved cased colored glass. The styles were copied by glassmakers in England, France, and America making the correct origin hard to determine.

Ludwig Moser has become one of the most well known of the many Bohemian glassmakers. He founded the Moser Glasswork in 1857 in Carlsbad. He created high-quality Art Nouveau perfume containers in enameled, intaglio cut, and iridescent glass. To insure authenticity look for signed pieces, since many items attributed to Moser are actually of French origin.

13. Japanese engraved brass scent bottle made for the English market. Circa 1895. (3").

14. Small marble glass scent bottle for the purse in a swirl pattern with adventurine inclusions. Attributed Italy. Circa 1860. (3").

15. English scent bottle in cobalt glass decorated with gilding showing only slight wear. Circa 1860. (4-1/2").

Most American manufacturers specialized in quantity production of bottles, often utilizing machinery, until the end of the century, when the remarkable achievements of both Frederick Carder and Louis Comfort Tiffany brought American art glass perfume bottles into competition with those of France and Bohemia.

Tiffany "Favrile" (meaning hand-made) glass perfume bottles, created in the Art Nouveau style, were marketed from 1893 until 1920 when the factory closed. Favrile, was characterised by a brillian iridescence with shimmering surface effects produced by spraying the hot exterior with metallic salts which were absorbed into the glass. The colors created were blue, green, gold, and pink. Favrile glass is marked and usually has a model number on the bottom.

Stunning cameo glass perfume and cologne bottles became extremely fashionable during the late 1800's. Cameo glass requires casing two or more layers of different colored glass together then carefully carving away pieces of the glass until the desired design emerges. The decoration on a fine piece of cameo glass should give the appearance of hand carving and stand out in deep relief against the darker ground. English cameo glass came in opaque yellow, aquamarine blue, rose pink, purple, red, and green, all cased with opaque white.

There were two periods in cameo glass. From 1870 thru 1880, pieces were mainly carved by hand tools, but from 1880 to 1910 acid etching and copper wheel engraving were used almost exclusively to meet the tremendous public demand. The English firms creating the greatest amount were Stevens & Williams and Thomas Webb & Sons.

In America similar bottles were produced by the firm of Gillinder & Sons of Philadelphia between 1890-1900. The cameo glass perfume bottles have a glass or silver stopper, a silver screw top, or a hinged lid of silver with an inner glass stopper. There was a rapid decline in demand for cameo glass around 1890 mainly due to the appearance from Bohemia, of a large quantity of poorly made imitations.

16. Dresser bottle in poppy design with raised gold enameled lines dividing the surface. Incised with the number 2302 1212 on bottom. Attributed Mt. Washington. Circa 1895. (6-3/4").

French cameo glass perfume bottles became fashionable in Europe about 1890 and continued in style until just before the First World War. The French and their imitators used acid-engraving to produce the cameo relief Art Nouveau designs of scenes or nature subjects on cased colored glass blanks with up to five layers. One of the most important creators of cameo glass in France was Emile Gallé. His firm, located in Nancy, fashioned beautiful cameo glass during the 1890's using a variety of technique. His firm also manufactured glass perfume bottles festooned with enameled decoration. Besides Gallé, Daum Nancy, De Vez, Legras, Baccarat (lightly etched cameo glass) and Val St. Lambert in Belgium produced cameo glass perfume bottles in the French manner.

Cranberry glass bottles, which are highly prized by collectors, were manufactured for middle-class markets throughout the 19th century in England, especially at Stourbridge, Europe, and the U.S.A. after 1850. The glass is named after its pale pink color which closely resembles cranberry juice. A tiny amount of gold was added to the glass batches to give this glass its color on reheating. Both free-blown and mould-blown bottles were made, occasionally embellished with trailed, enamelled, or moulded ornamentation.

The Brilliant Period of cut glass extended over a period of roughly 1890 to 1915 when the fashion conscious public turned to newer, less elaborate designs. The deeply cut patterns were only achieved on glass containing a high grade of lead that could withstand the necessary pressure. Cut glass dressing table accessories were quite often produced in matching sets of three to eight pieces, while cologne bottles, with a capacity of 3 to 18 ounces, were marketed singly or in pairs. Bottles may be globe-shaped, round, squat, square, cylindrical, or fancy shaped in many sizes. The cut glass patterns on bottles vary widely, including fans, hobstars, hobnails, strawberry diamonds, notched, cane pattern, or a combination of any of the various motifs. Occasionally, the stopper might be cut to match the bottle pattern or be made from silver. The English preferred hinged silver tops with inner glass stoppers. The rarest bottles were cased with transparent blue, red, green, or yellow glass with patterns cut through the colored layer. On cut glass bottles search for trademarks on the base or shank of the stopper.

Perfume and cologne bottles decorated with copper-wheel engraving in clear and colored glass were extremely popular in the United States from about 1900 to 1935. Engraved designs occasionally include berries, fruit, insects, and birds with flowers and geometric patterns being the most commonly found. The most valuable bottles are those which are either meticulously engraved, have unusual patterns, or are trademarked by manufacturers such as Hawkes or Sinclaire.

Toilet sets and cologne bottles in "Mary Gregory" glass were ornamented with poignant pictures of children, flowers, birds, or scenery in opaque white enamel between 1870-1900. The children are oftey portyrayed in silhouette holding a tennis racket, chasing butterflies, or playing. On a pair of cologne bottles one will often be a boy, the other a girl. Mary Gregory glass originated at the Hahn glassworks in Gablonz, Bohemia but was also made in England, U.S.A and elsewhere. The white enamelling was done on clear, ruby, cobalt, cranberry, amber, amethyst, green, black, and aquamarine glass. The quality of the enamelling varies considerably. Be aware that Mary Gregory glass has been reproduced and it is necessary to watch for imitations.

A large number of pretty dresser bottles in milk glass, an opaque milky white glass, were created in the 1890's and early 1900's. Bottles of fine glass that are well-patterned and desirable, for the majority of pieces are of inferior quality and poor workmanship. The average bottle shape is either square or round and ornamented with hand painting, embossed swirls and scrolls, or embossed portraits. The rarest examples of milk glass dresser bottles are those with cased glass pictures.

17. Clear ribbed crystal with applied gold iridescent drape pattern and English sterling top. Made in 1901 at Birmingham. (3-3/4'').

18. Lovely peachblow perfume bottle in matt satin finish made by Stevens & Williams. Circa 1885. (5'').

19. English perfume bottle shading from green to orange decorated with gold enameled ivy. A piece of carved ivory adorns the hinged silver top. Circa 1890. (4-1/2'').

20. Queen's Burmese Ware bottle in satin finish by Thomas Webb & Sons with silver screw on top. Made in 1892. (3-1/2").

21. Enameled bamboo pattern on satin finished ground. Attributed Mt. Washington. (4").

22. Unusual mould blown perfume bottle with classical face as decoration. Attributed Thomas Webb & Sons. Circa 1885. (5").

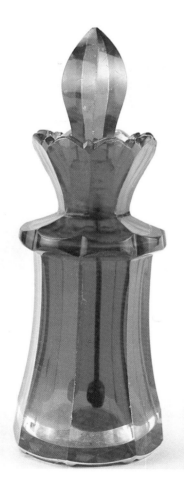

23. French red glass perfume bottle marked 22 on bottom. Stopper has original brass dapper with tiny sponge attached. (6").

24. French hand-painted scent bottle marked 10. on both bottle and stopper. Circa 1900. (4").

25. French opaline glass dresser bottle with ornate enameled decoration and red glass jewels. Circa 2nd half 19th century. (3-3/4").

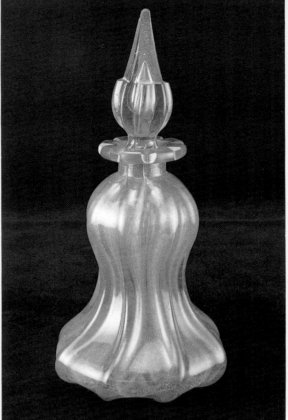

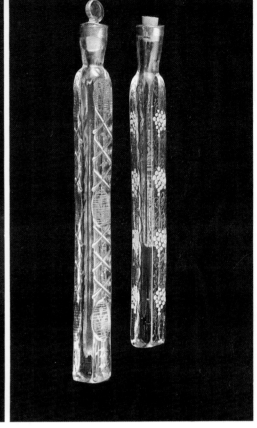

26. Opaline glass purse bottle for scent or smelling salts with plain brass top. Circa 2nd half 19th century. (3'').

27. Tall green glass mould blown cologne bottle. Attributed France. Circa 1890. (8'').

28. Two reclining bottles, one with a coursely cut geometric pattern, the other decorated with white enamel. They were made in France, Germany, and Bohemia to hold rose or lavender perfume oils. Circa 2nd half 19th century.

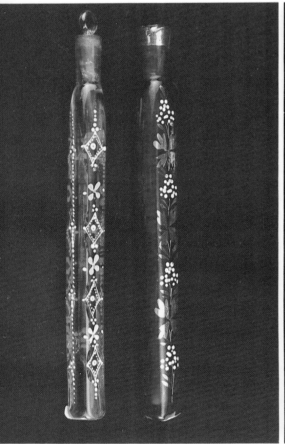

29. Reclining bottles in rare red and amber color with enamel decoration. Circa 2nd half 19th century.

30. Mould-blown French opaline glass dresser bottle with gold enamel trim. (6'').

31. Cobalt mould-blown French dresser bottle decorated with gold enameling marked 10 on bottom of stopper. (6'').

32. Yellow and white enamel on clear glass French cologne bottle marked 95.5 on bottom. Circa 1895. (6-1/2'').

34. Tall French dresser bottle decorated in Egyptian motif marked 22.00. Last quarter of the 19th century. (9-1/2'').

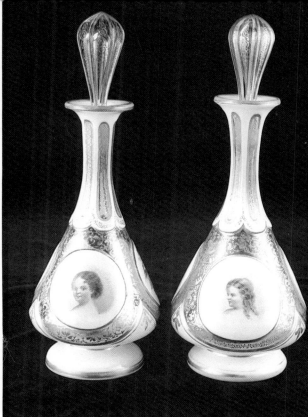

35. Rare pair of French cased and enameled colognes with children's portraits, marked 54 & 32. Circa 1870. (9-3/4'').

33. Ornate gold enameling festoons this French crystal bottle. Circa 1880. (6'').

Perfume bottles and dressing table sets of opaline glass were produced in France between 1825-1870 at Baccarat, Le Creusot, Bercy, Saint-Louis, Choisy-le-Roi, and other factories. Baccarat produced some of the best examples of opaline scent bottles. Opaline is a semi-opaque translucent glass, often with a milky-water appearance. After about 1835, the bottles were frequently embellished with gilding, enamellng, or applied trailing. White, green, and blue are the most common colors, while violet, mauve, yellow, turquoise, and rainbow hues were less often used. Opaline glass was also made in England, U.S.A., and Bohemia.

Mould-blown satin glass perfume bottles were made in the late 19th century and are very distinctive for their silky feel and matt finish which is achieved through the application of a hydrofluoric acid bath. The patterns for Mother of Pearl satin glass were created by trapping air pockets between two layers of glass to form regular patterns. Many patents for making satin and pearl satin glass were issued to factories in the U.S.A., Bohemia, and England in the 1880's. Some of the best examples of perfume bottles, in several soft colors, were made by the Mt. Washington Glass Co. of New Bedford, Mass. and the English firm of Stevens & Williams.

Elegant silver overlay perfume and cologne bottles have been made since the last quarter of the 19th century and continued to be popular well into this century. The bottles were decorated with patterns cut out of sterling silver, then applied to the surface of clear glass. The more intricate and detailed the pattern, the more valuable it is. Occasionally, there were colored glass bottles of red, green, and blue, often made by Steuben, decorated in this fashion.

Vaseline glass perfume bottles were manufactured in large quantities between 1835-1900 in England, France, America, and Bohemia. Vaseline is named for its oily, greenish-yellow color produced by the addition of uranium to the batch and will display a slight fluorescence when viewed in reflected light.

Some other popular types of glass, made here and abroad, used to make perfume bottles in the last quarter of the 19th century were: opalescent glass; spatter glass, characterized by its multicolor spatters; slag glass which resembles colored marble; and striped and filigree Venetian Glass.

The embellishment of a perfume bottle with enamelling, gilding, or cold-painting was usually done by a specialist decorator. Enamel is a lasting form of decoration made with a mixture of a fluxing substance, a water or oil base, and a powdered metallic coloring agent. After the bottle is painted, it is then fired so that the colors develop and fuse with the surface. When properly applied, this form of decoration is extremely durable and only abrasive substances or sharp tools can remove it.

Gilding involves applying gold as a paint, in powdered form, or as a thin foil to the surface of a perfume bottle, then firing it at low temperature to fuse it to the surface.

Hand painting, also known as cold-painting, uses colors with an oil or lacquer base with no subsequent firing. This method of decoration can be damaged or worn away easily. Many old perfume bottles that were cold-painted originally have lost their designs.

40. Art Nouveau style opaque glass bottle in a beautiful jade color. Often mistaken for an older piece, it is signed Czechoslovakia. Circa 1930. (6-1/2").

36. Saint Louie bottle with carved red florals against frosted acid etched background. (7").

38. Unusual long enameled chatelaine bottle in Bohemian style. (5-1/8").

41. Signed Moser purple to clear intaglio cut cologne bottle. (7-1/4").

37. Mould blown chatelaine bottle with Moser style enameling. (2-1/2").

39. Cased cranberry glass chatelaine bottle in Bohemian style with brass top. (3-1/2").

42. Red Bohemian cut to clear bottle with grape leaf motif. (5-1/2").

43. Bohemian ruby glass bottle decorated with gilt roses. Circa 1850. (5-1/4").

46. Louis Comfort Tiffany Favrile glass perfume bottle marked with style number 71888. Circa 1900. (8").

49. English cameo glass lay-down bottle in yellow. Circa 1885. (6-1/4").

44. Bohemian white overlay, cut to clear bottle with gilt and enamel decoration. Circa last quarter 19th century. (5-1/2").

47. Beautiful English cameo glass purse bottle by Thomas Webb & Son in 1884. (3-1/2").

50. Red English cameo glass dresser bottle with brass top. Circa 1885. (5").

45. Bohemian style opaque white overlay cut to blue glass cologne bottle with gilt decoration. Circa 1870. (10-1/2").

48. Thomas Webb & Son cameo glass dresser bottle. Circa 1880. (5-1/2").

51. Unusual tri-color English cameo glass perfume bottle shaped like an inkwell. Circa 1890. (4").

52. Signed Gallé French cameo glass perfume flacon with silver top. Circa 1900. (3-7/8'').

55. Perfume burner in French cameo glass decorated with a river scene, signed Gallé. Circa 1900. (7'').

58. Bleeding Heart Pattern French cameo glass atomizer signed Deque. Circa 1900. (7-3/4'').

53. French cameo glass bottle with matching stopper signed Gallé. Circa 1900. (4-3/4'').

56. French cameo glass atomizer signed Gallé. Circa 1900. (6-3/4'').
57. Atomizer of French cameo glass in a pine cone pattern signed Gauthier. Circa 1900. (6-3/4'').

59. Iris decorate this green perfume bottle signed Daum Nancy. Circa 1900. (8-1/4'').
60. Cranberry glass boudoir bottle. Attributed Bohemia. Circa 1850. (6-1/2'').

54. French style cameo glass with English atomizer top. Circa 1900. (5'').

64. Common American Brilliant Period cut glass bottle with hobstar pattern decoration. Circa 1890. (4").

61. Cranberry glass bottle with dark green pedestal base and gilt decoration. Circa 1850. (10").

67. American Brilliant Period perfume advertised in 1911 mail order catalog. (4-1/2").

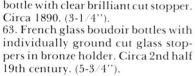

62. Cased cranberry glass perfume bottle with clear brilliant cut stopper. Circa 1890. (3-1/4").

63. French glass boudoir bottles with individually ground cut glass stoppers in bronze holder. Circa 2nd half 19th century. (5-3/4").

65. American Brilliant Period cut glass cologne with unusual teardrop stopper. Circa 1890. (8-1/2").

66. Fancy shaped American cut glass cologne bottle. (8").

68. Interesting bell-shaped American cut glass perfume bottle. Circa 1900. (5").

69. Libby cut glass cologne bottle. Circa 1905. (8").

70. American Brillian Period cologne with prism pattern. Circa 1908. (7").

73. Strawberry-diamond pattern cased with transparent green, with sterling silver top. (6-1/4").

74. Cut glass cologne cased with transparent green glass. (6-1/4").

75. Red and yellow cased cut glass cylinder shaped cologne. (5-3/4").

71. Tall cut and engraved cologne signed Hawkes. Circa 1900. (9-1/4").

72. American cut crystal with sterling top. (5").

76. Small cut glass cobalt blue perfume bottle with silver top. (3").

77. Rare Thomas Webb & Son rainbow cut glass cologne bottle. Circa 1900. (7'').

78. Cobalt blue cased cut glass cologne with gold enamel decoration made in England. (6-1/2'').

79. English cut glass with gold washed top. (6'').

80. English cut glass dresser bottle with sterling silver top. Circa 1890. (4-1/4'').

82. English cut glass dresser bottle with silver top. (4-3/4'').

81. Heart shaped English cut glass lay-down bottle with sterling silver top. (5-1/4'').

83. English cut glass dresser bottle with ornate sterling silver top and trim. (4-1/2'').

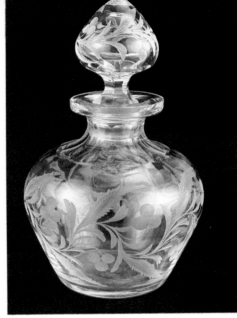

87. Signed "Sinclair" intaglio cut glass cologne bottle. Circa 1910. (6").

84. Edwardian cut glass perfume bottle with sterling silver bottle lip, trademarked 1908. (4-1/2").

88. Hallmarked English cut crystal perfume bottle with tortoise-shell top, made in Birmingham in 1902. (3").

85. Edwardian cut glass perfume bottle. Circa 1910. (3-1/4").

86. Edwardian cut glass perfume bottle. Circa 1910. (3-1/4").

89. Engraved perfume bottle with enamel top made in Birmingham, England in 1900. (4-1/2").

91. French cased, engraved, and gold enameled cologne bottle. Circa 1890. (7'').

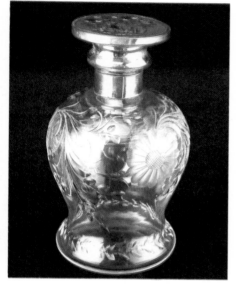

92. Signed ''Thomas Webb & Sons'' engraved cologne with enameled top. Circa 1910. (6'').

90. English bottle with engraved decoration and tortoise-shell top. Circa 1900. (4'').

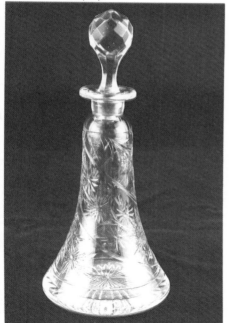

93. American engraved cologne bottle in a bell shape. Circa 1905. (8'').

94. Signed ''Hawkes'' engraved cologne bottle. Circa 1910. (7'').

95. Signed ''Hawkes'' engraved perfume bottle with silver trim. Circa 1915. (4-1/2'').

98. Amber color glass Mary Gregory cologne bottle with flower shaped stopper. Circa 1880. (5-1/2'').

99. Blue colored glass Mary Gregory cologne bottle. (5-3/4'').

96. Rare black Mary Gregory purse bottle. (2-3/4'').

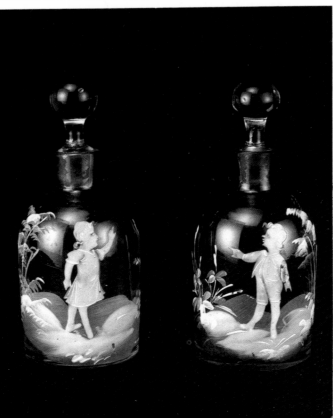

97. Pair of Mary Gregory bottles with a girl and a boy, in opaque white enamel, facing each other. Circa 1880. (5'').

100. Mould blown, milk glass perfume bottle with colorless cut glass stopper was made in the Midwestern U.S. about 1870. ''Lightner's White Rose Perfume'' is lettered on the underside of glass label which is set into a reserve space in the body of the bottle. Photo courtesy Huntington Galleries; gift of Mr. R.E. Wells. (19 cm).

(101. Marked "Thomas Webb & Son" mother-of-pearl satin glass with gold enamel decoration. Circa 1885. (2-3/4").

104. Extra fine Mary Gregory bottle in clear glass, probably Bohemian. Circa 1875. (4-1/2").

105. Blue satin glass bottle with sterling silver top by Stevens & Williams. Circa 1890. (2-3/4").

102. Blue, diamond-quilted pattern, mother-of-pearl satin glass bottle with gold washed top by Thomas Webb & Sons. Circa 1885. (4").

103. Satin glass bottle by Stevens & Williams in an unusual orange swirl design. Circa 1890. (5").

106. Sterling silver chatelaine bottle made into a necklace, hallmarked 1899. (2-1/4").

107. Chased silver heart bottle made by George Ward of Chester, England in 1895. (3-1/2").

108. & 109. Rare English sterling silver purse bottle made in 1903. (2-3/4").

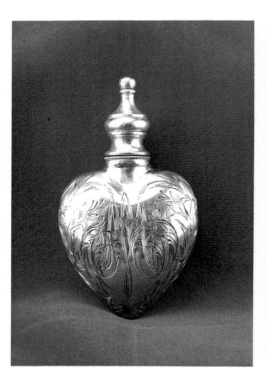

110. English engraved silver heart bottle with screw top for the purse. Circa 1900. (3-1/4").

111. Dutch silver and crystal perfume bottle with matching silver stopper made during last quarter of the 19th century. (3-3/4").

112. Ornate hallmarked English cut crystal and sterling silver bottle. Circa 1914. (6-1/2").

113. Silver over-lay purse bottle for scent or smelling salts. (2'').

114. Bell shaped silver over-lay bottle. (4-3/4'').
115. Silver over-lay bottle. (5'').

116. Silver over-lay bottle. (6'').

117. Silver over-lay bottle. (5/1/4'').

118. Silver over-lay green glass bottle. (4-1/2'').

120. Cobalt glass and silver over-lay purse bottle. (2-1/2'').

119. Silver over-lay red glass bottle. (5-1/2'').

121. Bohemian cut glass bottle in vaseline color. Circa 1850. (4-1/2'').

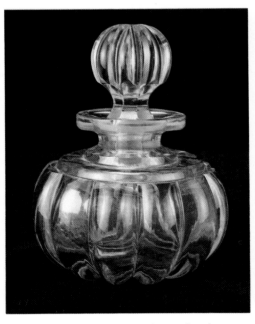

122. Vaseline glass cologne bottle. Attributed France. Circa 2nd half 19th century. (6'').

123. Cased splatter glass chatelaine bottle with brass top Circa 1885. (3-1/4'').

124. Venetian style blue swirl glass purse bottle with brass top. Circa 1890. (3-3/4'').

125. French "Old Paris" porcelain dresser bottle. Circa 1875. (7-1/2").

126. Pair Velux Paris cologne bottles with false chelsea mark. Circa 1890. (6-1/4").

127. French marble, glass, and metal carriage shaped perfume container. Circa 1910. (6-3/4").

128. Perfume necklace with mirror on back. Souvenir of 1889 Paris Exposition. (2-3/4").

129. Souvenir perfume bottle with cased glass picture of the Roman Colosseum. Circa 1885. (2-1/8").

130. Fin de Sìède style glass jewel decorated container with 4 crystal perfume bottles. Circa early 20th century. (5-1/4").

Chapter 3

Lalique

1. Metal face powder box designed by R. Lalique used by Rober & Gallet. (3" across)

2. Opalescent glass perfume burner by R. Lalique with a molded design of narrow entwined branches. (6-1/2")

The name Lalique invokes an almost instant vision of lyrical, artistic, well designed glass of the highest quality. One is frequently rewarded by finding his signature on bottles of exceptional beauty. His fame is firmly grounded on his mastery of techniques he refined as a jeweler and later converted to the production of glass.

Rene Lalique was born at Ay France on June 4, 1860. He showed an early aptitude for artistry. By the age of twelve he had won an important design award at the *Lycee Turgot* in Paris. He studied drawing there for four years. To earn money he painted ivory miniatures. In 1876 his father died, necessitating his learning a trade. Lalique apprenticed himself to a Paris silversmith, Louis Aucoc, and enrolled as a student at the Ecole des Arts Decoratifs.

In 1878, Lalique left Paris and went to England to study at a London Art college. This was the time period when Wlliam Morris and the Pre-Raphaelites were having a profound effect on the decorative arts. They believed that quality, beauty, and good design could be incorporated even in mass produced items. This movement was the forerunner to Art Nouveau which Lalique was to excel in.

After two years Lalique returned to Paris in order to freelance as a jewelry designer for several world-famous firms. In 1885 he opened his own Atelier in the Place Gaillon. He continued working for other houses for a time, but felt the creative urge to manufacture his own designs. It was during this time period that Lalique earnestly explored the potential of inexpensive materials outside those traditionally used by jewellers. In studying enameling, he invented superior ways of working with this material. Enamel being related to glass heightened his interest in the medium. Lalique set up his first small furnace to experiment with glass in 1890 in the Rue Therese, his new and larger quarters.

During the nineties Lalique exhibited his jewelry all over Europe winning personal success with his designs. The triumph of his pieces led to so many orders he was overwhelmed. During this period he designed the stage jewelry worn by the actress Sarah Bernhardt. He was awarded the Croix de Chevalier de la Legion d'Honneur in 1897 and at the Paris Exposition of 1900 his exhibition of jewelry won him international acclaim.

In 1902 Lalique went looking for new fields to explore and conquer. He was forty-two and at a time when he felt the need for a change in work or homelife. Renting a small workshop at Clairefontaine, he equipped it and hired four glass workers. One of a kind perfume bottles encased in silver were some of Lalique's earliest attempts. This interest was to occupy him, body and soul, for the remainder of his life.

Fate took a hand in 1907 when Francois Coty commissioned Lalique to design the labels for his perfume bottles. Lalique went one step further, he also designed the bottles! This relationship went on to become one of the most enduringly successful of all his commercial ventures. The glassworks of Legras and Cie executed the first bottles, but by 1909 he was manufacturing them himself at his glassworks in Combs, forty miles from Paris. Before this scent had been available in hand-made bottles that were sometimes more expensive to manufacture than their contents. Lalique found a way of

4. "Bouchon Eucalyptus"—Frosted tiara stopper molded as a cluster of fruit with long leaves tops the faceted bottle by R. Lalique. (5-1/4")

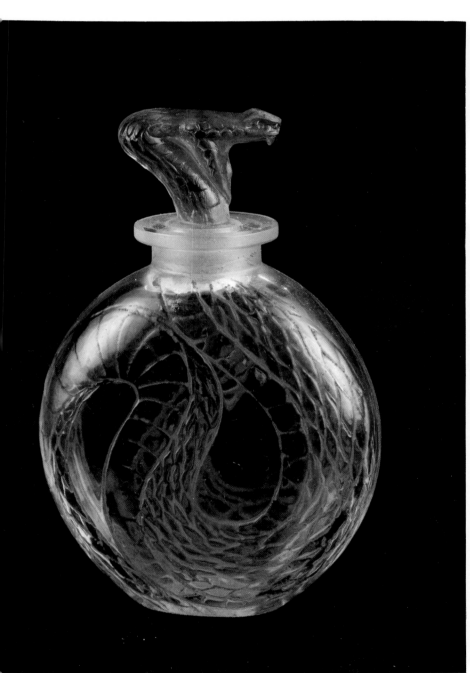

3. "Serpent"—Flask form R. Lalique scent bottle molded with the body of a serpent with the stopper shaped like a Cobra's head. (3-1/4")

5. "Olives"—Clear glass R. Lalique flacon molded with tear-shaped decoration on the bottle and stopper. (4-3/4")

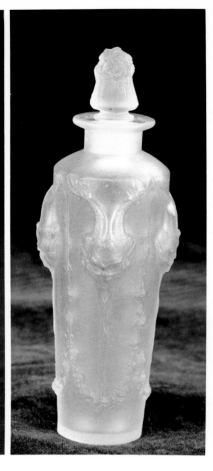

6. A. U.S. design patent was issued in 1924 to Jacques Worth of Paris, France for this "Dans La Nuit" bottled signed R. Lalique. (5-1/2").

7. Unusual 4-part mould bottle by R. Lalique for "Bouquet de Faunes" by Guerlain. Heads on the bottle match figures on the portico of the Guerlain building in Paris. U.S. introduction 1924. (3-3/4").

8. "Pan"—R. Lalique perfume bottle bearing four molded masks of Pan framed by festoons of flowers. (5")

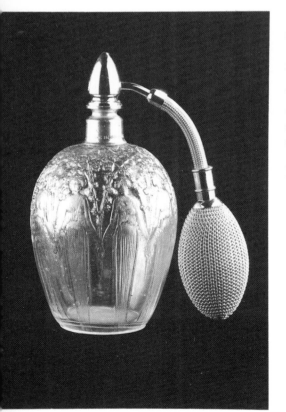

9. The Debans Importing Corporation of New York introduced this beautiful R. Lalique atomizer to the American public in 1923.

mass producing such bottles so that they appeared luxurious while being affordable to both the rich socialite and poor shop-girl alike. Involved in this process was what Lalique called "demi-crystal", more malleable and responsive than lead crystal.

The first flacon design Lalique made for Coty was known as "Libellule". This extremely rare bottle displayed an embossed dragonfly across the entire front of the bottle. A bottle for the scent "Amber Antique" made in amber colored glass ornamented with figures of Grecian women was also among the earliest.

Between 1910 and 1940 Lalique manufactured millions of bottles for French and American perfumers including:

Jay-Thorpe	Coty
Lournay	Guerlain
D'Orsay	Isabey
Arly	Lalo
Lentheric	Forvil
Corday	Roger et Gallet
Delettrez	Riquad
Gabilla	Riquad
Richard Hudnut	Worth
Lengyel	Houbigant
Molinard	Lucien Lelong
D'Heraud	Rosine
Volnay	Fioret
Gueldy	Burmann

His son, Mark Lalique, made bottles for Rochas, Nina Ricci, Raphael, and Lancome starting in the forties after World War II. This is not to say that the Laliques designed and made all the bottles for the above companies, but they produced at least one for each of the companies listed.

10. This ad appeared in 1927 for "Jaytho" by Jay-Thorpe, with bottle by Rene Lalique.

11. Hard to find "Sans Adieu" bottle marked R. Lalique. Circa 1929. (2-3/4").

12. "Capricorne"—Clear glass R. Lalique bottle molded with an insect design stained gray. (3")

Lalique used all colors of glass but the largest portion of his perfume bottles are of clear and frosted crystal. The hardest to find colors are red, blue, green, amber and black. Enameling, hand staining, and sandblasting contributed also to their beauty. Art Nouveau influenced much of his work which can be seen in the graceful nudes, insects, fish, flowers, birds, and animals on his flacons. The 1920's saw Lalique designs becoming more geometric and streamlined. He was an early leader of the Art Deco movement.

The mass produced flacons for perfumers were so successful that Lalique made perfume flacons a part of his own personal line. Garnitures de toilette, sets of co-ordinated containers designed for the dressing table for powder, cream, etc. were also included. Since the mid-nineteenth century dressing table sets of silver, cut crystal, and other expensive materials had been sold. The relatively inexpensive sets mass-produced in glass by Lalique were a wholesale success. There are at least six different patterns in the garniture sets. They include "Myosotis" a forget-me-not pattern, "Perles" with ropes of pearls, "Epines" a relief design of thorny branches, "Fleurettes" another flower design, "Duncan" with nude figures, and "Dahlia". The "Dahlia" pattern is still in production today after being revived by Marc Lalique after World War II.

In 1924 Roger et Gallet introduced to the U.S. "Le Jade" perfume in a moulded green flacon shaped like an oriental snuff bottle with a flying bird on it by Lalique. Houbigant introduced to the U.S. "La Bell Saison" in 1926. The square Lalique bottle has a profile of a girl framed in the center. Jay-Thorpe of New York used a Lalique bottle carved with tulips for "Jaytho" beginning in 1927. "Invalda" by Delettrez in a clear, round Deco flacon by Lalique was sold in the U.S. beginning 1935. In 1936 a crystal flacon with embossed double eagles and crown-like stopper by Lalique was used by Lengyal for the scent "Parfum Imperial". For Molinard, Lalique designed a doughnut shaped bottle with Etching in the center introduced to

13. Very rare figural dauber in the form of a nude woman enhances this plain cylindrical bottle by R. Lalique. (4-1/4")

the U.S. in 1937. Corday introduced "Tzigane" to the U.S. in 1938. The smoke colored Lalique glass has notches running up the sides. Ann Haviland of New York commissioned Lalique for the "Perhaps" bottle in 1940. A tower of a bottle, 10 1/2 inches tall, of clear crystal with an etched frosted stopper, it was among the last made by Rene Lalique before World War II shut the glass house down.

The U.S. patent office issued two design patents on January 19, 1932 to Rene Lalique of Paris, France. Both patents were assigned to Lucien Lelong who used them for his single letter perfumes beginning in 1930. One of the designs was eight pointed side flacon of clear glass and the other design had a pattern reminiscent of fish scales down the top and sides.

Some of the rarest and hardest to find flacons by Lalique are those with spreading, cresant-shaped stoppers. These designs are beautiful but awkward to handle which leads to breakage. "Satyre", the head of a satyr, and "Jeunessee" the body of a cherub, were two unusual bottles made with the figural stopper extending down into the bottle.

In his lifetime, Rene Lalique was crowned by the world as the most important designer of the 20th Century. He died at the age of eighty-five on May 5th 1945. Marc Lalique, who since the 20's had been in charge of production and the business end, took over the firm. All glass before 1945 is marked R. Lalique. All post 1945 glass is marked "Lalique France" dropping the use of the initial R.

14. Cylindrical R. Lalique atomizer molded with a design of all-over florettes stained blue. (4")

15. "Lotus"—R. Lalique perfume molded in the shape of a lotus flower. (2-1/2")

16. R. Lalique cylindrical perfume burner with a molded frieze of female dancers in the Egyptian Revival style enamelled in orange. (6")

17. "Amphytrite"—Green perfume flacon by R. Lalique molded in the form of a spiral shell with a figural stopper shaped like a kneeling sea nymph. (3-3/4")

18. Early R. Lalique screw top atomizer with nudes. The chain attached a cap over the spout to prevent evaporation of the contents. (3-3/4").

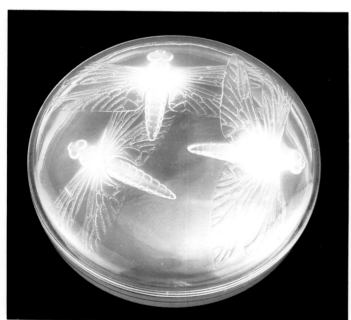

19. Beautiful opalescent box embellished with three molded dragonflies by R. Lalique. (6-1/2" diameter)

20. "Camille"—Vivid blue R. Lalique scent bottle molded with ribbed spiral fins on the globular body and stopper. (2-1/4")

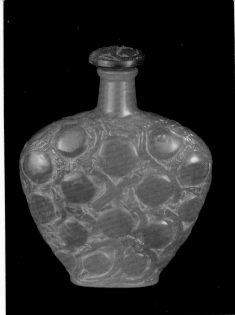

23. U.S. patent filed by Rene Lalique in 1931 for bottle used by Lucien Lelong.

22. "Salamandres"—Green R. Lalique scent flacon in flask form molded with an all-over design of salamanders. (3-3/4")

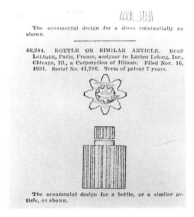

21. R. Lalique glass pendent molded with a nude surrounded by flowers was used by the company Fioret to decorate packages of its perfume. (1")

26. "Lentille"—Disk shaped R. Lalique scent bottle molded at the shoulder and below the neck with a band of stylized flowers. (2")

24. U.S. patent filed by Rene Lalique in 1931 for 8 point crystal bottle used by Lucien Lelong for "B" perfume.

25. Advertisement for "Parfum Imperial" by Lengyal introduced in 1936 in beautiful double eagle bottle by Rene Lalique.

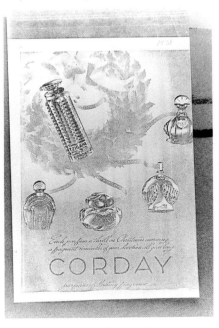

27. Ad for Corday in 1938 featuring the new perfume "Tzigane" in R. Lalique bottle.

28. Round tiered bottle with silver rims made for "Imprudence" by Worth, signed R. Lalique. U.S. introduction 1938. (3").

31. Large dresser bottle signed R. Lalique with interesting beaded swirls. (8-1/4").

29. "Meplat 490"—R. Lalique rectangular bottle with recessed oval panel molded with two naked women back to back. (5")

32. A "Spines" pattern dresser bottle with tan staining marked R. Lalique. (4").

33. "Cigales"—R. Lalique flacon with a cicada molded at each shoulder. (5-1/2")

30. "Lunaria"—Clear glass R. Lalique flacon with a design of opalescent leaves outlined in gray staining. (2-3/4")

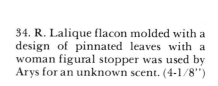

34. R. Lalique flacon molded with a design of pinnated leaves with a woman figural stopper was used by Arys for an unknown scent. (4-1/8")

35. R. Lalique designed this rectangular flacon with a molded rope design picked out in black enamel for the perfume "Les 5 Fleurs" by Forvil. (2-3/4")

38. Rare atomizer for the perfume "Calendal" by Molinard designed by R. Lalique. (5-1/2")

36. Ball-shaped bottle with molded rings of tiny flowers was created by R. Lalique for Arys. (3")

37. Tiny molded flowers cover the four arched sides of the flacon by R. Lalique for the perfume "Lilas" by Gabilla. Circa 1920's. (3-1/2")

39. R. Lalique flask form bottle held the perfume "Flausa" by Roger & Gallet. The molded kneeling nude is surrounded by flowers and foliage. Brown staining highlights the details. Circa 1910's. (4-7/8")

40. A molded frieze of dancing nudes below stylized flower heads decorate the flacon made by R. Lalique for the Molinard perfume "Calendal". Circa 1929. (4-1/2")

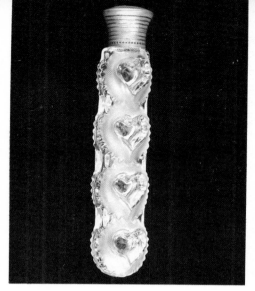

44. Rare Nina Ricci "Coeur-Joie" purse bottle with brass top, introduced to U.S. in 1951.

41. "Bouchon Mures"—R. Lalique red tiara stopper molded with mulberries sits atop a clear glass bottle with vertical red lines. (4-3/4")

45. Acorn bottle with gilt metal top was for "Replique" by Raphael. Lalique mark is under the cap. U.S. introduction 1951. (2").

46. Worth introduced three flower perfumes "Lilas", "Oeillet", and "Gardenia" in 1939 in this R. Lalique flacon with an all-over molded flower design. (3-1/4")

42. Introduced to the U.S. in 1952, the "Fillé d'Eve" by Nina Ricca bottle made by Lalique. (2").

43. "Coeur Joie" by Nina Ricci in the Lalique heart shaped bottle was introduced to the U.S. in 1951. (4").

47. Clear glass bottle with embossed design signed Lalique for Nina Ricci. (3-1/4'').

50. Clear glass commercial bottle with embossed wisteria signed R. Lalique. (3'').

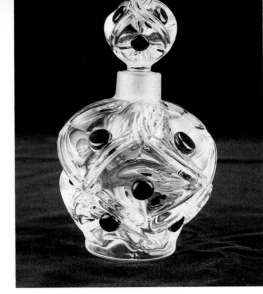

53. Clear glass dresser bottle decorated with black glass buttons. Paper sticker on bottom states, Cristal Lalique Paris.

48. Dresser bottle originally introduced to the U.S. in 1932, signed Lalique France. (5'').

51. Parfums De Volnay of Paris used this heart shaped flacon with molded coral pattern by R. Lalique. U.S. Introduction 1922. (3-1/2'')

54. Two Fleur Flacons with black enameled trim marked Lalique France. (3-1/2'').

49. Molded caryatid decorate the four sides of this black flacon by R. Lalique. It held the scent "Ambre" by D'Orsay. Circa 1920. (5-1/4'')

52. Clear glass Nina Ricci bottle made for European market by Lalique. (3-1/4'').

55. Frosted nudes framed with clear glass bottle with frosted stopper by Cristal Lalique. Circa 1984.

Chapter 4

Between the World Wars

The everday use of perfume by women from all levels of society emerged when the flapper era was ushered in. World War I had swept away much of the lingering Victorian morality which stigmatized perfume use as risque. With better sanitary facilities and more frequent bathing, women started using perfume to enhance their allure instead of masking unpleasant body odors.

Among the many perfume containers made during this time, some favorites are the so-called Depression glass bottles. Depression glass perfume bottles were made from an inexpensive, usually transparent glass in a rainbow of colors. Primarily machine made or mould-blown, they were sold near and during the Great Depression in the 20's and 30's. Many famous glass companies such as Cambridge, Duncan & Miller, Fenton, New Martinsville, Paden City, and U.S. Glass produced perfume bottles and vanity sets.

The majority of the Depression glass bottles were designed with simple, uncluttered lines enhanced only occasionally with etched or hand painted decoration. The most common colors found are green, pink, amber, and crystal. All companies at the time called their clear glass, crystal. The hardest to find bottle colors include red, cobalt blue, vaseline yellow, and opaque jade green. Many companies offered their transparent colored bottles in a satin finish. In the thicker sections of some bottles there is a tendency to appear darker in color.

Art glass of the highest quality, similar to Tiffany's Favrile, was made at the Steuben Glass Works of Corning, New York founded in 1903 by Frederick Carder and Thomas Hawkes. Frederick Carder was born in 1864 near Stourbridge, England. At the age of seventeen he became a designer for Stevens & Williams, where he remained until 1903 when he emigrated to the United States. Carder became art director of the Corning Glassworks, which absorbed the Steuben Company from 1918 to 1934, and designed all the glassware including perfume bottles.

Steuben Aurene, the specialty of Frederick Carder, was a lustrous, metallic, usually gold or blue glass introduced in 1904 and made until 1933. The premium labor force and the high-priced ingredients required to make Aurene resulted in a very expensive finished product. Steuben produced some lovely Verre de Soie glass which literally means, glass of silk. Perfume bottles made with this glass had a beautiful pearl-like lustre. Steuben also made perfume bottles in rosaline, silverene, alabaster, and Venetian glass.

Bottles made by Steuben are usually marked with their fleur-de-lis trademark or 'Steuben Aurene' in script with a stock number. Paper labels were also used. The lower the stock numbers on the glass, the older the bottle.

Orrefors of Sweden began making bottles and window glass around 1898. Consul Johan Ekman of Gothenburg purchased the glassworks and surrounding land in 1913. Wanting to raise the aesthetic and practical value of the glass Orrefors produced, Ekman went to the Swedish Society of Arts and Crafts for assistance. The society helped Ekman secure the services of two artists, Simon Gate in 1916 and Edward Hald in 1917. By the early 20's both Gate and Hald were making beautiful pieces of engraved glass including perfume and cologne bottles which are considered to be classics today.

1. Cambridge Glass Co. bottle in blue. Circa 1926. (5-1/2'').

Art Deco was a distinctive style movement of the 1920's and 30's which drew upon the French traditions of quality and elegance while responding to the demands of modern life. Art Deco was a hybrid style which can include as characteristics dynamic, streamlined, angular shapes; Oriental and African motifs; stylized surface decoration such as stars, nudes, flowers, greyhounds, and cars; and the repetition of geometric forms. The style has a tendency to be smart and sophisticated instead of just pretty.

Among the many manufacturers that made Art Deco perfume bottles were Val St. Lambert in Belgium; Orrefors, Hadelands, and Limmared in Sweden; Venini & Co. in Italy; Stevens & Williams in England; Steuben in the United States; Moser in Bohemia; Baccarat, Lalique, Daum, and Sabino in France; and J. & L. Lobmeyr in Austria.

Fashion magazines of the 1920's advised stylish women to carry their favorite perfume everywhere, so small bottles came in vogue. Enterprising manufacturers came up with an amazing array of perfume bottles for the purse in silver, porcelain, brass, wood, and of course glass.

In Germany during the 1920's and 1930's, these purse bottles were made in swirled, transparent, and opaque glass. The swirled glass bottles are often confused with English Nailsea or Venetian glass, but most are very clearly marked Germany somewhere on the bottle or top. There were three types of closures used: a round mercury or gold glass stopper; a small metal crown and cork; or a bent neck stopper. Some of these bottles have silver on the inside while others are of pastel shades.

Some beautiful porcelain perfume bottles and vanity sets were made from 1916 through the 1930's by Noritake. Noritake was a Japanese fine porcelain distributed by the Morimura Brothers with offices in N.Y. city. What makes these bottles so special is the fine, detailed, hand-painted decoration.

6. Cambridge Glass Co. bottle with modified bee-hive stopper. (5-1/4'').

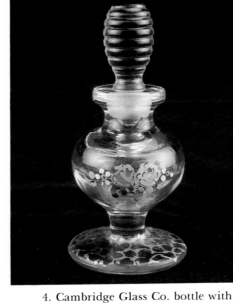

2. Cambridge Glass Co. bottle in amber. Circa 1924. (5'').
3. Cambridge Glass Co. bottle in a dark mulberry color. Circa 1924. (5'').

4. Cambridge Glass Co. bottle with bee-hive stopper. (4-1/4'').
5. Cambridge Glass Co. bottle with bee-hive stopper. (4-1/4'').

7. Cambridge Glass Co. bottle with damage. Circa 1924. (6-1/4'').

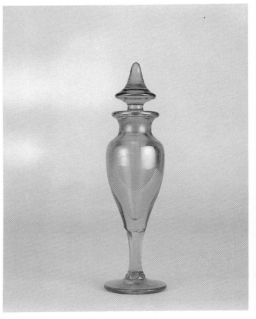

8. Fenton celeste blue cologne bottle. Circa 1924. (7'').

9. Fenton opalescent spiral cologne bottle with black glass stopper. Circa 1929. (5-3/4").

10. Fenton jade and black glass vanity set. Circa mid-20's. (Bottle 5").

12. Fostoria "Vanity" with original paper lable. Advertised 1924. (7-1/2").

11. Fenton "Moonstone" cologne with jade green stopper. Circa mid-20's. (5").

13. Fostoria bottle encrusted with coin gold. Advertised 1924. (5-1/4").

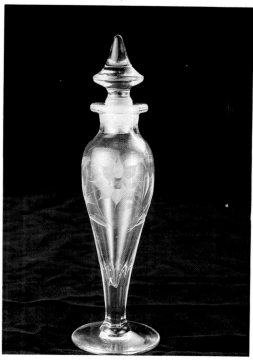

14. Fostoria etched crystal bottle. Circa 20's. (8").

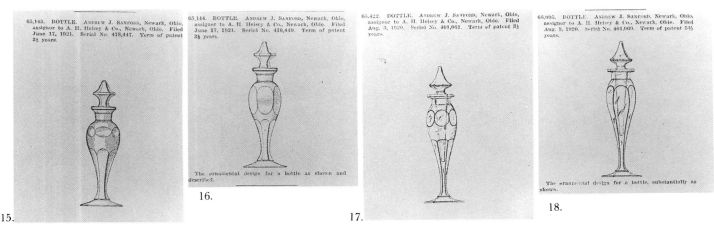

15—18. Patent drawings for Heisey cologne bottles filed: 15. June 17, 1921; 16. June 17, 1921; 17. August 3, 1920; and 18. August 3, 1920.

19. Marked Heisey cologne botle with gold trim. Circa early 20's. (7'').

20. Cologne bottle marked Heisey with red stopper. (5-1/4'').

21. Enameled roses on 22-karat gold background marked Heisey. (Wrong stopper.) Circa late 20's. (5-1/4'').

22. ''Cracked Ice'' by Indiana Glass Co. came in pink and green. Circa 30's. (5'').

23. New Martinsville Art Deco jade and black glass dresser set. Circa 1924. (6'').

24. Powder box and perfume bottle combined. Attributed New Martinsville. Circa 1920's. (5-1/2'').

27. "Queen Anne" dresser set by New Martinsville. Circa 1926. (6'').

25. "Geneva" by New Martinsville produced in green, rose, all crystal, and combinations of crystal with jade or black. Circa 30's. (7'').

28. "Leota" by New Martinsville in three color combinations. Circa 1933. (5'').

26. "Moondrops" pattern by New Martinsville. Circa 30's. (5-1/2'').

29. Cologne bottles by New Martinsville in unnamed pattern. Circa 1930. (5-3/8'').

31. No. 1926 vanity set by New Martinsville. Circa 1926. (4-3/4'').

30. ''Queen Anne' by New Martinsville in jade and black glass. Circa 1930. (6'').

33. No. 28 cologne bottle by New Martinsville. Circa 1930's. (6'').

35. ''Sun Set'' cologne by Paden City came in crystal or crystal base with stoppers in ruby, amber, blue, black, or green. Circa 1936. (5-1/4'').

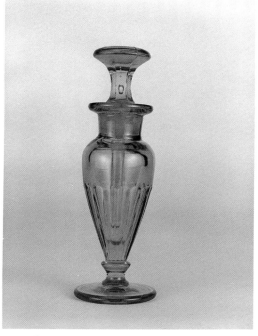

32. No. 1926 cologne bottle with gold decoration. (4-3/4'').

34. Paden City topaz No. 502 cologne bottle. Circa 1931. (6'').

36. ''Moonset'' by Paden City produced in same colors as ''Sun Set''. Circa 1936. (6'').

40. Canary satin finish bottle made by U.S. Glass also produced in red, emerald, and light blue. Circa 1924. (7'').

37. "Punch" by L.E. Smith, a colonial design available in crystal with black, green, or pink stoppers. Circa 1932. (6'').

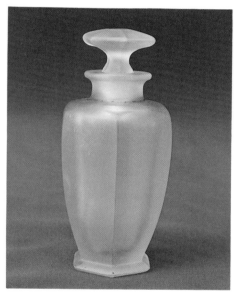

41. White satin finish "Classic Simplicity" bottle by U.S. Glass. Circa 1926. (4-1/2'').

42. Hand painted satin finish "Milady" cologne bottle by U.S. Glass. Circa 1926. (5-3/4'').

38. Black amethyst cologne bottle made by L.E. Smith. Circa 30's. (4'').
39. "Milady" cologne bottles by U.S. Glass Co. Circa 1926. (5-3/4'').

43. Complete dresser set in "Milady" by U.S. Glass. Circa 1926. (5-3/4'').

44. Red "Classic Simplicity" bottle by U.S. Glass also came in amber, green, canary, and blue. Circa 1926. (4-1/2").

47. "Scramble" pattern cologne by the Westmoreland Co. Circa 1924. (7").

48. Toilet bottle in jade green with original Westmoreland paper label. Circa 20's. (4-1/2").

45. Rare U.S. Glass cologne in amberina type glass. Circa 1924. (7").

49. Five piece vanity set advertised in 1926 mail order catalog. Came in amber, blue, pink and green. (5-1/2").

46. Another rare U.S. Glass cologne in amberina type glass. Circa 1924. (6").

50. Bohemian style, cut to clear, seven piece dresser set. Circa 1920. (6").

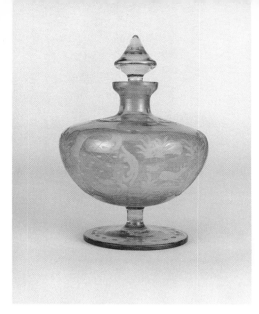

55. Rare cobalt blue cologne bottle by unknown maker. Circa 20's. (4-1/2'').

51. Bohemian style, cut to clear cologne bottle. Circa 1920. (6'').

54. Satin glass cologne bottle. Attributed Fenton. Circa 20's. (6'').

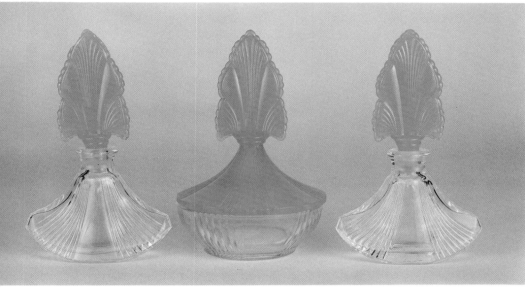

52. Unusual vanity set with jade glass tops and crystal bottoms. Circa 1930.

56. Crystal bottle with black glass stopper. Circa 1930's. (6-1/4'').

53. Three satin glass cologne bottles with hand painted decoration. Attributed Fenton. Circa 20's. (6'').

57. Crystal bottle with black glass stopper. Circa 1930's. (6'').

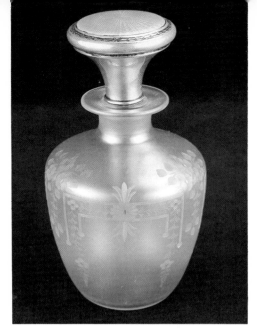

58. Crystal bottle with black glass stopper. Circa 1930's. (5'').

60. Signed Hawkes engraved Verre de Soie cologne bottle with sterling stopper. Circa 1920. (6-1/4'').

61. Engraved cologne bottle with silver top signed Hawkes. Circa 1920. (5-1/2'').

62. Engraved star pattern cologne bottle by Edward Hald for Orrefors. Circa 1918. (5-1/2'').

63. Signed Orrefors cologne bottle with dog design. Circa 1937. (6'').

59. Unusual star-shaped stopper tops this bottle. Circa 1930's.

64. Signed Steuben toilet bottle with applied glass thread decoration. (5-1/2").

67. Green signed Steuben bottle with alabaster stopper. (4-3/4").

68. Iridescent blue Aurene bottle signed Steuben. (4-1/4").

65. Rare cinnamon color cologne with gold mica flakes signed Steuben. (10").

66. Verre de Soie bottle with blue stopper signed Steuben. (4-3/4").

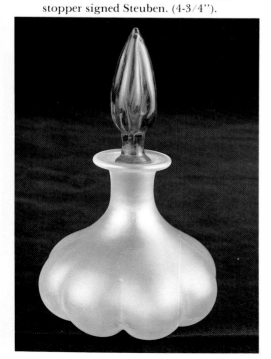

69. Iridescent gold Aurene bottle marked Steuben. (6").

70. Yellow Venetian glass perfume with black glass trim and flower stopper signed Steuben. (11-1/2'').

73. Gold Art Deco perfume bottle decorated with sleeping nude signed Austria. Circa 1925. (8'').

74. Opaque blue Art Deco perfume bottle with matching stopper. Circa 1930. (3-1/2'').

71. Art Deco perfume bottle with enameled copper base and cut crystal stopper. Circa 1930. (8'').

72. French Art Deco crystal bottle with black enameled decoration. Circa 30's. (6-1/4'').

75. Pink crystal with hand applied gray stain marked Austria. Similar bottles were also made in France. Circa 1925-1935. (5'').

76. Cute mould blown bottles with hand painted faces were made in Germany. Circa 1930. (1-3/4" and 1-7/8").

80. German mould blown purse bottle in blue milkglass. Circa 30's. (2-3/4").

77. Purse bottle in tortoise-shell glass with brass fittings. Circa 1925. (2-3/8").

78. Wooden clown case holds glass perfume bottle marked Austria. Circa 1920's. (3").

79. German swirled glass purse bottle also comes in other shapes. Circa 30's. (2-1/4").

81. Austrian purse bottle decorated with real petit point and rhinestones. Circa 1930. (2-1/8").

82. French silver filigree purse bottle with blue tassel. Circa 1920's. (1-7/8").

83. French cobalt glass and gold filigree purse bottle. Circa 1920's. (1-3/4'').

84. Set of four small hand enameled bottles signed HR. Circa 1920's. (2-1/4'').

86. Three sterling silver purse bottles. Circa 1920's. (Average h. 2-1/8'').

85. Engraved crystal purse bottle. Circa 1920's. (3'').

87. German porcelain purse atomizer. Circa 20's. (2-1/2'').

88. English nailsea atomizer for the purse. Circa 20's. (2-1/2'').

89. Evans purse atomizer shaped like a cigarette lighter in original box. Circa 1929. (2'').

90. Perfume bottle, pill box, and mirror in original presentation box. Circa 1920.

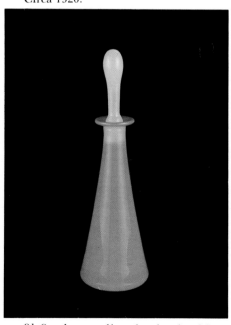

91. Steuben roseline glass bottle with alabaster stopper in modern design. Circa 20's. (7-1/2'').

92. Enamelled dots decorate this dresser bottle. Circa 30's.

93. French cased glass bottle with numbered bottle and stopper decorated with silver stars. Circa early 30's. (5-1/2'').

94. French bottle with unusual color glass and numbered stopper and bottom. Circa 1928. (5-1/4'').

95. Signed Baccaret bottle with grape-leaf decoration. Circa 20's. (3-3/4'').

96. Signed Val St. Lambert cologne bottle flashed yellow over clear. Circa 20's. (5-1/4'').

97. French cranberry glass with gold enameling marked 43 on stopper and bottle. Circa 20's. (4-1/8'').

98. French hand enameled bottle with hand stained stopper. Circa 20's. (2-1/2'').

101. English crystal and sterling bottle made in Birmingham during 1921. (6'').

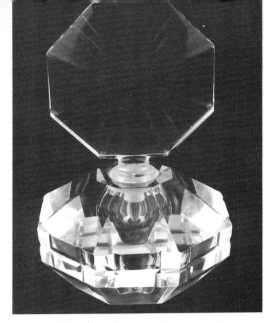

102. American Art Deco, hand cut, lead crystal perfume bottle with large starburst stopper. Circa 20's. (6'').

99. Iridescent swirl pattern cologne with enameled decoration and screw-on cap. Circa 1930. (5'').

103. Set of three Art Deco cut glass bottles with double stoppers. Circa 20's. (4-3/4'', 4'', 3-3/4'').

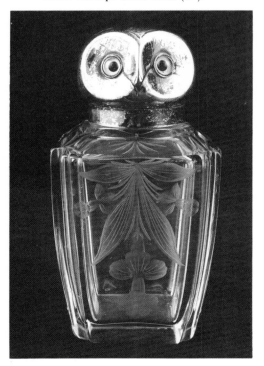

100. Engraved glass toilet bottle with silver plated owl's head stopper. Circa 1925. (5-1/4'').

104. Novelty shoe with two bottles made in Japan. Circa 1935. (3'').

105. Pressed glass double perfume bottle patented in 1937. (4").

106. Ornate bottle of frosted and clear glass. Circa 1930's. (8-1/4").

107. Frosted glass cat perfume bottle. Circa 20's. (3").

108. Marked Dresden porcelain purse bottle. Circa 1930. (2").

109. English porcelain purse bottle with shell decoration. Circa 1930. (2-1/2").

110. Green porcelain perfume bottle marked Bavaria. Circa 1930's. (5-1/2").

111. Imitation Capo de Monde bottle marked Germany. Circa 1930's. (6-3/4'').

114. Porcelain bottle with rose decoration marked R. S. Germany. Circa 1930. (6'').

118. Staffordshire bottle decorated with hand painted castle. Circa 1920's. (5-1/4'').

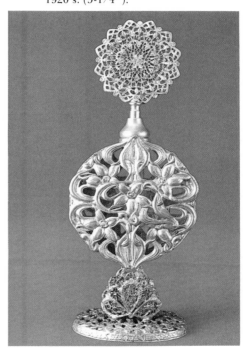

112. Wedgwood style perfume containers marked Germany. Circa 30's. (5-3/4'').

115. Hand painted porcelain bottle marked Noritake made in Japan. Circa 1925. (5-3/4'').

119. Art metal perfume bottle of European origin. Circa 1920's. (9'').

113. Porcelain bottle with applied flowers marked Germany. Circa 30's. (4-3/4'').

116. Purple and gold porcelain Noritake made in Japan bottle. Circa 1925. (6-1/2'').

117. Three porcelain bottles in metal holder marked Hand paint Made in Japan. Circa 1930's. (7'').

120. Art metal bottle with glass jewel decoration. Circa 1920's. (7-1/4'').

Chapter 5

Fan Stopper Bottles

The term "fan stopper" usually refers to pressed or mold-blown perfume and cologne bottles with large, ornate, glass stoppers made in the 1940's and early 1950's. The greatest number of these fanciful bottles were made in clear glass with geometric or flower motifs, although the occasional colored glass ones can be found.

With the onset of World War II, importers of perfume bottles and vanity items from Czechoslovakia, such as Irice (Irving W. Rice Co.) and Morlee (De Boer & Livingston, Inc.), had to seek alternative American sources to supply the demand. Irice turned to the Imperial Glass Co. of Wheeling, Ohio, to meet some of their needs. Imperial met the challenge and created many attractive bottles to be sold under the Irice sticker. In comparing the bottles shown in this chapter with the cut crystal bottles shown in chapter 7 on Czechoslovakia, one can see that many of the bottles made in America during the 1940's are almost direct copies of some of the Czech flacons made during the 1930's. The copies came in a limited range of colors including clear, pink, blue, and occasionally amber. American made reproductions of Czechoslovakian perfume bottles, boxes, and trays were also sold by Wondercraft, Luraline, American Cut Crystal Corporation, M.B. Daniels & Co., L. Luria & Son, Edward P. Paul & Co., Art Glow Creations, Block Mfg. Co., and Elbee Crystal.

Some mail-order catalogs and ads of the 1940's show a few of these bottles singularly and in four piece sets. For a small price of $2.19 you could purchase and become the proud owner of a mirror tray, two perfume bottles, and a matching powder jar. Most of the pieces shown in the ads were made to retail at $1.00 per piece.

A number of bottles have more than one stopper designed to be used with it. The decorative stopper was usually the most eye-catching feature of a bottle so consequently more emphasis was placed on its design. Sometimes the same basic stopper design was, added to or subtracted from, to achieve a different effect. An example of this can be seen on four bottles by the U.S. Glass Co. The same basic wreath pattern was used for each stopper with four different results. Some companies, such as the Imperial Glass Co., made their stoppers and bottles interchangeable.

Over the years many bottles have had stoppers broken, lost, or misplaced and then inaccurately replaced by careless or unconcerned people. To check the match of bottle to stopper you should see if the color, pattern, and type of glass used are all uniform and in balance with each other. Additional proof can be found in seeing the same combination of stopper and bottle used together in several places such as flea markets, antique shows, and shops.

1—9 Bottles made by Imperial Glass Co. for Irice during the early 1940's.

2.

5.

7.

3.

4.

6.

8.

9.

1—9. Bottles made by Imperial Glass
Co. for Irice during the early 1940's.

15. Dresser bottle sold in 1946 mail order catalog. (9-1/4").

10—13. Bottles made by U.S. Glass Co. using basic wreath motif on stopper. Circa 1940's. (Average h. 7-3/4").

14. Dresser set advertised in mail order catalog in 1944. (Bottle 7").

16. Perfume bottle seen in 1946 Christmas catalog. (7").

21. Tall Victorian inspired bottle. (10'').

17. Advertised in mail order catalog during the summer 1946 season. (7-1/2'').

18. Simple bird design stopper. (6-1/4'').

19. Hobnail bottle on small matching mirror tray sold in 1950 mail order catalog. (8'').

20. Interesting bottle sold through 1950 mail order catalog. (7-1/2'').

22. Tall Victorian inspired bottle. (10'').

23. Tall Victorian inspired bottle. (10-1/4'').

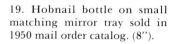

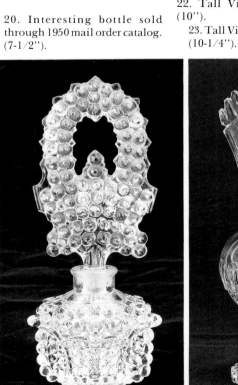

24. Frosted and clear glass Deco design. (8'').

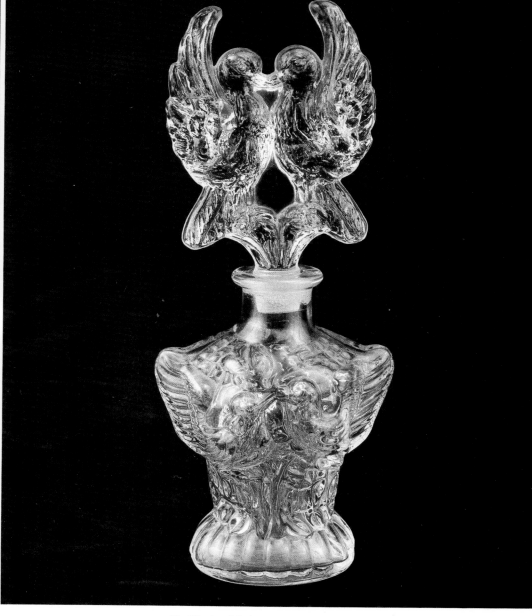

25. Frosted and clear glass flower design. (9-3/4'').

28. Kissing birds top this bottle seen in a catalog dated 1947. (7-1/4'').

26. Frosted and clear glass grape design. (9-3/4'').

27. Ornate bird design stopper. (7-1/2'').

29. Beaded oval design. (7-1/4'').

30. Geometric motif stopper. (7-1/4'').

32. Geometric design. (7-1/4'').

31. Rare bottle inspired by an inkwell.
(6'').

33. Geometric design. (7'').

34. Bird shaped stopper. (7-1/2").

35. Geometric design. (6-1/4").

36. Geometric design. (8").

37. Geometric design. (6'').

39. Geometric design. (6-1/2'').

40. Sun inspired stopper. (8-1/2'').

41. Star inspired stopper. (5'').

38. Geometric design. (6-1/4'').

42. Snowflake inspired stopper. (5-3/4'').

43. Geometric design. (7-3/4").

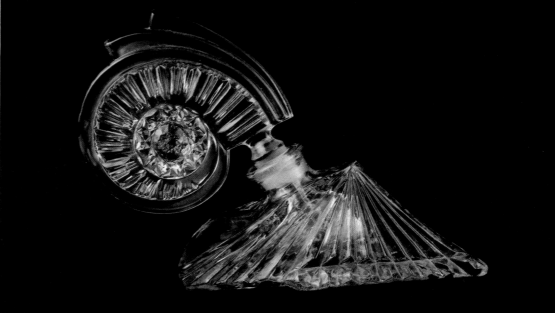

46. Rare blue glass inkwell bottle. (4-1/4").

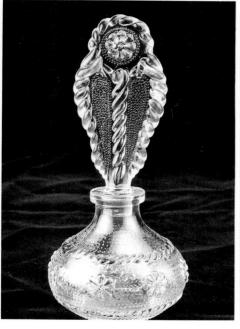

44. Flower and rope motif. (7").

47. Rare pink cornucopia bottle. (4-3/4").

45. Flower and geometric motif. (7").

48. Rare blue cornucopia bottle. (4-1/2").

Chapter VI

Perfume Atomizers

DeVilbiss, T.J. Holmes, and Others

1. Rare store display dummy bottle in orchid and gold marked 'made in U.S.A. DeVilbiss''. Circa 20's. (15'').

Atomization, simply described, is the process of reducing a liquid, such as perfume, to fine droplets by a mechanical means, usually using a gas such as air. A perfume atomizer can take a single drop and transform it into thousands of tiny fragrant atoms. Famous perfumers such as Coty, Caron, Guerlain, Houbigant, and others recommended spraying because they felt that it accentuated the rare, elusive qualities of a fragrance.

One of the largest and most successful makers of perfume atomizers in the United States was the DeVilbiss Co. of Toledo, Ohio. The company was originally founded by Dr. Allen DeVilbiss, a general practitioner with a specialty in nose and throat afflictions.

In the early 1880's the most common way a doctor treated a sore throat was by swabbing it with petroleum jelly or goose grease. There were atomizers sold at this time, but they were incapable of spraying the prescribed semi-solid remedies. Dr. DeVilbiss set about discovering a way to overcome this problem after contracting a throat infection from riding in an open sleigh to an emergency case during a snowstorm.

Dr. DeVilbiss set up a workshop in a wood shed behind his house in Toledo and through trial and error eventually came up with a perfected atomizer. It consisted of a small metal can containing vaseline, that could be held over an open flame to melt the contents, with a rubber bulb and tubing. Dr. DeVilbiss then added an adjustable tip for controlling the spray. This adjustable tip feature was the creative difference which made his atomizers unique enough to be patentable.

Collaborating with a top New York throat specialist, Dr. DeVilbiss created the first non-irritating light oil for nose and throat that could be sprayed, without heating, at room temperature to be used in his new atomizers.

The DeVilbiss Co. was founded in the original workshop behind the DeVilbiss home at 1941 Warren Street in 1888. This was rapidly outgrown so, in the early 1890's, the company erected its first factory at 1220 Jefferson Street in Toledo. Among the employees were the Doctor's two sons, Allen, Jr. and Thomas. They helped with the atomizer assembly and made company labels on a small hand press.

Thomas DeVilbiss bought a full partnership in the company in 1905. Shortly afterward, he took over the supervision and administration of the factory. Thomas' first suggestion was to add perfume atomizers to their repertoire, but Dr. DeVilbiss thought the idea frivolous and wanted nothing to do with it. Through years of much patience and tactful handling by Thomas, Doctor DeVilbiss finally gave his consent in 1907. Thomas modified the medical atomizer for perfume and on August 23, 1909 applied for his first patent which was granted on July 26, 1910.

The first perfume atomizers were an overnight success. They consisted of the special atomizer top fitted to ordinary salt-cellars made for table use and sold under the name, DeVilbiss Perfumizer. It was not long before the perfumizers outstripped the sales of the medical atomizers, proving Thomas' business acumen. The large orders necessitated a move to bigger quarters, so in 1910 the DeVilbiss Co. relocated to 1302 Dorr Street.

The beautiful glassware used by the DeVilbiss Co. came from glasshouses located in the United States and abroad. Thomas DeVilbiss made special

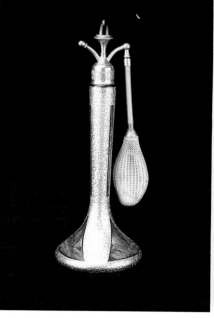

2. Copper wheel engraved Steuben gold Aurene bottle marked 'De Vilbiss'. Design patent for top filed June 1921. Circa 1924. (9-3/4'').

5. 22 karat gold encrusted bottle with engraved decoration. Circa 1924.(10'').

8. Opaque blue glass perfume bottle marked 'DeVilbiss' on bottom. Circa 20's. (6-1/4'').

11. Opaque pink Cambridge glass bottle with rubber bulb and gold plated top fittings has paper DeVilbiss sticker. Circa 1925. (4-1/4'').

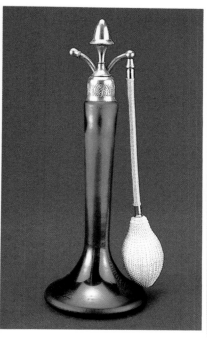

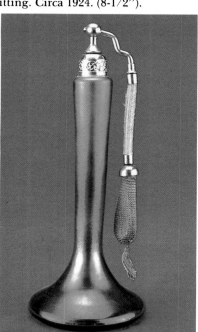

3. Steuben blue Aurene bottle for De Vilbiss. Circa 1924. (9-1/2''). 4. Frosted glass bottle with gold decoration and gold-plated top. Circa 1921. (9-1/4'').

6. Perfume bottle with long glass dapper in orchid glass. Marked 'DeVilbiss' in gold on bottom. Circa 20's. (6-1/4''). 7. Opaque black glass marked 'DeVilbiss' bottle with nickel-plated fittings. Circa 20's. (6'').

9. DeVilbiss atomizer with Steuben glass bottle shown in 1925 mail order catalog. (6-1/4''). 10. Opaque orange glass atomizer sold in mail order catalog during 1925 marked 'DeVilbiss made in U.S.A.' (6-1/2'').

12. Clear engraved glass bottle with blue enamelled foot marked 'De Vilbiss''. Circa 1925. (6-1/2''). 13. Blue Aurene bottle by Steuben for De Vilbiss with modified top fitting. Circa 1924. (8-1/2'').

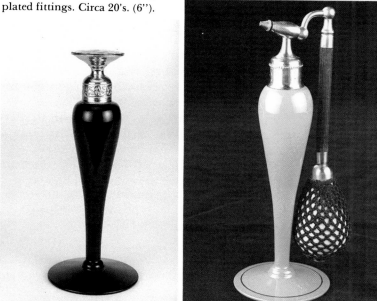

trips to Europe beginning in 1910 just to obtain glassware for his perfumizers. The well-known Steuben, Fenton, and Cambridge glass companies were among his American suppliers. The European bottles were made in France, Czechoslovakia, and Italy. In France the firm of Verreries Brosse supplied some of the atomizer bottles. From about the mid-twenties thru 1938 Czechoslovakia was supplying a large portion of the glass bottles. The final decoraton of the glass bottle blanks took place at the DeVilbiss manufacturing plant.

The top fittings were made of brass, then plated with gold or nichol. The most rare are those of sterling silver. In the thirties chrome fittings replaced the nichol ones. The atomizer bulbs were made of rubber, either left plain or covered with hand-crocheted silk web.

The perfumizers were categorized by the company under a letters system. The "A" series were of less expensive quality and marked only with a paper label. The "B" series were of fine quality and had the DeVilbiss name in gold or silver on the bottom of the bottle. The company name was also either moulded into the bottle glass, lettered on the metal collar, or embossed on the rubber bulb. The porcelain containers used in the sixties are marked with a "DEV" on the bottom.

The 1920's atomizers are characterized for the most part by tall, slender, and elegant shapes. By the early 1930's DeVilbiss started a heavy advertising campaign promoting new, stream-lined, Deco inspired bottles with shiny chrome or gold fittings. This campaign also included square, onyx looking atomizers in jade, rose, and black, and introduced a non-evaporating atomizer head. In 1934, DeVilbiss introduced their first atomizer made especially for cologne which would hold up to six ounces. Their sales promotion for the Christmas of 1934 included the line "imported and domestic glass, modern and period designs," indicating the wide variety of styles available. In 1936 covered atomizers shaped like urns or ginger jars were the new innovation. Also in 1936, beautiful, well-made Czechoslovakian cut crystal atomizers were introduced. During the years of World War II, DeVilbiss relied on U.S. companies such as Fenton to supply all the needed bottles. In 1928 the first ad for a DeVilbiss pump top spray bottle, with a classic 1920's shape, appeared. The late 1940's and 50's saw the inclusion of German made bottles and Murano glass bottles from Italy to the product line. China figural bottles made in Japan with DeVilbiss magic-mist bulbless atomizer tops were sold in the 1960's.

16. Engraved blue glass bottle for DeVilbiss by Steuben. Circa 1927. (6-1/4").

17. Amber glass bottle with modified DeVilbiss top fitting. Circa late 20's. (7").
18. Cranberry glass set with 22-karat gold encrusting marked 'DeVilbiss'. Circa 1928. (7").

14. Small blue Aurene bottle with nickelplated top by Steuben for DeVilbiss. Circa 1924. (6").

15. Pink cased glass atomizer with DeVilbiss marked on top fitting. Circa 1927. (4-1/2").

19. Gold Aurene bottle by Steuben for DeVilbiss with atomizer top patented in 1928. (7'').

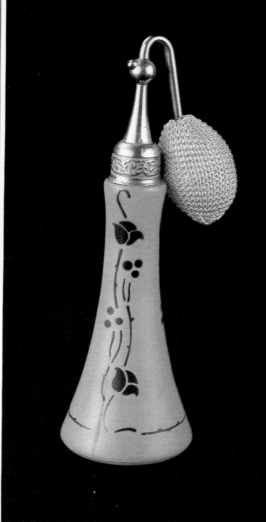

21. Opaque pink bottle with black Art Deco decoration and modified top marked 'DeVilbiss'. Circa late 20's. (7-1/4'').

23. The patent for the top on this engraved glass bottle was filed in February 1930. (6-1/2'').

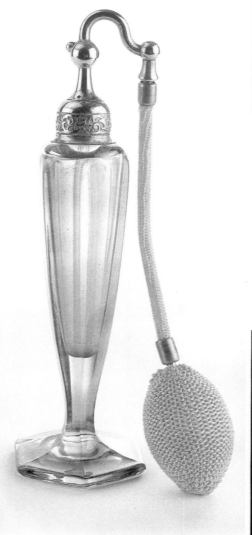

20. Orchid glass bottle with gold plated top fittings signed 'DeVilbiss'. Circa late 20's. (7'').

22. Rare marked 'DeVilbiss' vanity set encrusted with 22 karat gold and decorated with enameled roses. Circa 1924. (9-1/4'').

24. The rubber bulb on this atomizer is embossed with the name 'DeVilbiss'. Circa 1930. (6-1/2'').

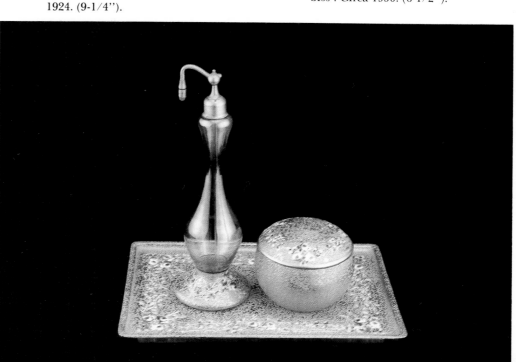

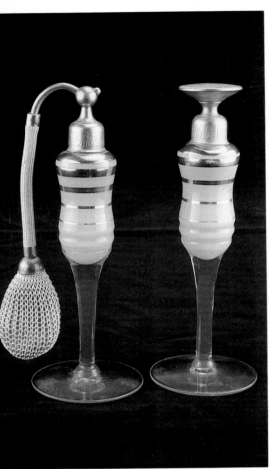

The DeVilbiss Co., which is still in business today, discontinued their atomizer line in 1969. They now manufacture fine paint sprayers, humidifiers, and other medical equipment.

The oldest, continuously operated atomizer company in the United States is the T.J. Holmes Co. founded in 1870 by Thomas Jefferson Holmes in Massachusetts. The company originally manufactured only medical atommizers for nose and throat spray applications, but on March 3, 1876 a patent for a perfume atomizer designed by Mr. Holmes was applied for. On May 1, 1876 a trademark was filed for the word "Favorite" to be used for perfumers and atomizers. The push to sell atomizers did not really begin, however, until the 1930's when Mr. Fred W. Lohse was president of the company.

Many patents for perfume atomizers were issued to Mr. Lohse during the 1930's. Another person who received patents for perfume atomizers and assigned them to the T.J. Holmes Co. was Mr. Fred R. High. Mr. High was born in Germany under the name Fritz Hoch and changed it after emigrating to the U.S. in the late 1930's. Mr. High was for many years the vice-president in charge of manufacturing for T.J. Holmes Co. and designed many of their atomizers during the 1940's, 1950's, and 1960's.

T.J. Holmes always manufactured the atomizer tops used on their products but purchased the glass bottles elsewhere. During the 1930's and 1940's all the glass used was purchased from U.S. companies such as Duncan & Miller. It became impossible in the early 1950's for them to obtain relatively *short production runs* of fancy bottles from U.S. manufacturers, so the company turned to Eastern Europe. During the 1950's and through much of the 1960's, most of their bottles were imported from West Germany, Austria, and Italy. During the 1970's the company imported bottles from Japan. In the company's current catalog they have over one

25. This set sold in mail order catalogs, was available in green, peach, coral, and black. Circa 1931. (6-1/2").

26. This ad cited the advantages of DeVilbiss atomizers in 1931.

27. 1931 advertisement featuring a Deco inspired DeVilbiss atomizer.

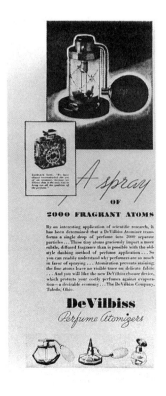

28. DeVilbiss advertisement in 1933 with an endorsement by Guerlain perfumes.

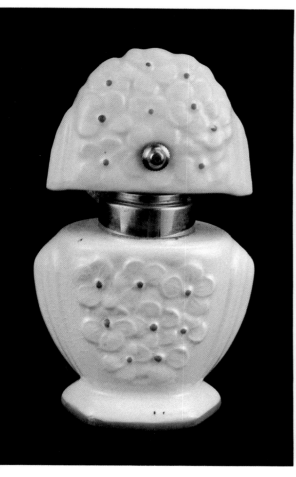

29. Lenox china made this bottle for DeVilbiss patented in 1936. (6-3/4'').

30. This cut glass atomizer, patented in 1936 by DeVilbiss, has an acid etched Czechoslovakian mark. (5-1/2'').

hundred different perfume bottles and atomizers, almost all in more than one color of glass, imported from Japan, Taiwan, and France.

T.J. Holmes atomizers can be identified by their trademark "Holmspray" etched on the metal fittings or a paper label attached to the bottom.

Bohemian glass makers made many beautifully embellished atomizer bottles from the last quarter of the 19th Century to about 1917. A vast number of imported Bohemian glass atomizers reached the American market, especially, between the years 1900-1916. Mail order and wholesale catalogues of this era show an interesting range of Bohemian atomizers costing, retail, as little as 39¢ to the large sum of $1.29 for a very ornate bottle. The bottles were ornately shaped, opaque or transparent colored glass with moulded, cut, gilt, enamel, or combined decoration. The bulbs were of plain rubber or covered with elegant silk net. The metal fittings were gilt or nickel-plated and occasionally had a bottle stand plated to match.

The best and easiest way of determining the age of an atomizer is by the style and type of glass used and more importantly the top fittings. The patents included in this book should be of an enormous help in dating your bottles accurately. The photographs shown of bottles with atomizer tops that were not patented were dated by using old catalogues, magazine ads, and articles. The older bottles will have a brass or glass perfume tube. Do not discard the broken atomizer top if you replace it with a new one. It is an original part of the atomizer adding to its value and makes dating at a later time that much simpler.

In addition, atomizers were made in France, England, Czechoslovakia, Italy, and the U.S. and also by manufacturers such as Baccaret, Wedgewood, D'Argental, Val St. Lambert, Marcel Franck, Lalique, Limoges, Moser, Fenton, Gallé, Steuben, Volupte, and Stevens & Williams.

32. Christmas 1937 ad showing a number of different DeVilbiss atomizers.

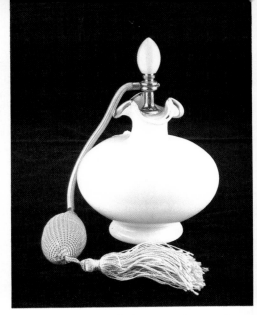

33. Opalescent glass atomizer bottle by Fenton Glass Co. for DeVilbiss marked 'made in U.S.A.' Circa 1941. (4'').

36. Clear atomizer with 'made in U.S.A. DeVilbiss' moulded on bottom of bottle. Circa 40's. (3'').

37. Pink cased glass atomizer made in France with gold plated fittings has paper DeVilbiss label. Circa 1950. (6'').

34. Coin dot pattern atomizer bottle by Fenton for DeVilbiss. Circa 1940's. (4-3/4'').

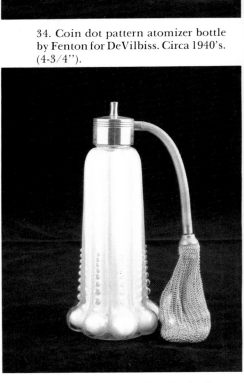

35. Cased glass atomizer bottle, by Fenton for DeVilbiss, advertised in 1947 fashion magazine. (6'').

38—41. Murano glass bottles from filigree pump spray covers. Paper labels marked 'Italy' and 'DeVilbiss'. Circa 1955.

39. Murano glass bottles.

41. Murano glass bottles.

42. DeVilbiss paper label identifies this hand decorated atomizer. Circa 1960. (4'').

43. Ball shaped, spiral pattern, pump spray atomizer with original paper label marked 'DeVilbiss made in Italy'. Circa 1960. (4-3/4'').

44. Three styles of the Japanese made DeVilbiss pump spray atomizer. Circa 60's. (a. h. 4-1/2'').

40. Murano glass bottles.

45. Opalescent glass bottle designed by F.R. Hoch for T.J. Holmes Co. was patented in 1941. (5'').

48. Three piece crystal dresser set marked 'Holmspray' on atomizer made in Eastern Europe. Circa 1955. (6'').

46. Patented in 1948 this American glass T.J. Holmes bottle was designed by F.R. High. (2-3/4'').

49. Blue crystal atomizer marked 'Holmspray' on the top made in Eastern Europe. Circa 1955. (3-1/2'').

50. Cobalt blue satin glass bottle made in Japan for T.J. Holmes Co. Circa 1985. (5-1/8'').

47. T.J. Holmes atomizer with embossed 'made in USA' on bottom of bottle. Circa 1950. (2-1/4'').

51. Black glass atomizer bottle made in Taiwan for T.J. Holmes Co. Circa 1985. (3-1/4'').

55. Green Wedgwood of England atomizer. Circa 1920's. (5-1/4").

52. Bohemian atomizer decorated with gold enameling. Circa 1900. (5").

56. Blue Wedgwood of England atomizer with Marcel Franck of France fittings. Circa 1940's. (3-1/2").

53. Bell-shaped Bohemian atomizer with enameled decoration. Circa 1900. (3-1/2").

54. Green glass Bohemian atomizer with gold enameling. Circa 1900. (4").

57. Tall cut glass atomizer with hand-tied silk bulb cover. Circa 1916. (5").

61. Baccarat blank with hand painted windmill scene. Circa 1917-1925. (6-3/4'').

58. Art Deco pyramid shaped cut glass atomizer. Circa 1930. (4-1/2'').

60. Hand painted atomizer bottle by the artist Malo on Baccarat blank. Circa 1917-1925. (8'').

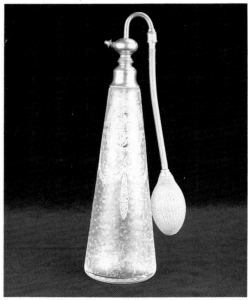

62. Atomizer with acid etched glass and gold decoration marked Baccarat. Circa 1926. (11'').

59. Swiss music boxes with atomizer tops were sold from the thirties to the early fifties. Circa 30's. (6'').

63. Baccarat marked bottle with etched decoration. Circa 1924. (5-1/4'').

64. Simple clear glass and gold atomizer marked Baccarat. Circa 1930's. (4-1/4").

65. Art Nouveau inspired French atomizer with dancing nude. Circa 1920. (6").

67. Porcelain atomizer decorated with Art Deco flowers signed 'Limoges France'. Circa 1920's. (6").

66. Unusual mottled glass cased with clear satin with top fittings marked 'made in France'. Circa 20's. (7-1/4").

68. Pink shading to clear glass atomizer with French atomizer top. Circa 20's. (7").

69. French atomizer with dancing ladies. Attributed Sabino. Circa 20's. (4-1/2").

75. Purse atomizer shaped like a cigarette lighter was by Elizabeth Ames. Circa 1952. (1-3/4'').

70. French atomizer with hand painted decoration. Circa 1918. (6'').

73. Brass purse atomizer decorated with mother-of-pearl was made in France. Circa 1924. (2-1/2'').

74. Purse atomizer by Marcel Franck was patented in the U.S. in 1949. (2-3/4'').

71. Red and black French style cameo glass atomizer. Circa 1915. (7'').

72. Marcel Franck atomizer made in France was patented in the U.S. in 1937. (3'').

76. Bohemian style glass atomizer bottle with French atomizer top. Circa 20's. (7-1/4'').

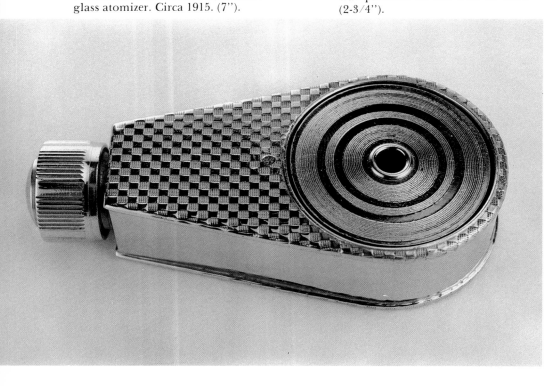

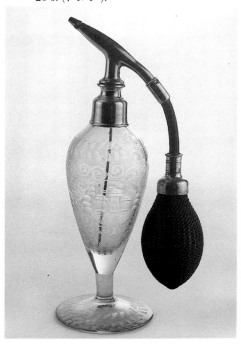

77. Bohemian style flashed, cut to clear bottle with fittings marked 'U.S.A.'. Circa 1920's. (7'').

78. Bohemian style cut to clear bottle with French atomizer top. Circa 1920's. (8-1/4'').

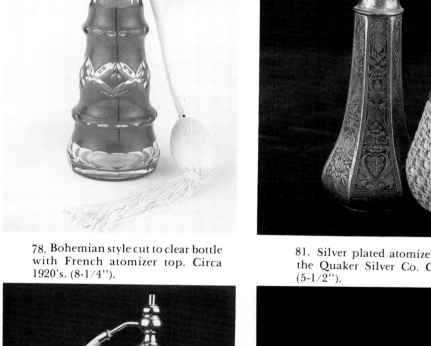

81. Silver plated atomizer bottle by the Quaker Silver Co. Circa 1925. (5-1/2'').

83. Pressed glass atomizer with stenciled heart decoration. Circa 1950's. (5-1/4'').

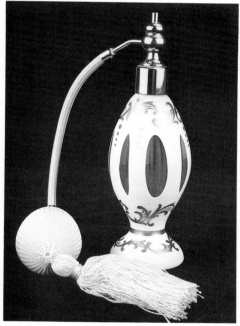

79. Opaque white cased over cranberry glass atomizer bottle. Circa 1900. (7-1/4'').

80. Cased glass atomizer with top fittings marked 'made in Germany'. Circa 1920's. (8-1/4'').

82. China poodle bottle with pump spray top made in Japan. Circa 1960. (4-3/4'').

84. Yellow glass bottle with flower pump spray top marked 'made in W. Germany'. Circa 1960. (7-1/4'').

86. Cut and enameled atomizer with applied glass flowers made in Murano, Italy. Circa 1950's. (6'').

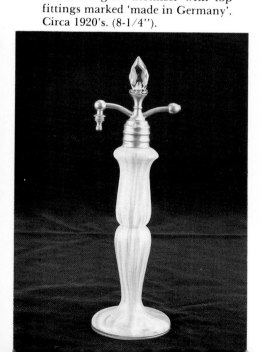

Chapter 7

Czechoslovakian Bottles

1. Rare, mould blown slag glass perfume bottle decorated with birds and flowers. Beside the acid-etched mark, the original 'Ingrid' importers paper label is on the bottom. (5").

To many collectors Czechoslovakian hand-cut crystal perfume bottles are the epitome of the bottle makers art. The attention to every detail from the raw blank to the finishing touches resulted in an almost flawless product. Made for only about twenty years (1918-1938), the individual makers and factories are shrouded in mystery, the information lost or destroyed during the struggle of World War II.

The nation of Czechoslovakia, comprising the Slovak and Czech provinces including Bohemia, formerly governed by the Austrian Hapsburgs, came into being in October, 1918, just before the surrender of Austria-Hungary in World War I. There were two main causes for the emergence of the new country: the wish of the allies to hasten the defeat of the Austro-Hungarian Empire by furthering the nationalist aspirations of the people, and the revolutionary stance of the people themselves. In 1919 Austria confirmed the independence of the new country by signing the Treaty of Saint-Germain. In 1920 the Czechoslovakian National Assembly formally established a government similar to that of France consisting of an elected president and legislature.

The State, proud of its rich and varied Bohemian glassmaking tradition, considered glassmaking to be Czechoslovakia's national art form. In 1920 there were three glassmaking schools in operation teaching and improving all aspects of the field. Before Hitler gained control of the country in 1939, over six hundred glass factories were in operation. In 1946, after the end of World War II, the New Communist Regime in Czechoslovakia nationalized the glass industry.

The importation of Czechoslovakian cut, mould-blown, and pressed glass perfume and atomizer bottles to the U.S. reached its peak between the years 1928-1938. Many American firms imported them including DeVilbiss, Wolflé, Morlee, Ingrid, E&JP, Tubby, E&TB, the Jones Co. of Chicago, Premire, Aristo, Paris decorators, Diamond Nasco, and of course Irice. Innumerable high quality bottles of different designs, decoration, and styles flowed into this nation's drug, department, and gift stores. The low prices some of these bottles sold for is truly amazing. In 1932, a Sears mail order catalog pictured a cut glass purse bottle for 47¢ and a beautiful cut glass dresser bottle for 98¢.

Besides a nearly infinite number of geometric patterns, many cut crystal bottles show the influence of the Art Nouveau and Art Deco style movements. Ruth A. Forsythe, in her book "Made In Czechoslovakia", lists the array of colors made and their rarity. The most common bottle colors used were clear crystal, then pink, blue, green, and amethyst. The rarest colors used were red, vaseline, heather, and clear crystal with a colored foot and stopper. In between the two came the bottle colors topaz, amber, transparent black, and opaque black. Many times the same bottle design was made with both colored crystal bases and clear crystal stoppers, and clear crystal bases with colored crystal stoppers. Some of the bases came in two separate pieces that were then glued together. The cut glass stoppers used with the bottles were hand ground to fit each bottle individually. A few of the stoppers were decorated with cutting on each side. The Czechoslovakian factories marked their bottles with either an acid etched or moulded mark on the bottom, a tiny metal plate, or an engraved signature on metal atomizer fittings.

2. In 1937 Marco Liquor Stores of Chicago imported thousands of Czechoslovakian and French perfume bottles to the U.S. This hand blown bottle was made in Czechoslovakia. (2-1/4").

3. Czechoslovakian perfume bottle used to hold imported liquers by Marco Liquor Stores of Chicago. The bottle is handblown with ground stopper and has paper label marked 'made in Czechoslovakia.' Circa 1937. (2-3/4").

4. Pressed clear glass perfume bottle with opaque black stopper. (5").

Czechoslovakian perfume bottles were also used for commercial purposes. Elsa Schiaparelli introduced her "Shocking" perfume in hand-etched bottles made in Czechoslovakia and the French perfume "Triomphe", introduced to the U.S. in 1934, was bottled in hand-cut crystal. In 1937 Marco Liquor Stores of Chicago imported thousands of Czechoslovakian and French perfume bottles to hold liqueurs. The bottles were hand blown and had ground stoppers. There are a few three and four part mould bottles. There appears to be a minimum of at least sixteen styles in all. The Marco liqueur perfume bottles have an oval with numbers embossed on the bottom and a paper label that has "made in Czechoslovakia" on it.

9—23. Atomizers made in Czecho-slovakia.

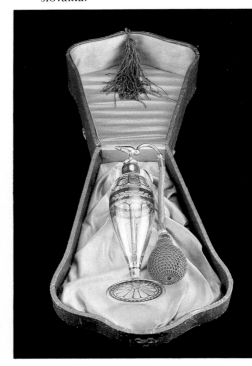

9. 7-1/4"

5. Tall Depression era type perfume bottle with hand painted decoration. (6-1/4").

7. Mould blown bottle, hand decorated in white and red. (6").

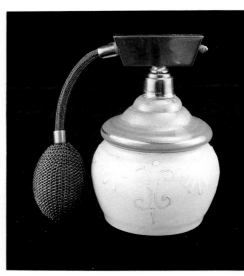

10. 4-1/2"

6. Faceted crystal dresser bottle with pink and white hand enameled decoration. Numbered stopper. (7-1/2").

8. Heavy Czechoslovakian paper weight bottle has a bird on a ball stopper. Similar stoppers were made by Imperial and Pairpoint in the 1940's. (7-1/2").

11. 4"

12.

15. 6-3/4''

18. 7-1/2''

13. 4-1/2''

16. 7-1/2''

17. 7-1/2''

19. 7-1/2''

20. 5-1/2''

14. 8-1/2''

24—26. Perfume bottles with long glass dappers were usually made to match an atomizer.

24. 7"

21. 4"

25. 6-1/2"

26. 5-1/4"

22. 7-1/2"

23. 4"

31. Unusual purse bottle with red fox head top. Embossed 'Irice' on the bottom. (3'').

32. Engraved crystal purse bottle with jeweled top. (3'').

27—28. Cased glass miniature perfume bottles with opaque black cut glass stoppers are hand painted. (2-1/2'').

29. Pair of small purse bottles decorated with jewel tops and beads on a chain. (2-1/4'').

30. Pair of hand painted miniature crystal bottles. (2-1/2'').

33. Triangular purse bottle decorated with glass jewels and filigree. Small metal Czechoslovakian tag is visible on the cap. Purse bottles are usually marked in this manner. (3'').

34. Three filigree purse bottles. (2-1/2'').

35. Three filigree purse bottles. (2-1/4'').

36. Purple and clear cut glass miniature set with matching tray. (2'').

37. Four cut glass purse bottles. (a.h. 2'').

38. Rare miniature cut glass bottle set with stoppers shaped like the four card suits. (2-1/2'').

39. Three cut glass purse bottles. (2'').

40. Cut glass purse or miniatue bottle with red stopper. (2'').

41—155. Cut crystal perfume bottles all acid etched marked 'Czechoslovakia.'　　41. 4-3/4''

42. 6''

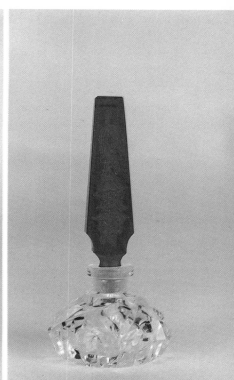

43. 6-1/2"

45. 4"

48. 4-1/4"

44. 6"

46. 4-1/2"

49. 5"

47. 6-1/2"

50.5''

53. 4-1/4''

55. 4-1/2''

51. 5-3/4''

54. 4-1/2''

52. 4-1/4''

56. 5-1/4''

57. 7-1/2''

59. 6-1/4''

58. 6''

60.

61. 3-3/4''

64. 6''

66. 4-1/4''

62. 5-1/2''

65. 3-1/4''

67. 6-1/4''

68. 5''

69. 5''

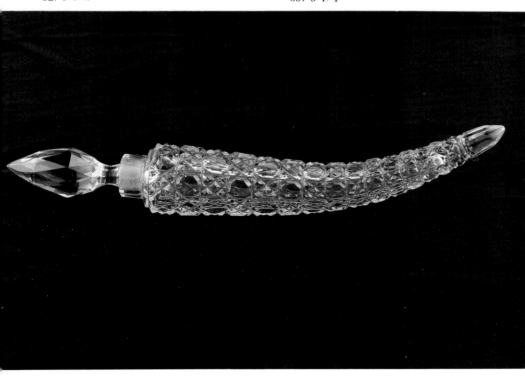

70. 5-1/2"

73. 5"

71. 6"

72. 5-3/4"

74. 4-7/8"

75. 4-3/4"

76. 4-1/2''

79. 8''

80. 4-3/4''

77. 4-1/2''

78. 4-3/4''

81. 8-1/2''

82. 7''

83. 5-3/4''

84. 7''

85. 5''

86. 6-3/4''

87. 7''

88. 4-1/2''

89. 9-3/8''

90. 7-1/4''

91. 4-3/4''

93. 5- 3/4''

96. 6- 3/4''

92. 4-1/2''

94. 6''

95. 5-3/4''

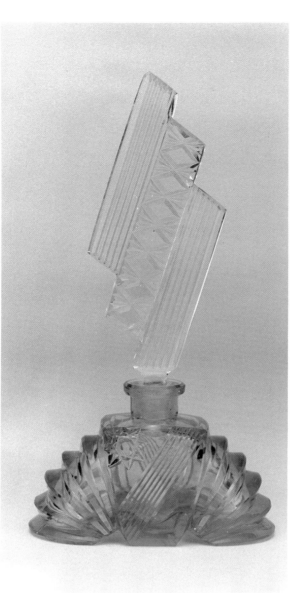

100. 6-1/2''

98. 7''

101. 7''

97. 6''

99. 6-1/4''

102. 5-1/4''

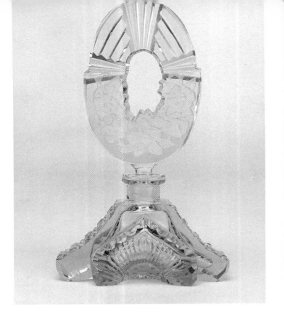

103. 5-3/4''

104. 5-3/4''

107. 5-3/4''

105. 3''   106. 5-1/2''

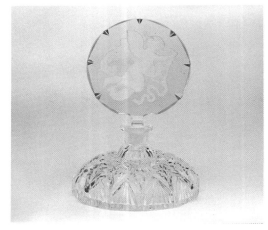

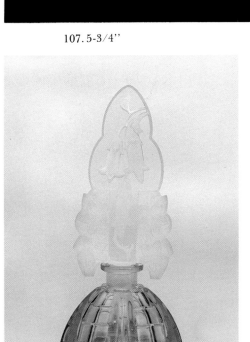

108. 7-1/4''

109. 7-1/4''

110. 3- 1/4''

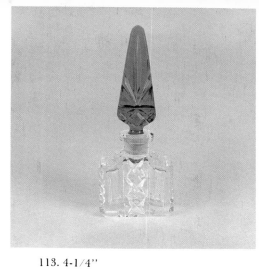

113. 4-1/4''

114. 8-1/4''

111. 5''

112. 6-3/4''

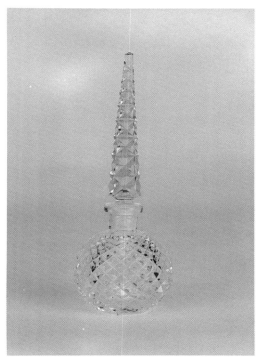

115. 5-1/2''

116. 6-1/4''

118. 6''

120. 4-1/2''

117. 7-3/4''

119. 5-1/8''

121. 5-1/4''

122. 5-1/2''

123. 5-3/4''

124. 7-3/4''

125. 5-3/4''

128. 6-3/4''

127. 5-1/2''

129. 6-3/4''

130. 6-1/2''

132. 6-3/4''

131. 6- 1/2''

133. 6-1/2"

135. 4-3/4"

134. 7-1/2"

136. 5-3/4''

138. 5-3/4''

140. 6-1/2''

137. 5-1/2''

139. 5-3/4''

141. 6-1/2''

142. 6-3/4''

143. 7''

144. 6-7/8''

146. 6-3/4''

148. 4-3/4''

145. 7-1/4''

147. 5''

149. 4-3/4''

117

150. 4-3/4"

152. 5"

154. 5-3/4"

151. 4-3/4"

153. 5-1/2"

155. 5-3/4"

Commercial Bottles

In today's collectibles market there is a rapidly growing interest in commercial perfume bottles. The decoration and designs that have been used for commercial perfume bottles is almost limitless. For each new perfume or cologne marketed, a wide range of containers were needed from small sample bottles to deluxe presentation bottles. It was in the last century that the practice of commissioning the design of a bottle to hold a particular perfume by a specific company began. Two advances in bottle making helped make it possible to standardize the bottles used for perfumes and colognes.

The first advance was the accomplishment of mechanizing the mould blown glass method of manufacture beginning in the 1880's. The glass was gathered automatically or by the glassworker's rod and placed in the blank mould where it was blown by compressed air. The blank was then hand transferred from the blank mould to the second, finishing mould. After cooling, the bottle surface was polished with felt polishing wheels or by hand with cork to bring forth the sparkle and clarity of the glass. Even today, the highest quality perfume bottles are still made semi-automatically.

The second advance was the invention of an automatic bottle making machine patented in 1891 by J. Michael Owens. The machine accomplished every step from shaping the molten glass to cooling the completed bottle. By the early 1900's much of the commercial bottle manufacturing in America had become automated. As advances were made in automatic production a greater range of shapes became available, but the semi-automatic technique was still the only way to manufacture prestigious, heavy weight flacons.

Advances in the perfume trade from 1870 on were also taking place. Chemists were discovering amazing synthetic fragrance chemicals to replace some of the expensive natural essential oils needed in perfume manufacturing. The synthetics helped lower the price of the finished product thus expanding the market of purchasers. From about 1900 on, the majority of perfumes were made with a combination of both artificial and natural products.

In Europe at the beginning of the century the perfume trade was dominated by only a small number of makers such as Lubin, L.T. Piver, Houbigant, and Guerlain. Within a few short years two new firms, Coty and Caron, were to open and challenge the leadership of the perfume market.

The name Guerlain has been associated with fine perfumes for over 150 years. The original founder of the company was Pierre Francois Guerlain from Picardy. He opened his first shop selling smelling salts, soaps, and fragrances in 1828 in Paris on the Rue de Rivoli. He became so successful that in 1848 the shop was moved to the fashion center of Paris on the Rue de la Paix. Guerlain was appointed perfumer to the Court of Napoleon II and Empress Eugéie in 1853. "Eue Imperiale" was created especially for the Empress by Guerlain around 1853. His son Aimée Guerlain, applied for their first U.S. trademark for the perfume "Eau Imperiale" label on February 25, 1875. The firm of Park and Tilford of New York became Guerlain's agents in the U.S. in 1884.

Pierre Guerlain's sons Aimée and Gabriel took over control of the firm in 1890. In 1889 Aimée created "Jicky", one of the first modern perfumes to

1. Geisha Girl brand perfume was made by Japanese Mfrs. of Chicago. Circa 1900. (3-1/2").

2. English commercial wheelbarrow bottle used to hold either perfume or smelling salts. Circa 1885. (3-1/2" long).

5. Tappan of New York sold cologne in this hand shaped bottle. Circa 1900. (5" long).

3. Typical commercial bottle of the turn-of-the-century has paper label reading 'A. P. Babcock Co. New York'. (6-1/2").

6. Caron of Paris made the perfume "Le Narcisse Noir" originally for export to other countries. U.S. introduction 1912. (2-1/2", 3-1/2", 5-1/2").

4. Theo Ricksecker of New York started making perfume in 1881. This handpainted heart perfume bottle necklace is marked 'Ricksecker perfumer N.Y.'. (2-1/2").

7. Guerlain used the same Baccaret bottle for "L'Heure Bleue" introduced to the U.S. in 1913 and "Mitsouko" introduced to the U.S. in 1922. (5-1/4").

8. Houbigant of Paris, France established in 1775 introduced "Quelques Fleurs" to the U.S. in 1913.

9. Vivaudou's "Mavis" perfume was U.S. trademarked in 1915 and the bottle patented in 1916. (8-1/2").

12. This frosted bottle of "Jonteel" perfume was sold exclusively through the Rexall drug stores. Circa 1918. (3-3/4").

13. A bottle of "Juneve' by Langloois with the original box. Langlois was a brand name trademarked by the United Drug Co. of Boston, Massachusetts in 1918. Circa 1920. (5-1/2").

14. Houbigant travel set with the perfumes "Quelques Fleurs" and "Ideal" in a red leather case. Circa 20's. (3").

10. Another exported perfume by Caron was "Petit Mimosa" introduced to the U.S. in 1917. (3-3/4").

11. Hand painted lacquer box made in Japan held two Vantine of N.Y. perfume bottles. Circa 1917. (2").

15. Frosted glass bottle decorated with moulded nude has paper sticker reading "Wildewood Toilet Water" on it. Circa 1920. (6-1/2").

16. This bottle made in France with a figural stopper was for "Glyciane" by Favolys. The name J. Viard is embossed on the bottom of the bottle. Circa 1920's. (3-1/2").

17. "Le Golliwogg" by Vigny has a black glass head stopper topped with fur for hair. Bottle and name are based on a character created by Florence K. Upton around the turn of the century. The bottle was made by Verreries Brosse. U.S. introduction 1922. (3-1/2").

contain synthetic oils. Gabriel Guerlain contributed by designing the bottle made by Baccarat.

Jacques Guerlain, Pierre Guelain's grandson, became a creative director for the firm early in this century. He is responsible for some of Guerlain's best selling perfumes. Jacques created "L'Heure Bleue" introduced to the U.S. in 1913, and "Shalimar" introduced to the U.S. in 1926.

A beautiful collection of perfume bottles can be made just from the bottles produced for Guerlain. The most sought-after bottle is the one for "Champs Elysées" made and designed by Baccarat. Collectors have nicknamed it the "turtle" bottle. Shaped like a turtle in clear faceted crystal the bottle has a flat space on the front on which a label was placed. The bottle was introduced about 1904.

The firm of Houbigant, one of the biggest perfume producers in the United States today, was originally founded in 1775 by Jean-Francois Houbigant in Paris. Houbigant opened his master perfumer's shop at 19, Faubourg Saint-Honoré under a sign meaning 'The Flower Basket'. France was under the rule of Louis XVI at the time, and Houbigant sold wig powder, perfume, pommade, fans, and gloves. He soon became the fashionable perfumer and enjoyed the patronage of both the nobility and clergy. Armand-Gustave Houbigant, Jean-Francois' son, took over control of the business in 1807. Regimes and clienteles changed but the firm served them all beautifully. Among Houbigant's most successful perfumes were "Ideal" introduced in 1900, "Coeur de Jeannette" introduced in 1899, and "Quelques Fleurs" created by Robert Bienaimé in 1912. Many of the bottles used by Houbigant were made by Baccarat, Lalique, and recently Saint Gobain Desjonquères.

The famous perfume house of Coty was founded by Francois Sportuno of Corsica. He learned how to compound perfumes from an apothecary named Raymond Goery in his spare time. He furthered his education in the perfume trade by a visit to the Grasse distilleries. Coty opened his first shop in Paris on the Rue de la Boétie with money borrowed from his family and wholesale perfume houses. About this time Francois Sportuno changed his name to Coty, thinking it would be easier for his customers to say and remember. His first perfume was "La Rose Jacqueminot", a cabbage rose scent named for a well-known general. In 1904 Coty approached a large store in Paris attempting to sell his perfume. He was turned away before he had an opportunity to demonstrate his fragrances. However, Coty happened to break a bottle of his perfume in the store, allowing the clientel to experience one of his scents. The store then revised its decision and began to sell Coty fragrances.

Many factors contributed to Coty's phenomenal success in the perfume business. He was among the first to market small bottles of his perfumes at prices the working class could afford. Coty teamed up with the innovative designer René Lalique so that the bottles mass produced for his perfumes were of the highest quality. Coty was also among the first of the French perfume houses to perceive and exploit the large U.S. marketplace.

The well-known perfume house of Caron was started in 1903 by Ernest Daltroff. Daltroff was fascinated by scent, so he purchased a perfumery in Asnières not far from Paris. He also bought out the rights and shop of one Anna-Marie Caron and kept the name, thinking it would sound and look better on packaging. In 1904 Daltroff met Fèlicie Vanpouille, a young dressmaker. She designed the bottle for the Caron perfume "Chantecler" in 1906. Vanpouille gave up dressmaking and became Daltroff's lover and active business partner, taking charge of design and packaging. Many of the bottles used by Caron were designed by her. In 1939, with war on the horizon, Daltroff, a Jew, left Paris for Canada. In 1941 he died of cancer and Félicie Vanpouille became the sole owner of the firm they built.

The Caron company, right from the start, exported their products abroad. Throughout its history the vast majority of its products went from France to foreign markets such as the U.S., England, and South America. Not until the 1930's were Caron perfumes easily attainable in France.

The easiest to recognize of Caron's perfume bottles is the squatty clear bottle with the opaque black flower stopper used for "Narcisse Noir" (Black

Narcissus) made and designed by Baccarat and introduced in 1912. The unpatented "Narcisse Noir" bottle design was widely copied by other firms. There would be differences in the stopper color or design but at first glance the copies would fool the eye. The copied bottles used by other companies almost always held a narcissus perfume. Caron learned a valuable lesson and from then on usually patented the bottle designs.

In America during the last quarter of the 19th century there were many native perfume houses competing with the European houses for customers. Some of the American perfume makers were Larkin of Buffalo, N.Y., McKesson & Robbins, Theo Ricksecker of New York, Eastman of Philadelphia, Herman Tappan, Colgate, Palmer, Richard Hudnut, Percy E. Page, and the Andrew Jergens Co. These companies used a variety of bottles in many different styles and shapes including figurals. Figural bottles were made in hundreds of patterns in America and in Europe. The perfumes were marketed almost exclusively by Retail druggists throughout the U.S.

Richard Hudnut was one of the most important founding fathers of the American cosmetics and perfume industry. As the son of a New York druggist he was familiar with the typical marketing of scent and perfume products in the late 19th century. After graduating from college he traveled to Paris. Here he noted the extensive and tasteful use of cosmetics and perfumes by all classes of women, unlike their American counterparts. Hudnut realized that if these products were correctly presented to American women a vast, virtually untapped market would open up. In the 1890's he converted the family drug store at Broadway and Ann Streets into an elegant show case for beauty products. No expense was spared and the shop fittings included marble floors, mahogany counters, and cut crystal chandeliers. At about the same time Hudnut's first fragrance "Violet Sec", trademarked in 1896, made its debut. The shop was very successful and attracted a large clientele. The wholesale end of the company eventually became so profitable that Hudnut closed his retail store. One of his best selling lines "Three Flowers" was introduced in 1915. Richard Hudnut sold the thriving business and retired a very wealthy man in 1916.

The twentieth century was to see the long-lasting marriage between high fashion and perfume occur. The couturier that started the trend of marketing fragrances to harmonize with his designs was Paul Poiret. A design genius, Poiret studied under both Worth and Doucet. He opened up his own couture salon in 1903 at the age of twenty-four and soon his colorful, exotic, fluid designs became the rage of fashion conscious Paris. In 1910 Poiret created the company Parfums Rosine, named after his small daughter, to produce perfume. He created his perfumes with the help of M. Schaller, a perfumer. The exotic packaging and bottles used by Rosine were designed by such well-known artists as Erté, Paul Iribe, George Lapape, Raoul Duffy, and Sonia Delaunay. A real push to capture an American market for Rosine perfumes was not made until the middle 1920's when the company opened an office in New York at 20 West 37th St.

With the ending of World War I the fragrance market entered a period of unprecedented growth that continued throughout the 1920's. Many factors contributed to the vogue for perfume including: vastly increased advertising, women holding jobs in ever increasing numbers, the shattering of the tabu against nice women using cosmetics, a change in the stereotype of the ideal woman from the passive, demure Victorian to the sophisticated, assertive flapper, and the popularity of moving pictures which created a desire for glamour. Also, other Paris fashion houses started to follow the lead set by Poiret in 1910 and began introducing perfumes under their labels. Among the houses that introduced fragrances were Nicole Groult, Weil, Worth, Callot, Chanel, Bechoff, Jean Patou, J. Suzanne Talbot, Martial et Armand, Lucien LeLong, Drecoll, Lenief, Molyneux, Lanvin, Kondazian, and Reboux. Some houses created a single perfume, while others evolved whole collections. Practically all of the large houses became known as parfumeurs de luxe, as well as dressmakers, and many houses of lesser size and fame added their contributions to the perfumes of the 1920's. The fitting-room in Paris was not considered complete without its atomizer bottle of the house perfume.

18. Travel set in original box of Richard Hudnut's "Three Flowers" products including tiny bottle of perfume. Circa 20's.

19. A Langlois bottle made in France with an inner glass stopper under the metal cap. Circa 1920's. (5").

20. A mushroom shaped stopper tops this bottle made by Baccarat for "Rue de La Paix" by Guerlain. U.S. introduction about 1922. (4").

23. An ad for the Houbigant perfume "Parfum d'Argeville" appeared in a 1922 fashion magazine. The bottle, possibly made by Baccarat, has a numbered stopper. (4-1/4").

26. Crystal bottle by Baccarat held the scent "Etre Aimée" by Gellé Frères of France. Circa 1920's. (3-3/4").

21. A cone-shaped bottle decorated with a spiral of vivid blue was made by Baccart for the Mury perfume "Jasmin". The container is of gold satin. U.S. introduction 1922. (4").

24. Houbigant filed for a U.S. patent in 1922 for this crystal purse bottle with brass top designed by Pierre Bassaler. (2-3/4").

25. "Nuit de Noel" introduced in 1922 by Caron was bottled in opaque black glass and packaged in a green-tasselled cardboard box covered with paper imitating shagreen. (4-5/8").

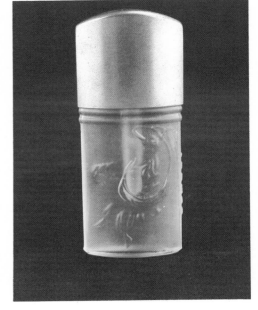

27. Miniature frosted purse flacons made in France called "Lionettes" contained different Vigny perfumes. A brass top covers an inner glass stopper. U.S. introduction 1923. (2-1/2").

22. Cobalt blue bottle made by Rene Lalique for "Canarina" perfume is decorated with a moulded eye pattern. Circa 1920's. (2").

28. A Christmas advertisement in 1924 identified this presentation bottle of "Lybis" toilet water by Luxor. (5-1/2").

29. A Baccarat glass Buddha contained "Subtilite" by Houbigant introduced to the U.S. in 1924. It was also produced in a less expensive clear glass bottle. (3-1/4").

31. Three sizes of "Chevalier De La Nuit" by Ciro of Paris, France. The bottle was designed by Guy T. Gibson and granted U.S. patent 68,779 on November 17, 1925. (4-3/4", 4", 3-1/4").

30. Shooting stars decorate this Verreries Brosse bottle for "Nuit Romantique" by Delyna of France. Circa 1920's. Photo courtesy Brosse U.S.A. Inc.

32. Black opaque glass bottle for "Chevalier De La Nuit" by Ciro shows superb detailing. (4-3/4").

33. Opaque black glass bottle with handsome gilded detailing was made by Verreries Brosse for "Nuit Romantique" by Delyna of France. Circa 1920's. (5-1/4").

One of the most chic and trend-setting perfumes introduced in the 1920's was "Chanel No. 5" blended by Ernest Beaux for Chanel. Gabrielle (Coco) Chanel was born in the French province of Auvergne in 1883. In 1914 she moved to Paris and opened a millinery shop. In 1916 she designed and presented her first complete fashion collection. By the mid-1920's she had established her reputation internationally and was generally considered to be the most important figure in the world of haute couture. As a couturier she usually emphasized a comfortable, easy to wear, classic costume consisting of a cardigan with turned-up sleeves, a full-cut skirt, loads of costume jewelry, short cut hair, and a sailor hat. In 1921 she brought out her first perfume "Chanel No. 5" named for her lucky number. The clear bottle, made by Brosse, had a simplicity and purity of line that is considered a classic today. In 1959 the bottle was honored by being placed in the New York's Museum of Modern Art's permanent collection.

For the most part, the couturiers and perfumers during the 1920's and 1930's dressed their perfume creations in elegant containers. During this time it was quite common for the most respected painters, sculptors, and decorators to design flacons for the perfume trade. A short list can include such illustrious artists as Gallé, Lalique, Dali, Léger, Picart, Lepape, Pegnet, Helleu, and Marie Laurencin. The chic bottles were made by companies in France like Lalique, Sue et Mare, J. Viard, Sabino, Verreries Brosse, Boutet de Monvel, Baccarat, Pochet et du Courval, and Daum. Beautiful commercial flacons were also made in Germany, Murano and Czechoslovakia. In America the firms of Wheaton and Carr-Lowry produced high quality bottles for the perfume trade. The final cost of the bottle may have been many times the cost of the perfume it held. The best made French perfume bottles usually had matching numbers or marks on both the bottle and stopper. They were put there by workmen in the glass houses and indicate that the bottle and stopper were made for each other.

Crystal perfume bottles signed Baccarat are among the most avidly sought by collectors. The Cristallenie de Baccarat was founded in 1822 in France and from the beginning produced beautiful, well-made perfume

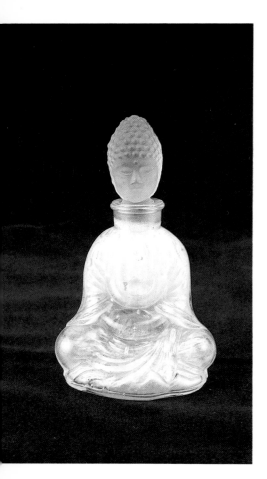

34. Budda figural bottle with frosted glass head has no marks or labels. Circa 1920's. (4'').

35. An ad appearing in 1923 for the Ramsès "Secret du Sphinx" perfume introduced in 1919.

36. In 1923 this ad appeared for the new Veolay (Violet) perfume "Les Sylvies".

Parfum--Les Sylvies -- a new Veolay *odeur* which Paris has acclaimed with delight.

37. A 1924 advertisement for Vigny of Paris perfumes featuring three of their best selling items. The bottles were made by Verreries Brosse.

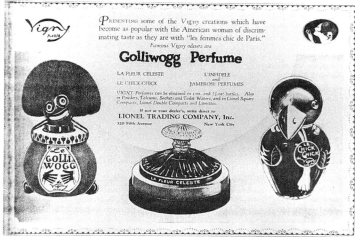

flacons. Between the years 1916-1970 many of the commercial bottles made by Baccarat were designed by George Chevalier. Among the many companies Baccarat has made perfume flacons for are Guerlain, Corday, Lentheric, Houbigant, Coty, Gellé Frères, Suzanne, Forest, Schiaparelli, Caron, Elizabeth Arden, Christian Dior, Richard Jaeckel, Lasco, Jean Patou, Molinard, and D'Orsay.

The Carr-Lowry Glass Co. was started in 1889 in the state of Maryland. From its inception until the 1950's, a special division of the glassworks made better hand-ground stoppered commercial bottles for the perfume trade. Among the many companies Carr-Lowry manufactures fully-automatic bottles for today are Geoffrey Beane, Lagerfeld, Avon, Guerlain, Chanel, Elizabeth Arden, Estee Lauder, and Warner.

The Wheaton glassworks in Milleville, New Jersey were started in 1888 by a pharmacist, Dr. T.C. Wheaton. The firm manufactured fully hand-blown bottles with ground-to-fit stoppers for the perfume trade until around World War II when the glassworks became fully automatic. Today the company, still family owned and controlled, produces bottles for such leading firms as Avon, Estee Lauder, Warner, Lancome, Coty, Dana, Max Factor, Elizabeth Arden, Revlon, Jovan, and Houbigant. The Wheaton trademark is W inside a circle.

After World War I there were two approaches used by European perfumers to market their products in America. The first was to appoint an agent or importing company in the U.S. to handle all sales, advertising, and promotion. Some examples are: Lionel N.Y. for Corday; M.C.M. Co. Inc., N.Y. for Mury; Harold F. Ritchie N.Y. for Grenoville; and the Chandon Co., N.Y. for Lubin. If a bottle has an importers label usually it means it was made in the 1920's or thereabouts. The second marketing approach used was for the perfume company to open an office or daughter company in the U.S. This proved most satisfactory in terms of marketing and sales so by the 1930's most companies had switched to this method.

American couture was quick to follow the Parisian fashion and introduce perfumes under their own names. The most successful of these was the New

40. Figural perfume bottle made in France and designed by Albert Mosheim for the Tre-Jur of New York company. Received U.S. patent 68,726 on November 10, 1925. (2-1/2").

38. An advertisement from 1926 showing four Grenoville of Paris, France products. Many of the Grenoville bottles were made by Verreries Brosse.

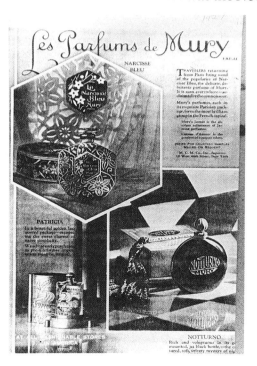

39. Advertisement used in 1927 by Mury of Paris to show three of their perfumes. Many of the Mury bottles were made by Verreries Brosse.

41. Molinard of France used this advertisement in 1937 to promote their perfumes in the U.S.

127

45. Fan decorated bottle with black glass fan stopper was made by Verreries Brosse for "Miracle" by Lentheric. The bottle was designed by Pierre de Wagner. It received U.S. patent 70,320 on June 8, 1926. (2-1/2").

42. Rare black opaque glass sailing ship bottle trimmed in gold for "Caravelle" by Marcel Guerlain of Paris, France. Circa 1924. (5").

46. Introduced to the U.S. in 1926, this crystal bottle made by Daum Nancy for "Toujours Fidèle" by D'Orsay has a bull dog stopper. (3-1/2").

43. Raquel of New York introduced this bottle for the fragrance "Olor de la Noche" in 1925. During the 1940's Massenet used a similar bottle for their perfumes. (5-3/4").

44. Easy to recognize, flattened, urn-shaped "Shalimar" by Guerlain bottle with blue stopper received U.S. patent 71,108 on September 21, 1926. The bottle was designed by Raymond Guerlain and made by Baccarat. Three other bottles for "Shalimar" have been used. (3-1/8").

47. "Chaine D'Or" by Grenoville introduced in the U.S. in 1926 is encased in a beige tasselled cardboard box covered with imitation shagreen. (2-3/4").

48. Beautiful jade green flacon for "Femme de Paris" by **YBRY** received U.S. patent 70,116 filed on October 15, 1925. The same bottle design by Simon Jaroslawski was used for "Dèsir du Coeur" in ruby and "Mon Ame" in amethyst. A less costly clear crystal bottle was added in 1934. (2-3/4").

49. The thick cut crystal bottle with a pedestal base and green enameled top held "Pois de senteur de Chez Moi" by Caron introduced in 1927. The smaller all crystal bottle was seen in a 1947 advertisement. A similar cut glass bottle is now being used to hold "Eau de Caron" introduced in 1980. (6" and 4").

50. Bottle with waffle design on the sides and frosted stopper was made by Verreries Brosse to hold "April Showers" by Cheramy introduced to the U.S. in 1927. Photo courtesy Brosse USA, Inc.

51. Jet black bottle held the fragrance "Byzance" by Grenoville introduced in the U.S. in 1926. The bottle was by Verreries Brosse. (2-1/2").

52. Bottle made by Verreries Brosse to hold "Le Narcisse Bleu" by Mury introduced to the U.S. in 1927. The bottle was copied in 1982 to hold "Ombre Rose" by Jean-Charles Brosseau. Photo courtesy Brosse USA, Inc.

53. Félicie Vanpouille, co-owner of Caron perfumes, designed many of the companies' bottles including this one for "Bellodgia" in 1927. (3-3/4").

54. This hand gilded and painted perfume bottle has a label on the bottom reading 'John Wanamaker Philadelphia Performie'. Circa 1920's. (3-1/4'').

55. Basic clear and gold Prince Matchabelli crown bottle was patented in 1927. An azure-blue crown for "Beloved" was introduced in 1950, a green crown bottle for "Wind Song" in 1953, and a red tinted bottle for "Added Attraction" in 1956.

York couturier Hattie Carnegie who had a salon on E. 49th Street in the 1920's. Her first perfume, introduced in 1928, was called simply "Hattie Carnegie". It was packaged in a charming black bottle similar to an inkwell decorated with small gold nosegays. The interesting portrait bottle used to hold several Hattie Carnegie perfumes was designed by Tommi Parzinger in 1937 and received U.S. patent 109,618.

In the 1920's two noted American based cosmetic firms entered the perfume field. They were Elizabeth Arden and Helena Rubinstein. The firm of Elizabeth Arden was founded by a Canadian nurse named Florence Graham of Woodbridge, Ontario. She opened her first beauty salon in 1910 in New York City. The salon approached hair and skin care scientifically and clients could buy the recommended beauty products to take home with them. By the early 1920's over 600 shops in the U.S. carried her products and Elizabeth Arden salons were operating in London, Paris, Boston, Chicago, Detroit, Washington, and San Francisco. In the beginning her salons sold fragrances by other companies such as Babani of Paris. By the late 1920's Elizabeth Arden was having perfumes blended in France especially for her company. Elizabeth Arden's best selling perfume was "Blue Grass" introduced in 1934. Elizabeth Arden perfumes were packaged, for the most part, in bottles made in France by such companies as Baccarat and Verreries Brosse. Two of my favorite bottles are the fan shaped flacon for "Cyclamen" introduced in 1938 and the hand holding torch flacon for "It's Your" introduced in 1939.

During the late 1920's the Polish born Helena Rubinstein was to expand her American salon and cosmetic business to include perfumes under her label. They proved to be a financial asset to her fast-growing beauty empire. Among the many bottles produced for Helena Rubinstein, is the ballerina bottle designed by Ladislas Medgyes for "Gala Performance" in 1940. Another interesting bottle shaped like a skyscraper was designed by Walter Nuckols in 1937. It held the perfume "715" named after the address on Fifth Avenue in New York of a Helena Rubinstein salon.

In America during the 1920's and 1930's many shops and department stores entered the competition with perfumes blended in France to sell under their company label. Russeks on Fifth Avenue in New York advertised in 1926 two Paris perfumes "Bon Jour Toi" and "Marylin" blended exclusively for its label. Jay-Thorpe on 57th Street in New York had a wonderful carved tulips bottle by René Lalique made to hold "Jaytho", its house perfume. Some others who had perfumes created for them were John Wanamaker in Philadelphia, Bonwit Teller in New York, and Marshall Field in Chicago.

This trend started in the 1920's, continued in the 1930's with Jean Desprez, Jean Dessès, Marcel Rochas, Elsa Schiaparelli, and two furriers Revillon and Richard Jaeckel. The perfume "Are Jay" introduced to the U.S. by Richard Jaeckel in 1938 in a Baccarat crystal bottle was said to have a special affinity for furs. Revillon marketed his first perfume "Carnet de Bal", introduced to the U.S. in 1938, in an amusing Verreries Brosse bottle which, when turned upside down, proved to be a brandy sniffer.

Elsa Schiaparelli was an inventive, cultured designer who brought a refreshing sense of humour, daring, and Bohemian outlook to the fashion industry. Born into a prominent Roman family in 1890, she opened her first Paris salon in 1927. Among her many friends were such famous surrealists as Salvador Dali, Schlemberger, and Man Ray. Her first perfume "Salut" created in 1931 was not marketed in the U.S. until 1934. The bet known of her perfumes, "Shocking", was an instant hit when introduced in 1937. The bottle of hand-etched Bohemian crystal designed by Schiaparelli was inspired by the dressmaker's dummy that she used when making clothes for Mae West. Elsa Schiaparelli filed for a U.S. patent on September 17, 1936 for the bottle, several months before the perfume made its debut. In 1938, Schiaparelli introduced a smaller, less expensive torso bottle to reach a larger market.

The bottles for all of Schiaparelli's perfumes have been truly innovative and therefore highly collectible today. In 1939 "Sleeping", advertised as a night perfume, was introduced in a crystal candle in holder bottle made by

Baccarat and designed by Elsa Schiaparelli. She received U.S. patent 116,055 on August 8, 1939 for the bottle design. Also in 1939, her "Snuff" perfume for men was presented in a crystal pipe shaped bottle. Salvador Dali designed the gorgeous sun ray stopper bottle in crystal made by Baccarat in 1946 for the Schiapareli fragrance called "Roi Soleil". The bottle for "Zut" presented to the U.S. market in 1949 was shaped like a woman's body from the waist down, dressed only in a pair of painted-on panties. The bottle was so offensive to the typical American woman of the day that the perfume was only marketed in the U.S. for about two years. Another unusual Schiaparelli bottle, that looked like a gilt-veined ivy leaf, was made for the fragrance "Succès Fou" introduced to the U.S. in 1953.

The 1930's in America saw many cosmetic firms, and couture house introducing perfumes. Among them were Hedwig Orlik, John Frederics, Eisenberg of Chicago, Henri Bendel, Kathleen Mary Quinlan, Barbara Gould, Frances Denny, and Dorothy Gray. For the most part, the better American lines were still being made in France. In fact, ads of the time made a point of saying this.

The firm of Mary Chess started in a small shop in New York that specialized in perfume and perfume related items such as sachets, perfume lamps, scented jewelry, and even scented paint. Saks Fifth Avenue became a client and her business boomed. The name Mary Chess was given a U.S. trademark in 1932. Her business became so successful she moved to 334 Park Avenue in 1938. The wonderful bottles shaped like different chess pieces designed by Grace Chess Robinson came into use in the late 1930's but were not patented until 1941.

World War II cast a blight over the French perfume industry. The clearing-house or assembly point for the scores of costly ingredients that make up perfume shifted from Paris across the Atlantic to New York in the early 1940's. The war did not come suddenly, and the U.S. representatives of the famous French perfume houses were forewarned enough to stock up heavily on essential oils and started duplicating exact replicas of perfumes in America when France fell. The 1940's were to see many American firms introducing perfumes for the first time including Lilly Daché, Maurice Rentner, Sherry Dunn, Ellyn Deleith, and Nettie Rosenstein.

After World War II, France was prepared to retake the honour of being the perfume capital of the world. During the mid to late 40's and the 1950's many couturiers introduced perfumes blended especially for their house label for the first time. Among the famous designers were Cristobal Balenciaga, Pierre Balmain, Carven, Christian Dior, Nina Ricci, Robert Piguet, Givenchy, Grès, Kislav, and Suzy (a milliner). The most influential of these was Christian Dior.

Born in 1905 in Granville, Christian Dior was originally educated to enter the diplomatic service at the Ecole des Sciences Politiques. He began in the 1930's working in the fashion industry, first as a fashion illustrator for Le Figaro Illustré and then as an assistant to Robert Piquet. In 1946 Dior opened the doors to his own salon in Paris at No. 30 Avenue Montaigne. Dior in 1947 premiered the so-called new look, featuring a long, full-cut skirt. It totally revolutionized women's dress and reestablished Paris as the center of the fashion world. In the same year "Miss Dior," created by Edmond Roudnitska for the House of Dior was presented. The bottles for the Dior perfumes made by Baccarat were designed by Serge Heftler Louiche and patented in the United States.

The late 1950's and 1960's were to experience a decline in the quality of bottles used to house perfume. Few companies would pay the ever increasing cost of hand grinding bottle and stopper to match. Gone also were the opulent, luxurious, dramatic colors, designs and hand finishes that had reached their heyday in the 1920's and had made these bottles works of art. By the early sixties, interchangeable, machine ground glass to glass stoppers had become the norm. All plastic screw tops became common to see on even the better perfumes.

You could call the 1970's the decade of the designer perfume. Both French and American designers such as Gucci, Ralph Lauren, Karl Lagerfeld,

56. Art Deco bottle with a brass and cork stopper held "Jasmin" toilet water by Spencer of South Bend, Indiana. Circa 1927. (6").

57. This clear and frosted glass bottle with numbered stopper appeared in a 1928 ad for "Karess" by Woodworth. (5").

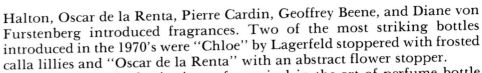

Halton, Oscar de la Renta, Pierre Cardin, Geoffrey Beene, and Diane von Furstenberg introduced fragrances. Two of the most striking bottles introduced in the 1970's were "Chloe" by Lagerfeld stoppered with frosted calla lillies and "Oscar de la Renta" with an abstract flower stopper.

The 70's saw the beginnings of a revival in the art of perfume bottle design and making. The sophisticated perfume purchasing public was insisting on the luxury of better quality flacons. Through the use of advanced semi-automatic and fully-automatic techniques, such glass houses as Saint Gobain Desjonquères, Verreries Brosse, and Pochet et du Courval have been answering the public demand.

Founded in 1854, the French company of Verreries Brosse et Cie originally built its excellent reputation on quality hand crafted bottles, glass, and crystal. In 1919, Emile Barre bought out the remaining partners and became sole owner of Verreries Brosse. Barre, recognizing the importance of the revolution taking place in perfume packaging in the 1920's, converted his entire factory to the manufacture of customized, luxury perfume bottles. Brosse was soon supplying high quality semi-automatic bottles to such noted perfumers as Coty, Guerlain, Patou, Lanvin, Chanel, Bourjois, Ciro, Vigny, Bienaime, Mury, Grenoville, Forvil, Lubin, Roger & Gallet, Lentheric, Worth, Caron, and D'Orsay. In 1963 Brosse switched from hand grinding stoppers to precision machine grinding. In 1976 Verreries Brosse patented two new stopper innovations. The first is a ring made of polypropylene with horizontal joints placed on the stopper dowel. The second is a polypropylene coating of the stopper dowel designed with internal friction teeth. Today Brosse makes the highest quality, stoppered, semi-automatic bottles for such firms as Giorgio of Beverly Hills, Hermes, Desprez, Carven, Chanel, Guy Laroche, Warner, Yves St. Laurent, Nini Ricci, Ungaro, Gres, and Guerlain. The Brosse trademark on a bottle is a VB or

The firm of Saint Gobain was founded in 1665 under the patronage of the French King Louis XIV. This glasshouse has been making flacons for perfumers for centuries. In the 1950's Saint Gobain acquired the Desjonqueres glass company. The Desjonqueres factory was completely destroyed by bombs during World War II. After the war, under the Marshall Plan, the factory was rebuilt and equipped with modern fully-automatic machinery with the help of the Wheaton glassworks of New Jersey. In 1979 Saint Gobain Desjonquères introduced a plastic covered dowel stopper. An exciting innovation developed by Saint Gobain Desjonquères was fully automatic lead crystal introduced in 1984 with the "Diamella" by Yves Rocher bottle. Saint Gobain Desjonquères is now the largest producer of

58. "Le Dèbut" by Richard Hudnut, available in four fragrances and four bottle colors including blue, clear, black, and green. Introduced to the U.S. in 1927. (2").

59. Early cobalt blue "Evening in Paris" purse bottle marked 'Made in Austria'. (2").

60. Bourjois's "Evening in Paris" was introduced in the U.S. in 1929. The cobalt blue bottle was designed by Jean Helleu and made by Verreries Brosse. (2-3/4").

perfume bottles in the world. They can number among their clients Halston, Guy Laroche, Cardin, Gucci, Dior, Avon, Yardley, Estee Lauder, Warner, Kenzo, Elizabeth Arden, Givenchy, Yves Saint Laurent, Chanel, Niki de Saint-Phalle, Ted Lapidus, and Rochas. Occasionally you can find the Saint Gobain Desjonquères trademark **S** or SGD on the bottom of bottles made by this firm.

The French glassworks of Pouchet et du Corval started in 1623 in upper Normandy has a long history of making quality perfume bottles. In 1930 Pouchet built its first semi-automatic factory. Today Pouchet makes both traditional semi-automatic and modern fully-automatic flacons for the commercial perfume market. Pouchet et du Courval's trademark on bottles is a H P or **HP**

Two of the best contemporary bottle designers to emerge in our time are Pierre Dinand and Serge Mansau. The French born Pierre Dinand was working in an advertising agency when asked by Hélène Rochas to design a bottle for "Madame Rochas" in 1959. Now head of his own design firm in New York and Paris he has created the striking packaging for such perfumes as "Magie Noire", "Opium", "Ivoire", "Calandre", and "Ysatis". Serge Mansau, also a Frenchman, was a sculptor well before becoming a bottle designer. Some of the bottles he has created include "Oscar de la Renta", "Infini", "Fidji", "Diorella", and "Vivre". Some other noteworthy modern bottle designers are Jacques Llorente, Joël Desgrippes, Robert Du Grenier, Joseph Messina, and Ira Levy.

The commercial bottle collector has a wide range from which to choose. A collection can consist of bottles of all types, such as those from only a certain time period, or a certain size, a particular perfume company, a special bottle maker, or a particular design such as figurals. A bottle with the original label intact is more valuable than a similar bottle without the label. Perfume bottles in their original boxes are a true find. Usually the boxes were thrown away or destroyed over the passage of years. Many times the boxes have information about the company that the bottles don't carry.

The following perfume directory is the result of extensive research using trademarks, patents, magazines, catalogs, and company information. The U.S. introduction dates have been used whenever possible because of the large gap that often occurred between the European and American introduction of a fragrance. When the exact date of introduction could not be determined, the oldest advertisement or catalog date was used. The following information will be helpful to the readers in dating their commercial bottles.

62. Often mistaken for a perfume, this bottle which came in three sizes actually held "Duska" skin tonic. (2").

61. Deluxe presentation flacon in sterling silver with ivory top for an unknown Roger & Gallet perfume. Circa 1920's. (2-1/2").

63. Made in France for the Vantine Co., this bottle and metal Art Deco holder was signed by the artist A. Ouveb. Circa 1920's. (7-1/2").

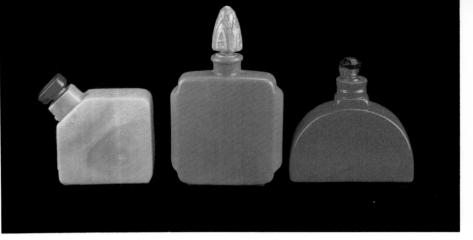

64. Opaque and slag glass perfume bottles were popular in the 1920's and early 1930's. The orange bottle was used by **YBRY**, the green Renaud, and the red by an unknown maker. Circa late 1920's. (1-1/2'', 2-1/2'', 1-3/4'').

69. Oval shaped crystal bottle with the D'Orsay seal on the stopper contained "Duo". Introduced in 1930. The bottle was by Verreries Brosse. (2'').

65. Frosted and clear glass bottle which held a flower scent was bought in the Philippines in the 1930's. (4-1/4'').

67. Bright ochre yellow cylinder bottle of opaque glass with brass screw top was patented in the U.S. by Renaud in 1931. (3-3/4'').

70. Elizabeth Arden introduced "Blue Grass" in 1934 however this bottle with a horse on a blue glass stopper cover was not introduced until about 1936. The bottle was made in France by Verreries Brosse. (2-3/4'').

71. Baccarat made the crystal bottle for "L'Ardente Nuit" by Corday introduced in 1930. It was imported to the U.S. by Lionel, New York. (4-3/4'').

66. Parfum-cologne bottle made by Verreries Brosse used by Jean Patou to hold several fragrances. The bottle was introduced in the late 1920's. (5-1/2'').

68. This purse size bottle of "L'Origan" by Coty in a metal case was advertised in a 1930 mail-order catalog. (2-1/2'').

72. Elizabeth Arden used this bottle made by Verreries Brosse to hold "Blue Grass" eau de toilette. The bottle received U.S. patent 98,040 filed November 7, 1935. Photo courtesy Brosse USA, Inc.

73. Pineapple shaped bottle made by Verreries Brosse held the perfume "Heure Intime" by Vigny. U.S. introduction 1933. Photo courtesy Brosse USA, Inc.

74. Shown in a 1932 article this black, white, and crystal bottle with cut crystal stopper held the perfume "Lili" from Bermuda by an unknown maker. (3-3/4'').

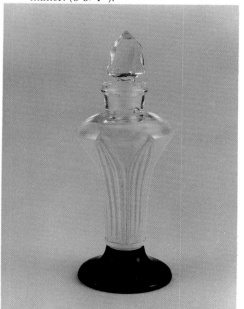

75. Lucien Lelong's crystal bottle for the scent "Mon Image" was introduced in 1933 and received U.S. patent 91,504 on February 13, 1934. The bottle was designed by Joseph S. Stein. (2-3/4'').

76. Pale blue purse bottle with tassel was made in Bavaria for Blue Kamel perfumes. Retail price for the bottle containing perfume in 1933 was 29¢. (3'').

77. Beautiful cobalt blue and gold perfume bottle for an unknown scent has a numbered stopper and is marked 'A-E made in France'. Circa 1930's. (3-3/4'').

78. Commercial purse bottle with aluminum top and inner glass stopper is marked 'made in Germany'. Circa 1930's. (2-1/2'').

79. Du-Bé of New York used this Deco bottle in various colors to hold different scents. Circa 1940's. (2-1/2'').

81. Chanel "Petite" bottles were originally introduced in the U.S. in 1934. Sets of miniature bottles by various perfumers became popular during the 1930's and remain popular. (2-1/2'').

80. Faceted crystal prism bottle with an atomizer top, shown in it's velvet lined box, held "Essence Rare" by Houbigant. U.S. introduction 1929. (3-1/2'').

82. Cobalt blue bottle for Guerlain's "Verveine" was granted U.S. patent 100,424 in 1936. The bottle was inspired by the arc lights of Paris. (4'').

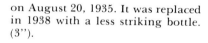

86. A frosted crown bottle used by Prince Matchabelli for the perfumes "Ave Maria" and "Duchess of York". Circa late 1930's and early 1940's. (4").

83. Lucien Lelong's unusual crystal pyramid bottle for the perfume "Opening Night" was introduced in 1935 and received U.S. patent 96,615 on August 20, 1935. It was replaced in 1938 with a less striking bottle. (3").

87. The name "Vermeil" by Bienaimé of France was U.S. trademarked in 1935. This "Vermeil" bottle has 'made in France' embossed on the bottom, and was made by Verreries Brosse. (2-1/2").

88. Even though the frosted glass draperies bottle for "Indiscret" by Lucien Lelong received U.S. patent 97,332 in 1935, it wasn't put on the U.S. market until 1936. The bottle was made by Verreries Brosse. (3-1/2").

84. Frosted flacon moulded with a flower design by Verreries Brosse contained the Oriental scent "Kobako" by Bourjois introduced to the U.S. in 1936. Photo courtesy Brosse USA, Inc.

85. Clear and frosted flacon by Verreries Brosse held the perfume "Miracle" by Lentheric. The bottle designed by Frank McIntosh received U.S. patent 100,434 filed May 27, 1936. Photo courtesy Brosse USA, Inc.

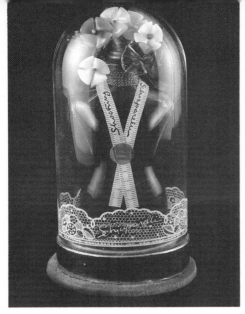

89. Dressmaker's flacon designed by Elsa Schiaparelli for "Shocking" perfume was granted U.S. patent 102,172 on December 1, 1936. This surreal bottle was originally of hand-etched Bohemian crystal with glass flowers typifying the escaping fragrance. (5'').

90. Original travel size bottle for "Shocking" by Schiaparelli. Circa late 1930's. (3'').

91. Suzanne's "Secret de Suzanne" perfume was originally introduced to the U.S. in 1924. (2-3/4'').

92. Frosted glass mannequin bottle held the perfume "847" by the dressmakers Eisenberg Et Sons of Chicago, Ill. Introduced in 1938. Ads claimed the name had numerological fashion power. (3-1/2'').

93. S.A. Ogden designed this metal and glass purse bottle for Mary Dunhill, Inc. The design received U.S. patent 105,298 filed May 26, 1937. (2'').

94. To appeal to the outdoor girl "Grand Prix" by Charbert came in a leather boot designed by Otto S. Garry and Percy M. Brown patented in the U.S. in 1938. (3-1/4'').

97. French-blue package decorated with scenes of Paris was introduced in 1938 to house the already classic perfume "Paris" by Coty. (3").

95. Lace trimmed pedestal and satin quilted box encased a perfume made by Prince George of Russia. Circa 1938. (4").

98. Miniature crystal flacon, which held various Jean Patou perfume was introduced to the U.S. in 1938. (2-1/4").

96. Scalloped fan-shaped stopper tops this bottle of "Mais Oui" by Bourjois. Introduced to the U.S. in 1938. (3-1/2").

99. Famous dress-designer Hattie Carnegie was assigned patent 109,618 on May 10, 1938 for this portrait bottle that held various scents. The bottle was designed by Tommi Parzinger. (4-1/4", 3-1/4").

100. Architecturally inspired "Danger" by Ciro bottle with black glass top was granted U.S. patent 113,549 filed on July of 1938. The bottle was made by Verreries Brosse. (3-1/4").

103. English perfume house Floris of London, established in 1730, introduced their perfume "Lily of the Valley" to the U.S. in 1938. (3").

105. Clear ribbed glass bottle held the perfume "Tailspin" by Lucien Lelong. The bottle designed by John D. Buckingham received U.S. patent 111,954, filed September 2, 1938. (3-1/2").

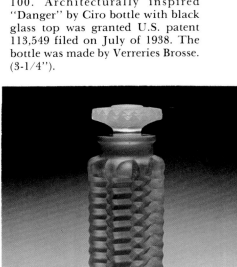

101. Interesting moulded glass bottle designed by Rene Lalique held the perfume "Tzigane" by Corday. U.S. introduction 1938. Photo courtesy of Brosse USA, Inc.

104. Angel bottle introduced in 1938 held a night perfume called "Slumber Song" by Helena Rubinstein. The bottle was granted U.S. patent 114,659 on May 9, 1939. (6-1/2").

106. Opaque white glass bottle with stopper shaped like a hand holding a bouquet of ribbon was made by Verreries Brosse for "Belle de Jour" by D'Orsay. The bottle designed by Jacques Guerin received U.S. patent 112,638 filed October 15, 1938. Photo courtesy Brosse USA, Inc.

107. Introduced in 1931, "Joy" by Jean Patou was originally packaged in a cut crystal bottle made by Baccarat. Verreries Brosse also made "Joy" bottles. (2").

102. Cobalt blue bow-tie bottle made by Baccarat held the perfume "COQUE D'OR" by Guerlain introduced to the U.S. in 1938. The bottle

was given U.S. patent 110,302 on June 28, 1938. There is also a gilded version of the bottle.

108. Opaque black glass bottle with red and black stopper was made in France to hold "Joy" by Jean Patou. (2-1/4").

109. Clear glass bottle shaped like a Mayan templer contained the scent "Ballad" by Avon Products, Inc. Circa 1939. (1-3/4").

110. Smallest candlestick bottle used for the night perfume "Sleeping" by Schiaparelli. U.S. patent 116,055 was granted for the bottle on August 8, 1939. (3-1/8").

111. "It's You" by Elizabeth Arden introduced in 1939 came in the bottle shown or had a golden torch in an opaque white hand. The bottle made by Baccarat was granted U.S. patent 110,870. (7-1/2").

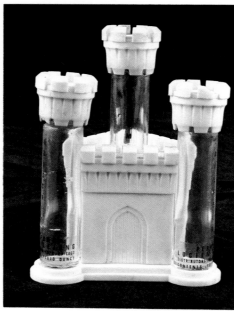

112. "Le Castel" introduced and patented in 1940 held four different Lucien Lelong perfumes. The bottle display unit was designed by John D. Buckingham. (3-3/4").

113. Figural commercial bottle for an unknown scent came in blue, greeen, and frosted white. It has an acid-etched Czechoslovakia mark. Circa 30's. (8").

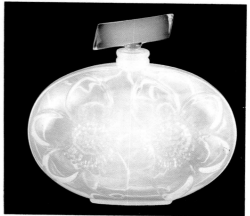

114. Gorgeous opalescent glass double flower bottle used for "Voeu de Noël" by Caron was introduced and patented in 1939. The bottle was designed by Felicie Bergaud and manufactured by Lalique. (3-3/4").

115. Charming white and pink Charles of the Ritz "Moss Rose" cologne bottle designed by Lawrence Colwell received U.S. patent 124,017 on December 17, 1940. (7-1/2").

116. An advertisement for "Sinful Soul" perfume by Gabilla of Paris, France appeared in an American fashion magazine in 1940. (6").

119. Mary Chess miniature bottle gift set included five different perfumes in bottles shaped like chess pieces. Circa 1940's. (2-3/4").

117. Dressed in clothes of the 19th century, this figural bottle held an unidentified scent by Pinaud. Circa 1940's. (7").

118. Store tester display used in France held four different Bourjois scents including "Evening in Paris" and "Kobako". Circa 1940's.

120. Clear bottle decorated with moulded glass ruffle and bow topped stopper held "Confetti" by Lentheric cologne. The cologne bottle was patented in 1941 and a similar cylinder shaped perfume bottle was patented in 1940. (6-1/2").

122. Barbara Gould of New York introduced "Skylark" in this clear ribbed bottle with frosted flower stopper in 1941. (3").

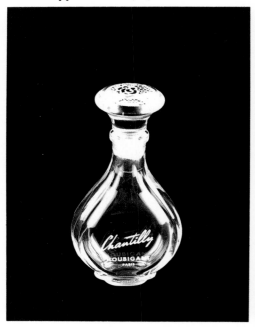

121. Violin shaped sample bottle of "Tabu" by Dana perfume. "Tabu" was presented to the American market in the 1930's. (2").

123. In 1941 "Chantilly" became Houbigant's newest perfume. This clear glass bottle has a fancy lace design painted on the top. (4-1/4").

124. Store tester bottle for Houbigant's Chantilly perfume. Circa 1940's. (2-3/8'').

127. Renooir Parfums, Ltd., New York received U.S. patent 131,361 on February 10, 1942 for this heart-shaped bottle on a frosted ruffled pedestal used for "Chi Chi" perfume. Another version with the heart on a ribbed pedestal can be found. The bottle was designed by Felix Levy-hawkes. (4'').

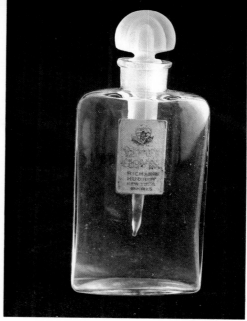

128. The perfume "Yanky Clover" by Richard Hudnut appeared in a 1944 Sears mail-order catalog. (3'').

129. An elegant, clear, cut glass flask holds "Intoxication" by D'Orsay first introduced to the U.S. in 1942. Later versions may have a lucite instead of glass top. The bottle was made by Verreries Brosse. (5'').

125. Gilded swirls surround the bottle for "Balalaika" by Lucien Lelong. Introduced in 1941, the bottle received U.S. patent 131,830 on March 31, 1942. The bottle shown is missing it's stopper cover. (2-3/4'').

126. Victorian inspired metal stand holds bottles of "Jolie" and "Captive" by Rawlings of New York. Circa 1941. (3-1/2'').

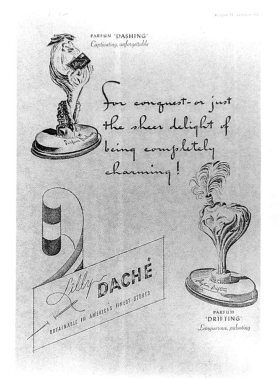

130. A 1943 advertisement for the perfumes "Dashing" and "Drifting" by Lily Dache which were introduced in 1941.

132. The classic ball bottle designed by Paul Iribe in 1925 for Lanvin perfumes was originally in clear crystal. The black bottles made their first appearance in America right after World War II. The bottles were made in France by Verreries Brosse.

131. Nattie Rosenstein received a U.S. trademark for the name "Odalisque" in 1946. The bottles are marked made in France. (3-1/4", 4-1/2").

133. This frosted glass figural bottle made in France which held "On dit" by Elizabeth Arden received patent 144,619 on May 7, 1946. "On dit" also came in 1-1/4 oz. round crystal bottle and a 1/8 oz. gold flashed flacon. (4").

134. Cobalt blue "Evening in Paris" bottle with gold plastic cap was introduced about 1947.

135. Large doorknob type stopper topped this bottle of "A" by Gres of Paris introduced in the U.S. in 1947. (4-1/4").

136. Modern flacon made by Verreries Brosse to hold the perfume "Nostalgia" by Germaine Monteil. U.S. introduction 1947. Photo courtesy Brosse USA, Inc.

137. Fancy oval stopper on a crystal bottle made in France for Suzanne Thierry held "Ondine". Circa 1950's. (4-1/4").

145

141. "Diorama" by Christian Dior. 3-1/2". Circa 1948.

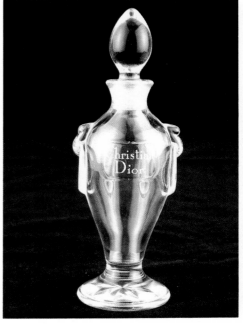

138. Heart bottle with heart shaped stopper designed by Adele Simpson received U.S. patent 150,037 filed on January 17, 1947. The bottle was assigned to Renoir Parfums, Ltd. N.Y., yet the bottle in the picture has an Elizabeth Arden "White Orchid" label. (4").

142. Urn shaped bottle held "Miss Dior" by Christian Dior which was introduced to the U.S. in 1948. The bottle received U.S. patent 156,002 on November 15, 1949. The design was by Serge Heftler-Louiche. (5-1/2").

143. Corday's "zigane" perfume came in a violin-shaped bottle made by Verreries Brosse. U.S. introduction 1949. Photo courtesy Brosse USA, Inc.

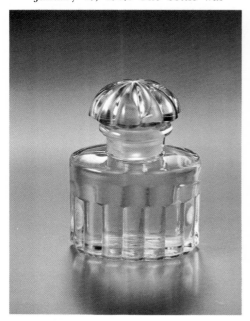

139. Balenciaga introduced "Le Dix" perfume to the U.S. in 1947 in an oval shaped bottle. Photo courtesy of Brosse USA, Inc.

140. Frank McIntosh designed this cylinder shaped bottle made by Verreries Brosse to hold "Repartee" by Lentheric. The bottle received U.S. patent 160,407 filed November 16, 1949. Photo courtesy Brosse USA, Inc.

144. Only a few thousand bottles were made with the insect stopper for "Or et Noir" by Caron. U.S. introduction 1949. (4-1/8").

145. Yardley of London introduced the prismatic "Lotus" perfume to the U.S. in 1949. (3-1/4").

146. Odd-shaped clear glass bottle held the fragrance "Acclaim" by Ciro of Paris, France. The perfume was introduced to the U.S. in 1950. (3-1/4").

147. The Corday bottle for "Toujours Toi" introduced in 1951 is covered with gold leaf and stoppered with gilt lace on glass. The bottle is exactly like the one for "Toujours Moi" patented in 1925. (3").

148. A moulded leaf pattern decorates this bottle of "Cachet" by Lucien Lelong introduced to the U.S. in 1949. (4").

149. Fabergé introduced "Woodhue" to the American market in the late 1940's. (3").

150. The name "Mouche" was trade-marked by Marcel Rochas of Paris, France in the U.S. in 1948. (3-1/4").

151. Advertisement for "Zut" perfume by Schiaparelli was introduced to the U.S. in 1949. The bottle was shaped like a woman's body from the waist down wearing painted panties.

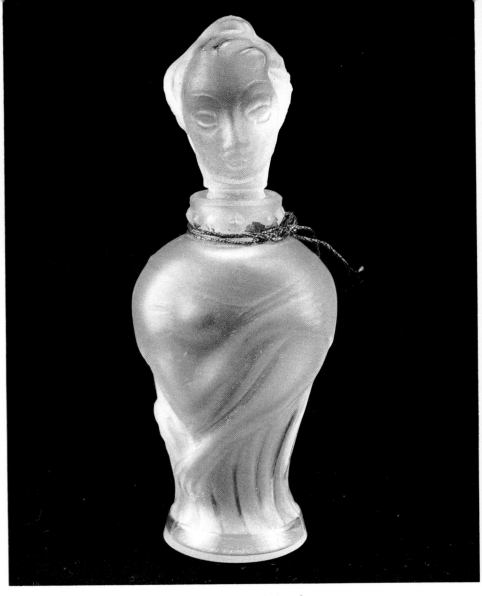

153. Beautifully sculptured, hand-blown bottle made in France was for the Elizabeth Arden perfume "On dit". Circa 1952. (2-5/8").

152. Evyan tectured glass, heart-shaped sample bottle for "Most Precious" introduced in 1947. The bottle is marked 'not for sale'. (2-1/4").

154. Store tester bottle for "Rigolade" by Germaine Montiel has long glass dapper. An advertisement for the perfume appeared in a 1952 fashion magazine. (2-3/4").

155. Carven's "Ma Griffe" bottle introduced to the U.S. in 1946 is decorated with a gold and green ribbon label. The bottle was made by Verreries Brosse. (3-1/4").

159. "Dykil" by Lenthéric of Paris is packaged in pink and the clear bottle has a smart, grey metal stopper cover. Circa 1935. (2-1/4").

160. An advertisement for "Succès Fou" by Schiaparelli which appeared in a 1953 Vogue magazine.

156. Christian Dior's perfume "Diorissimo" arrived in America during 1957 packaged in a Baccarat flacon stoppered with gilt flowers. (8").

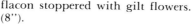

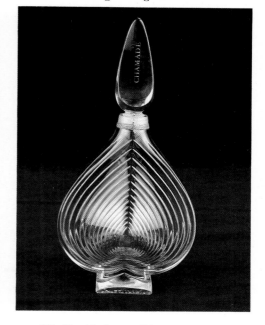

157. Frosted glass bottle decorated with a raised star pattern was made in France to hold "Magie" by Lancome of Paris. The perfume was introduced to the U.S. in 1952. (5").

158. The perfume "Antilope" by Weil of Paris was introduced to the U.S. in 1935. (5"). (5").

161. Upside down ribbed heart bottle on a pedestal base, made in France to hold the perfume "Chamade" by Guerlain introduced in 1969. (8-3/4").

162. Lenel introduced "Bellezza" to the American market in this crystal pedestal bottle with squared stopper about 1956. (3").

164. "Casaque" by Jean d'Albert, once a favorite scent of writer George Sand, was introduced to American women in 1957 in the same bottle used for "Ecusson" perfume. (3-1/4").

166. A gold plastic shoe holds a small bottle of "Emeraude" by Coty perfume. Circa 1940's. (2-3/4").

163. Clear glass bottle draped with frosted glass with a flower bud shaped stopper held "Ode" perfume by Guerlain. The same bottle can also be found with a "Shalimar" label. U.S. introduction 1956. (4-1/2").

165. Presentation bottle in a gold satin lined silk brocade box holds "Bal á Versailles" introduced in 1962 by Jean Desprez of Paris. A painting by Fragonard decorates the label. (2-1/2").

167. An unusual stopper tops this bottle of "Parure" by Guerlain introduced in 1975. (4").

168. "Isadora" perfume was introduced in the U.S. in 1979. The bottle was originally designed by Rene Lalique to honor the famous dancer Isadora Duncan in the 1920's but with her untimely death in 1927 it was not released to the market. (3").

169. Special acid etched crystal bottle was made in France for Avon in 1963. (4-1/2").

170. Opaque black, round crown-shaped bottles with cut glass stoppers held the perfume "Incanto" by Simonetta of Rome. The scent was introduced to the U.S. in 1955. (2", 3").

171. Ribbed crystal bottle with gilt stopper marked Daum Nancy was possibly a commercial bottle. (4-1/4").

172. Marquay's of Paris bottle for "Prince Douka" perfume has a frosted glass head-shaped stopper with jeweled turban and wears a satin cape which came in blue, white, or rose. The "Prince Douka" name was trademarked in 1951 and the bottle received U.S. patent 171,824 filed on November 18, 1952.

173. Verreries Brosse made this bottle beginning in 1957 for the perfume "FLeur Sauvage" by Germaine Monteil. Photo courtesy Brosse USA, Inc.

174. Frosted and clear hand-finished three part bottle made by Verreries Brosse for "Paloma Picasso" by Warner. Introduced in 1984 the bottle was designed by the Primary Design Group of New York and Robert Du Grenier for Brosse. (3-1/4").

176. Three similar small gilt purse bottles decorated with imitation jewels were made in France for Givenchy, Caron, and an unknown maker. Circa 1960's. (2-1/4", 2-3/4", 2-1/4").

177. Made in France for the perfume "F#" by Fabergé, this bottle made by Verreries Brosse has an unusual screw-shaped inner glass dapper. Circa 1950's. (2-1/2").

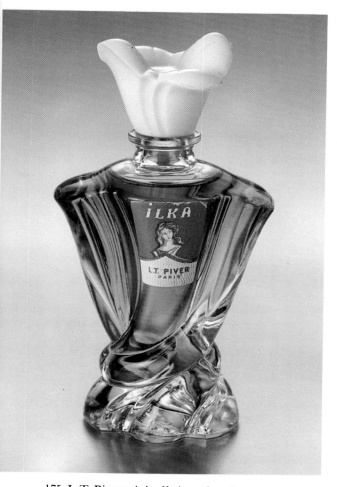

175. L.T. Piver originally introduced "Ilka" to the U.S. in 1912. The bottle pictured was made by Verreries Brosse in the 1950's. Photo courtesy Brosse USA, Inc.

See page 220 for Chapter 8 patents.

Chapter 9

Dime Store Novelties

During the 1920's and 1930's variety chain stores, which were then almost exclusively five and ten cent stores, were rapidly increasing in number. These stores catered to the mass market, to consumers in the vast low income group. Among the array of products they carried were inexpensive perfumes, colognes, and toilet waters including some in *"cute"* glass figural bottles or novel containers. The largest purchasers of the dime-store novelty perfumes were children and teenagers who, attracted by the toy-like bottles, bought them as gifts to give their mothers, friends, and teachers. The many companies who made novelty perfumes were very aware of this and kept the retail price at one dollar or lower to fit the pocket money of this age group. The business grew by leaps and bounds in the late 1930's and 1940's, continuing strong in the 1950's. By the 1960's, with the rising costs of plastic moulding, the retail prices could no longer be kept under a dollar, so the novelty perfume market started to die.

The American capitol of the dime-store perfume business was Jersey City, New Jersey. While most of the companies had offices in New York or another large city, the bulk of the perfume manufacturing occurred in New Jersey. The bottles used were bought in the thousands of dozens from such glass companies as J.T. & A. Hamilton of Pittsburg, T.B. Brauner, Owens-Illinois, Carr-Lowry, Wheaton, and Hazel-Atlas.

Some of the hardest to find novelty bottles are very thin and fragile free-blown bottles made in Germany. Imported into this country from the early 1900's to the 1930's, few have survived the years. The bottles, which held flower scents, portrayed various tiny figures such as birds, insects, and animals. The hand detailing seen on most of the bottles is excellent. An article in a 1922 Vogue magazine showed an assortment of these figurals holding French perfumes by Mingot.

One of the largest producers of dime-store novelty perfumes was the Stuart Products Co. of St. Paul, Minnesota started by William B. Cohen in 1935. The company sold its products to variety stores, drug stores, and mail order firms. The company's first big success was "Floral Quintuplets" designed by Robert B. Karoff in 1936. The set of five bottles, each with a cute

1. Pink blown glass elephant on ball made in France to hold "Rose" perfume. Circa late 1920's. (4-1/4").

2. Close up of blown glass perfume flask made in Germany in the shape of a deer. It contained "Lilas" perfume. (2").

3. Blown in German, fragile glass animal forms held different floral scents. A 1922 article appearing in Vogue showed the deer and fox holding French perfumes by Mingot. (1"-2").

handpainted, wood, screw top and ruffled collar, retailed for about 39¢. Stuart Products Co. continued to manufacture imaginative, well-made, yet inexpensive, perfume novelties until 1946. In 1947 the name of the company was shortened to the Stuart Co., which was in operation throughout the 1950's.

Three of the most prized dime-store novelties sought by collectors were marketed by the same company, Babs Creations, Inc. started in 1939 at 136 W. 52 St. in New York City. Imitating the successful "Shocking" by Schiaparelli packaging, Babs also marketed its perfumes in unique bottles, showcased on pedestals covered by glass domes. In the early 1940's "Forever Yours" was presented in a heart-shaped bottle held by two painted metal hands. A figural bottle shaped like a young girl holding an umbrella was designed by Walter Hershfield for "Yesteryear" cologne by Babs Creations in 1939. The ornate "Tic toc" perfume bottle, designed by Charles H. Foster, was marketed by Babs in 1941.

Maison Joubert Inc. of New York, a large firm started in the 1920's, produced several moulded glass figural perfumes for the variety store market. Joubert also manufactured perfume under two other brand names, Duchess of Paris and Blue Waltz. Lawrence J. Kihn designed several figural bottles used by Joubert starting in 1938, including a Betty Boop, a three-piece suited man, and a double bell. Blue Waltz put out a heart-shaped bottle which contained 5/8 oz. of "Key to my Heart" perfume in the 1930's. The original bottles had a light-weight chain with a lock and key attached to the red bakelite screw-on closure. Duchess of Paris introduced "Queenly Moment" in the late 1930's in portrait bottles representing famous queens of history.

The Lander Co., which is still in operation today, was founded by 22-year-old Charles H. Oestreich and two partners in 1920. Oestreich devised many innovative ways of manufacturing and distributing good, inexpensive cosmetics, toiletries, and perfumes aimed at women in the lower income groups. The company was the first cosmetic manufacturing firm to base its prices on the cost and overhead of an item instead of what it could bring in the marketplace. The Lander Co. started marketing perfumes heavily in the 1930's and 1940's. Among the perfumes they introduced were "Romantic Days" in 1939, "The Untamed Perfume" in 1943, and "Samezi-Soir" in 1950. By the 1950's the Lander Co. owned and controlled over thirty brand names and four subsidiaries including Lundborg Perfumers Inc. and McGregor Men's Toiletries Inc.

A European contender for the American dime-store novelty perfume market was S. Kleinkramer of Bergen-Op-Zoom, Holland. Kleinkramer introduced over a dozen different moulded glass figural bottles containing a children's cologne to the United States in the late 1940's. A delightful dog shaped bottle used by Kleinkramer was granted patent 152,431 filed Septemgber 12, 1947. The bottles are embossed with "Holland" on the bottom and many times the original paper Kleinkramer label is still on them. Some of the figurals are copies of 1930's Garnier Liquor bottles

5. Insect bottle blown in Germany decorated with feathers. Original label is unreadable. (2-1/4" long).

FLORAL QUINTUPLETS

Miss Gardenia Miss Rose Miss Violet Miss Sweet Pea Miss Chypre

4. "Floral Quintuplets" by the Stuart Products Co. of St. Paul, Minnesota was granted patent 99,623 in 1936. Each hand painted wood capped bottle held a different scent. (2-5/8").

6. Blown glass perfume bottle in the shape of a green, imaginary creature has a clear glass stand. Country of origin unknown. Circa late 1920's. (4").

7. "Perfume O'Clock," a plastic grandfather's clock containing a bottle with a clock face by the Stuart Co. Circa 1950's. (5-1/4").

which will be embossed "France" or "Germany".

Around 1940 Robert B. Karoff, who had designed novelty perfume containers for the Stuart Products Co. in St. Paul, opened his own firm called Karoff Creations Inc. at 347 5th Avenue in New York City. One of his first creations for the variety store market was a brass and plastic lamp that held three tiny bottles of perfume. The design was granted patent 126,397 filed December 20, 1940. The inventive mind of Karoff was to produce many more novelty perfume containers including a tennis racket bottle in 1941 and a cannon bottle in 1943.

Some of the other companies that marketed dime-store novelty perfumes in the 1930's and 1940's were Cardinal, the George W. Button Co., Bija, and De Marsay. The George W. Button Co., started in the 1920's, also produced perfumes under the brand name Bouton which was trademarked in 1934. De Marsay Inc. made a series of animal novelties with perfume bottles attached by ribbons that were designed by Jean Vivadou.

Collecting the appealing, whimsical novelty perfumes is fun and still relatively inexpensive to do. Although many of the bottles were made of poor quality glass and the perfume leaves much to be desired, the bottles make for an interesting addition to any collection. The collector does need to be on the alert when buying moulded glass or free-blown figurals since many were also used as miniature liquor bottles. When no descriptive labels are left on the bottles, sniffing the contents may help to determine the original use.

8. Stuart Products Co. of St. Paul, Minnesota made this copper and brass cart with small padlock to hold five bottles of perfume. Circa early 1940's. (3-1/4").

9. Babs Creations of New York presented "Forever Yours" in a cute heart shaped bottle with brass top and chain. The bottle is held by two painted metal arms trimmed with cuffs of pink velvet and lace. The arms are screwed to a heavy metal base. Circa early 1940's. (3-1/2").

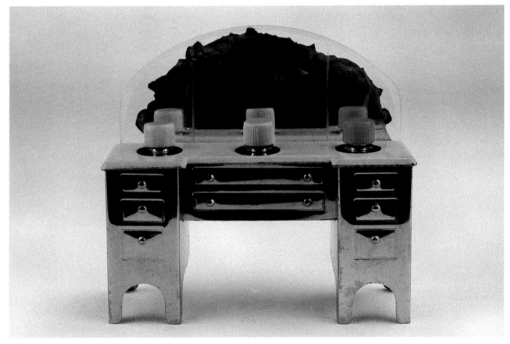

10. Brass vanity with hinged top and mirror holding three miniature perfume bottles was called "Perfume Vanette" by the Stuart Products Co. Circa early 1940's. (4-1/4").

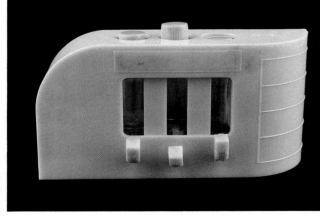

11. Push the button on this pink plastic radio by the Stuart Co., a perfume bottle pops up. Circa 1950's. (2-1/2").

12. Bottle decorated with filigree and clock on a pressed fiber base held "Tic-Toc" perfume by Babs Creations, Inc. New York. The bottle was granted patent 127,737 filed March 20, 1941. (3-1/2").

14. Figural bottle of girl holding an umbrella designed by Walter Hershfield for "Yesteryear" cologne by Babs Creations. Granted patent 116,845 filed April 21, 1939. (4-1/4").

16. Betty Boop cologne bottle was granted U.S. patent 109,326 filed February 19, 1938. The bottle patent was assigned to Joubert Inc. New York. The bottle was also used by Manhattan Dist. Inc. of Miami to hold liquor in the early 1940's. (4-1/4").

13. Joubert Inc. of New York was assigned patent 109,325 filed February 19, 1938 for this hand painted toilet bottle. The painting can vary making the same bottle look very different. This figural bottle was also used to hold liquor. (3-3/8").

15. Heart shaped bottle held "Key to my Heart" perfume by Blue Waltz of Jersey City, New Jersey. Blue Waltz was a brand name used by Joubert Inc. Circa 1930's. (3-3/4").

17. The double bell bottle with bow and brass screw top held "Blasco" by Joubert Inc. New York. The bottle was granted a U.S. patent in 1938. (2-3/4").

18. "Queenly Moment" by Duchess of Paris of Jersey City, N.J. came in portrait bottles representing famous Queens of history. The bottles in the picture include Queen Elizabeth, Queen Victoria, and Queen Marie Antoinette. Circa late 1930's and early 1940's. (Ave. Height 3-1/4").

19. Small bottle of "Gardenia Time" perfume by Lander of New York has a bright red holder. Circa late 40's. (2-1/4").

20. Close up picture of the Queen Elizabeth of England bottle used by Duchess of Paris to hold "Queenly Moment" perfume. (3-1/4").

21. Both Lander of New York and Jolind of Jersey City, N.J. used this figural bottle to hold perfume. It was also used by Manhattan of Miami to hold liquor. Circa 1940's. (3-5/8").

22. Twisted candle bottle with red plastic flame shaped screw-on cap was used by the Lander Co. in the 1950's. (3").

23. Three moulded glass figural perfume bottles embossed "Holland" with paper tags reading 'S. Kleinkramer Bergen op Zoom Holland'. The dog bottle was granted patent 152,431 filed September 12, 1947. Circa late 1940's. (2-1/4", 2-3/4", 2-1/2").

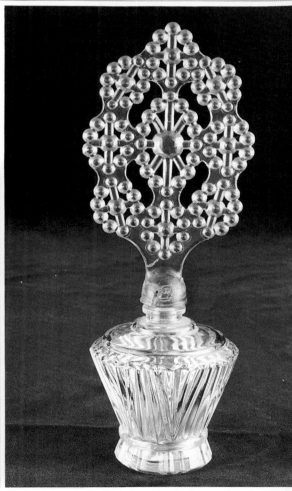

24. Glass lamp bottle with hard plastic shade was used by the Lander Co. to hold both "Gardenia" and "Apple Blossom" perfume. Circa 1950's. (4").

25. "Little Miss" cologne by the Lander Co. has a porcelain doll head placed on top of a bottle shaped to resemble an old-fashioned hoop skirt. The porcelain heads came in assorted designs. Circa 1957 and 1958. (3-1/2").

26. A Lander Co. 2-5/8 oz. toilet water bottle with a jewel style plastic finial top. The tops came in an assortment of colors and styles. A similar 1/2 oz. perfume bottle was also marketed. Circa 1954-1957. (8").

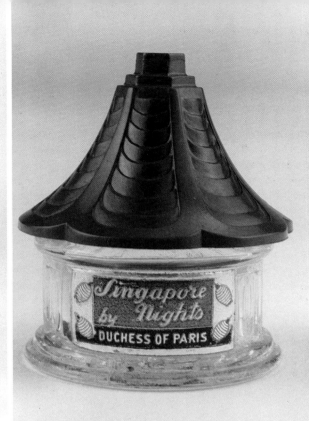

27. Brass floor lamp with silk screened glass shade held three miniature perfume bottles lowered by pulling a chain. The set was called "Perfume Hi-lights" by the Stuart Products Co. Circa 1939. (5-1/2").

29. This metal shelf holding three different tiny bottles of perfume was called "What Not" by the Stuart Products Co. Circa early 1940's. (6").

31. Pagoda bottle designed by Yasuhisa Mogi was granted patent 103,160 filed December 18, 1936. It was used by Duchess of Paris to hold the scent "Singapore Nights". (1-3/4").

28. Plastic drum shaped box with wooden drumsticks on top held "Drum Majorettes" by the Stuart Products Co. Each bottle had a hand painted wood cap. Circa 1937. (2-3/4").

30. Floor lamp of brass and plastic holding three tiny perfume bottles was called "Aromalite" by Karoff of New York. The perfume container was granted patent 126,397 filed December 20, 1940. (6").

32. Moulded glass, hand painted beetle bottle has paper label marked 'Maiglockchen' which means lily of the vally in German. (2").

33. A man smoking pipe, girl with lollipop, and clown moulded glass figural perfume bottles were made in Holland for S. Kleinkramer. Circa late 1940's. (3-1/4", 3-1/4", 3-1/2").

34. A Dutch boy, policeman, and Dutch girl moulded glass figural perfume bottles were made in Holland for S. Kleinkramer. Circa late 1940's. (2-3/4"), 3", 2-1/2").

35. An owl, duck, and bear moulded glass figural perfume bottles with handpainted decoration were made for Kamaya and Co. of Tokyo, Japan. Circa 1950's. (2-1/2", 2-3/4", 2-1/2").

36. The top of this presse material grandfather clock co to reveal the perfume bottl printed clock weight label. used to hold "Gala Night" b Button Co. of New York. Circa (6-3/4").

39. Pressed fiber material piano holding two bottles with keyboard printed labels contained "Springtime Fragrance" by Bouton of New York. Circa 1940's. (2-3/4").

37. Wood champagne bucket, rock salt imitation ice, and small perfume bottle was called "Minute Cocktail" by the Karoff Co. of New York. Circa early 1940's. (3-1/4").

40. Three book shaped bottles fit into a brass holder shaped like three books on a stand. The bottles held "Gardenia", "Bouquet", and "Chypre" scents by Cardinal of New York. Circa 1940's. (Bottle 2", stand 3").

38. Table lamp bottle with plastic shade was called "Perfume-A-Lite" by Karoff of New York. This bottle held orchid perfume. Circa 1940's. (2-3/4").

41. Brass stand with guard rail and hinged top holds three small bottles of perfume by Cardinal of New York. Circa 1940's. (1-3/4" bottle, 2-1/4" stand).

42. Purple porcelain candlestick decorated with a pink rose was made in Germany to hold a candle bottle with gold flame stopper that held "Rose" perfume by Duvinne of Paris and New York. Circa 1930's. (4-1/4").

44. This combined perfume bottle and holder in the form of a dog standing on a basket with a bottle tied around its neck was granted patent 123,439 filed August 29, 1940. It was designed by Jean Vivaudou for De Marsay Inc. (4").

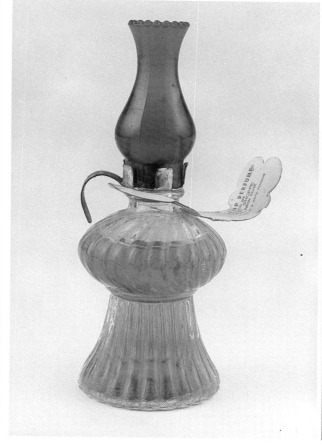

43. Hurricane lamp bottle with glass base and red plastic shade held "Colonial Lamp" perfume distributed by The Antique Shoppe, 5th Ave., New York. Circa 1950's. (3-1/2").

45. Silver metal tray with guard rail and mirror holds three bottles of "Flowers of the Morning" perfume by Pickwick Cosmetic Corp. of New York, N.Y. Circa late 1930's or early 1940's. (Bottle 2-1/2", stand 3-3/4").

46. Metal chest made in the U.S.A. containing three small perfume bottles was called "Treasure Chest" by Bija Inc. of New York City. It received a U.S. patent in 1939. (Bottles 1-1/4").

49. Green painted wood telephone with glass bottle in the middle held "Florale" by Robinson Cosmetic Co. of New York City. Circa 1940's. (3").

47. Figural bottle of a man in Turkish costume with hand painted face and a black screw top resembling a hat held "Oriental Lure" by Lioret of Jersey City, N.J. (3-1/2").

48. Red painted wood pole is the base for a bottle of "Stoplight Perfume" by an unknown maker. (6-1/2").

50. Toilet shaped glass bottle with red plastic seat was used by H. Fishlove & Co. of Chicago to hold "Real Toilet Water". Circa 1948. (1-3/4").

51. Figural perfume bottle in the form of a dressmaker's dummy has a painted lace-up corset with glass ruffle. The bottle held the scent "Imagination" by Lioret of Jersey City, New Jersey. Circa 1940's. (3-1/2").

53. Little girl in pinafore figural perfume bottle has hand painted details. The company who used it is unknown. Circa 1940's. (3-1/4").

55. Hand painted Santa Claus bottle was used by Delavelle of London, England and was distributed in the U.S. by Wallner & Mayer Inc. of New York City. (3-1/2").

52. Frosted glass Christmas tree bottle has green painted branches and toys lying at the base of the tree. The red hard plastic screw cap has an opening so that the bottle could be used for a tree ornament. The bottle is marked "made in Roumania MS1096". (3-3/4").

54. A girl with hand painted details wearing a black hat cap holds "Devon Voilets" made by Lownds Pateman of Torquay, England. Circa 1970's. (3-1/4").

56. Gold metal stand holds a square bottle with a red cap that has an opening in it so that it can hang from the stand. The set was called "Parfum-Cage" by Le Sager Inc. New York. Circa 1940's. (4").

57. Silver plastic candelabra holding three glass candle bottles with red plastic flame shaped caps has original F.W. Woolworth price tag of 49¢. Circa 1950's. (6'').

59. A cute clown bottle wearing a large ruffle around his neck was made in West Germany. (4-1/2'').

See page 230 for Chapter 9 patents.

58. Eiffel tower and windmill perfume bottles were made in France. Circa 1950's. (2-1/2'', 3-1/4'').

Chapter 10

Porcelain Figurals

A vogue for pretty or amusing, yet practical, porcelain figurines started around the turn of this century and reached its peak during the 1920's and 1930's. Among the fashionable articles made were mass produced perfume bottles in the forms of clowns, pretty ladies, animals, birds, cupids, children, flowers, and people dressed in native or exotic costumes. Since porcelain could be controlled to a greater extent than many other materials at the time, these factory made figurals are of superior quality, detail, and color. Some of the perfume bottles were parts of matching dresser sets that included pieces like powder boxes, pincushions, trays, brushes, and lamps.

The most popular type were the bottles representing ladies dressed in eighteenth-century full-skirted costumes, sporting elegant hair-dos or wigs. Their lovely hands usually held a fan, flowers, or an urn. Oriental figures and women dressed in the flapper mode of the roaring 20's were also much in demand. Hundreds of different animal shaped bottles were also made, ranging from the ordinary dog or cat to the unusual mythological beast.

Germany and Bavaria were the largest producers of the porcelain and ceramic figural perfumes, but many delightful bottles were also manufactured in Japan, England, Austria, and France. Some of the bottles can be found with the original importers stamp or label still on them. Among the importers were Lisette, Fireside, Coronet, L&R, and Irice. The George Borfeldt Co. of New York started using the trademark of a crown within a wreath and the word Coronet starting around 1902. Other bottles will only have the country of origin, maker's trademark, or simply a number stamped or incised on the bottom. Many bottles had nothing marked on them giving the collector no definite clue to their origin.

The state of Thuringia, in the green heart or forest region of Germany, was the home of many porcelain houses that produced novelties including figural perfume bottles. Three of these companies marked their bottles with a trademark. They were the Sitzendorf Porcelain Manufacturing, the Schafer & Vater Porcelain Factory, and Carl Schneider's Erben (Carl Schneider's Heirs). The Sitzendorf Porcelain Manufactory was founded in about 1902 by Alfred Voight in Sitzendorf, Germany. The company manufactured decorative porcelain, figurines, and novelties in the Meissen style. The manufactory marked its bottles with an "S" under a crown. The Schafer & Vater Porcelain Factory was located in Rudolstradt, Germany and was in operation from about 1896 until the 1920's. The firm specialized in novelties including atomizer and figural perfume bottles. An incised mark of an "R" inside a nine-pointed star was used to mark its products. The company of Carl Schneider's Erben, started in 1887, was actually a continuation of the firm Unger, Schneider, & Cie founded in 1861. The company made souvenirs, figurines, dolls heads, and figural perfume bottles. The company mark was a "G" (sometimes mistaken for a "C") with two vertical slashes through it.

Bavaria was also the home of many porcelain houses that produced figural perfume bottles including some wonderful pieces in the Deco style. Most of the companies did not mark their bottles with a trademark but one famous exception was Goebel. Franz Detleff Goebel and his son William applied for a permit in 1871 to open a porcelain factory in Oeslau, Bavaria. The necessary permission was slow in coming and wasn't granted until

1. Porcelain Oriental lady's head by Schaffer & Vater of Germany is the bottle for an atomizer. Circa 1896. (4-1/2").

2. Unmarked lady with snowman was probably made in Germany. Circa 1900. (4-1/4").

1879. From the year 1900, the company included novelties, figurines, and gift articles in its line. Most of the porcelain figural perfume bottles found today by Goebel were made in the 1930's. Goebel's trademark was a "G" with a "W" over it, under a crown.

The Japanese entered the porcelain figural perfume bottle field during World War I when the importation of bottles made in the Germanic states was obstructed. Many of the bottles made were of as high a quality as their German counterparts. An example of this is a darling bottle shaped like a girl in a clown outfit, painted in cheerful colors, that was sold in a 1930 Sears mail order catalog. Some of the Japanese made ware was also used as commercial perfume bottles by such companies as Lioret and Delinet.

Starting a porcelain figural perfume bottle collection ten or fifteen years ago was fairly inexpensive and easy to do. Today, as more and more collectors are attracted by these quaint bottles, they are becoming scarce and the prices continue to escalate.

3. A well-made cat bottle, probably German. Circa 1910. (2-1/4").

4. A porcelain figural perfume bottle tops this pincushion covered with shirred rayon. It originally sold for 69¢ in a 1928 mail order catalog. (4").

5. Set of three bottles including a Dutch boy, boat, and Dutch girl were used to hold eau de cologne by J.C. Boldoot of Amsterdam. (3-1/4").

7. Original box that held set of three bottles by J.C. Boldoot of Amsterdam. The box states a gold medal was won in Paris in 1900.

8. Set of four porcelain bottles made in Germany with flapper girl head stoppers, used to hold "Canadian Beauty Revue Parfum". (2-1/2").

9. Set of four porcelain bottles made in Germany with bellboy stoppers, used to hold "Canadian Club" men's cologne. (3-1/4").

6. Queen Elizabeth perfume bottle made in England by Crown Staffordshire. Circa 1930's. (6-1/4").

10. Cute girl in clown outfit with incised Carl Schneider's Erben of Germany mark. (5-1/4'').

13. Lady in 18th century costume made by Carl Schneider's Erben of Germany. (3-1/2'').

11. Girl with flapper hairdo. Carl Schneider's Erben of Germany mark incised on bottom of bottle. (4-3/4'').

12. Carl Schneider's Erben of Germany made this peasant girl figural perfume. (3-3/4'').

14. Girl holding a flower basket made by Carl Schneider's Erben of Germany. (3/8'').

15. The Sitzendorf Porcelain Manufacturing of Germany made this lady in Spanish costume. Similar jar seen in 1922 fashion magazine. (3-1/2'').

19. Woman in harem costume holding an urn by the Sitzendorf Porcelain Manufacturing of Germany. (2-3/4'').

16. Lady in 18th century costume by the Sitzendorf Porcelain Manufacturing of Germany. (4-1/2'').

20. Child holding bouquet of flowers was made by the Sitzendorf Porcelain Manufacturing of Germany. (2'').

17. Lady holding flowers and fan made by the Sitzendorf Porcelain Manufacturing of Germany. (4-1/2'').

18. Deco inspired lady with neck ruff by Sitzendorf Porcelain Manufacturing of Germany. (3-1/4'').

21. Comic green dog was made by the Sitzendorf Porcelain Manufacturing of Germany. (2-3/4'').

22. Blue cat with black bow is marked
L & R Germany on the bottom.
(1-7/8'').

25. Smiling Oriental figure by the
Sitzendorf Porcelain Manufacturing
of Germany. (3-1/4'').

26. Dutch lady holding flowers made
by Goebel. Circa 1934. (3'').
27. Gentleman in powdered wig has
paper importer's tag marked Lisette
made in Germany. (3-1/4'').

23. Pair of Oriental figural perfumes
by the Sitzendorf Porcelain Manufacturing of Germany. (3'').

24. Three Deco inspired perfume
bottles marked Germany. (2-1/2'').

28. Lady in 18th century ball dress made by Goebel. Circa 1934. (3-3/8").

31. This little boy holding his hat marked Germany is the bottle for an atomizer. (8").

29. Little girl in Dutch costume made by Goebel. Circa 1935. (3").

30. Curtsying lady marked Coronet Registered Germany imported by the George Borgfeldt Corp. of New York Ctiy. (6").

32. Imported by the George Borgfeldt Corp. of New York City, this lady holding a parrot is marked Coronet Registered Germany. (6").

33. Lady with neck ruff is marked on bottom, Lisette made in Germany. (3-3/8").

34. Girl leaning against a column is marked, Lisette made in Germany. (3'').

37. This swirl glass bottle marked Germany has a porcelain devil's head stopper. Circa 30's. (2-3/4'').

38. Marked Bavaria, this Art Deco porcelain figural also came in green. (6'').

39. Pair of kewpie perfume bottles marked Germany. The original kewpies by Rose O'Neill were introduced in a Ladies' Home Journal story in 1909. (2-3/4'').

35. Brightly dressed girl holding a vase has paper sticker reading Ninon Paris and incised Germany mark on bottom. (3'').

36. Only part of the original paper label with Waterbury Conn. on it marks this black page bottle. (3-3/4'').

40. Little girl holding her cat is marked Bavaria. (3-1/4'').

41. Harlequin perfume bottle with original Irice importer's sticker is marked Bavaria. (5'').

42. Young boy in striped pants and green top hat is marked Bavaria. (3-1/8'').

43. Yellow cat and a blue dog are marked Bavaria. (3-1/4'').

44. This girl in a clown costume marked 'Hand Paint made in Japan' was sold by Sears in 1930 for 19¢. (3-1/2'').

45. Winking cat perfume bottle marked 'Hand Paint made in Japan' was used by Lioret as a commercial perfume bottle. (3-1/4'').

46. Lioret used this rooster bottle made in Japan to hold Narcisse perfume. (3-1/4'').

48. Delinet also used attractive Japanese porcelain bottles to help sell their perfume. The name Delinet was trademarked in 1927. (3-1/4'').

49. Lady in yellow with purple fan is marked 'Gold Castle Hand Paint Made in Japan'. (3-3/4'').

47. Marked 'Germany' porcelain perfume bottles. (2-3/4'').

50. Dancing lady is marked 'Gold Castle Hand Painted Made in Japan'. (4'').

51. Flower seller has paper label marked jasmin and the number 8182 incised on bottom. (3'').

52. Unusual girl holding her cat bottle marked only with the number 1656. (3-1/4").

55. Unmarked cat, frog, and dog perfume bottles. (2" a.h.)

53. Cherub playing the drum bottle is marked 6201 on the bottom. (3-1/4").

54. A pair of bellboys carrying flowers are marked 64 & 50 respectively. (2-3/4").

56. Lay-down bottle in the shape of a flapper's head is unmarked. (2-3/4").

57. Porcelain figural of girl holding hat marked 'M4'. Circa 1950's. (5").

59. Lady in hat and gloves marked 'Napco made in Japan'. Circa 1958. (4-1/4").

60-71. Marked 'Germany' porcelain perfume bottles. 60. 3"

58. Marked 'Germany' porcelain perfume bottle. (5").

61. 3"

62. 3-1/4"

63. 2-1/2"

64. 3"

66. 2-3/4"

65. 2-1/2"

67. 2-3/8"

68. 4-3/4"

69. 1-3/4''

70. 2-3/4''

72. Porcelain figural bottle marked 'Mocco made in Occupied Japan'. Circa 1946-52. (2-1/2'').

71. 4-3/4''

73-96. Marked 'Germany' porcelain perfume bottles. 73. 1-7/8''

74. 4-1/2''

75. 2-1/4''

78. 3''

81. --

76. 2-1/4''

79. 2-3/4''

82. 4''

77. 1-7/8''

80. 3-3/8''

83. 3-1/8''

84. 4''

87. 3-1/2''

88. 2-3/4''

85. 3''

86. 3-1/2''

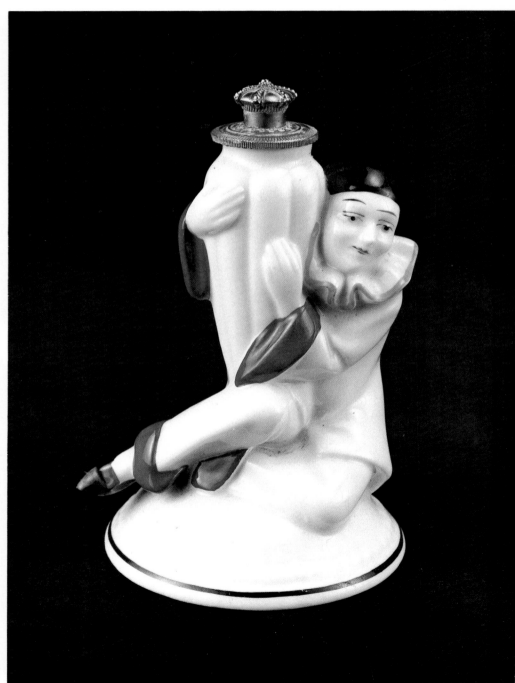

89. 4-1/4''

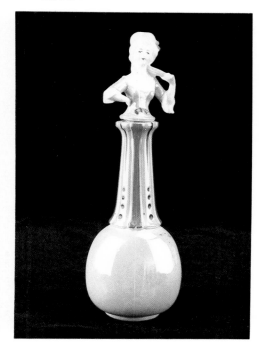

96. 2-1/4'' h.

97. Marked 'Japan' porcelain perfume bottle. (3-3/4'')

98. Marked 'Germany' porcelain perfume bottle. (5-1/4'').

99. Marked 'Japan' porcelain perfume bottle. (4'').

100. Marked 'Germany' porcelain perfume bottle. (6'').

101. Marked 'Germany' porcelain perfume bottle. (2-7/8'').

102. Marked 'Germany' porcelain perfume bottle. (3-1/2'').

103-107. Marked 'Japan' porcelain perfume bottles.   103. 4-1/4''

104. 3-3/8''

105. 3- 1/4''

106. 3-1/2''

109. 3''

110. 2-3/4''

107. ——

108-122. Bottles marked only with numbers.   108. 4-1/2''

111. 2-7/8''

112. 3-5/8''

115. 3-1/4''

116. 3-1/2''

113. 3-1/2''

114. 3-1/2''

117. 3''

118. 4-1/2''

119. 3-1/4''

121. 3-1/2''

120. 3-3/4''

122. 3-1/2''

123. Unmarked porcelain perfume bottle. (4-1/2'').

127-141 Unmarked porcelain perfume bottles.   127. 3-5/8''

124-126. Bottles marked only with numbers.   124. 2''

128. 4-3/4''

125. 2-3/8''

126. 2-1/2''

129. 4-1/2''

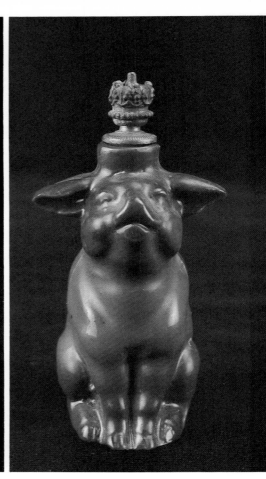

130. 2-1/2''

131. 2-3/8''

132. 2-1/2''

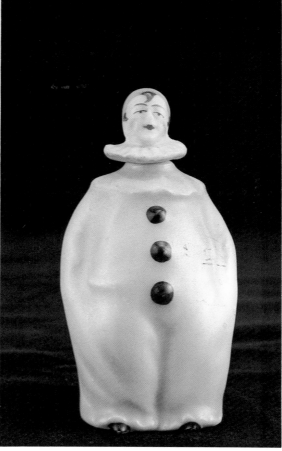

133. 3-3/4''

134. 2-3/4''

135. 2''

136. 4-1/2''

137. 3-3/4''

138. 4-1/4''

139. 4-1/2''

140. 4-1/4''

141. 2-1/4''

Nineteen-forties to Nineteen-eighties

1. Introduced in 1940, Baccarat's "Rose teinte" bottles were press-moulded in a beautiful amberina-like glass. The bottles were made in three patterns: helical twist, pinwheel, and laurel. Atomizer bottles were also made. (6-1/4").

The early 1940's ushered in a period of prosperity and high productivity for the American bottle makers. The endless variety of perfume and cologne bottles that flowed into the U.S. from European and Japanese producers during the 1920's and 1930's came to a sudden standstill with the onset of World War II. The many U.S. companies that depended on these sources for their supplies had to scramble to find American manufacturers to replace them. The Irving W. Rice Co. turned to the Imperial Art Glass Co. of Ohio and the Gundersen-Pairpoint Glass Works in New Bedford, Massachusetts. The DeVilbiss Co. of Toledo, Ohio asked Fenton Art Glass of Williamstown, West Virginia to supply them.

Fenton Art Glass Co., following the fashionable and patriotic trend of the 1940's for Early American and Victorian designs and colors, introduced an array of hand-made cologne bottles in hobnail and opalescent glass. According to William Heacock in his many definitive books and articles on Fenton glass, the first hobnail bottles made by Fenton were a special commercial run for the Wrisley Co. in 1939. The bottle was so popular with consumers Fenton added hobnail bottles to their own product line in 1940. The hobnail bottles sold well into the 1950's with only variations in the stopper design. Fenton was also approached by the DeVilbiss Co. to make atomizer and cologne bottles for them in the early 1940's. Many beautiful art glass bottles with interesting designs and finishes were produced by Fenton to sell under the DeVilbiss name.

In the early 1940's the Irving W. Rice Co. of New York approached the Gundersen-Pairpoint Glass Works in New Bedford, Massachusetts to make perfume bottles to sell under the Irice label. Guided by designer Floyd F. Cary, the glass-blowers at Gundersen-Pairpoint created lead crystal bottles of unsurpassed brilliance, workmanship, and quality. A large number of the bottle bases were decorated with ribbing, trapped air bubbles, or colored threading. The heavy, high lead content bottles were in direct contrast with the airy and fragile, ground to fit stoppers shaped like fantastic flowers or abstract sculpture that topped many of them. The other stoppers used were more conventional and matched or complemented the overall bottle design. The fantasy stoppers are the most difficult to find in mint condition since the delicate decoration was easily broken. A 1943 Irice advertisement pictured two of these bottles with a matching powder box and tray, proving complete sets were also made. The ad proclaimed the set added "an air of luxury and good taste to the vanity table." The sets were sold by fine stores and better gift shops.

With the end of World War II, the American occupation of the Japanese islands took place. The occupation was to last from September 1945 to April 1952. One of the main objectives of the occupation policy was the reestablishment of a peacetime industrial economy sufficient for the Japanese population. All items made in Japan for export during this time period were required to carry the mark "Made in Occupied Japan". Among the many items produced for export were inexpensive perfume bottles. The majority of the perfume bottles and sets made were of cheap, cloudy, bubbly pressed glass in clear or pastel colors. The main attraction for a collector is the historical significance of the embossed mark or label on the bottom of the bottle. Very occasionally a bottle or atomizer will also be found marked

2. Dresser set in blue opalescent hobnail glass with two perfume bottles and powder jar made by Fenton Art Glass of Williamstown, West Virginia. The set also came in white, cranberry, topaz, and green opalescent glass. The line was introduced in 1940. (4-1/2'').

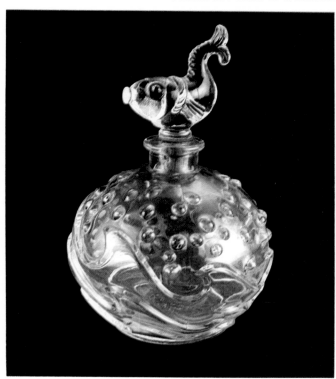

3. Unusual pressed glass round cologne bottle with a pattern of waves and bubbles has a fish shaped stopper. The words 'Des Reg U.S. Pat Office' are embossed on the bottom. The design was patented in 1942 by Alfred A. Flaster. (5-3/4'').

4. Attributed to the Imperial Art Glass Co. this cologne bottle has a pair of perching birds on a ball stopper. Circa early 1940's. (8-1/4'').

"Germany Occupied West Zone", made when American, British, and French troops occupied West Germany. The German bottles are of much higher quality than the Japanese ones.

By the 1950's, with the cost of short runs of special, fancy bottles made by American manufacturers becoming prohibitive, companies such as Irice and DeVilbiss turned once again to Europe. Perfume and cologne bottles flowed into this country from Italy, West Germany, England, and France.

In the late 1940's and 1950's handmade perfume bottles from Murano, Italy were exported in vast quantities to the United States. Many of the perfume bottles were very heavy in weight with hand polished bottoms, and the surfaces had a smooth, oily feel to the touch. A large number of the bottles were decorated with trapped air bubbles and silver or gold mica blown through the second layer of glass. Some of the companies in Italy who made bottles for export to the U.S. were Cesare Toso, Archimede Seguso, Vetrerie Artistiche Toscane, and Arturo Zaniol. Archimede Seguso specialized in beautiful lace-glass dressing table accessories and Arturo Zaniol in gild adorned perfume bottles. A paper label on a bottle stating its origin is the only sure way of knowing that it is a genuine piece of Murano glass.

The 1960's and early 1970's were a low point in the art and manufacture of the perfume bottle. Changing tastes, higher costs, and women's liberation threatened to end such frivolities as the luxurious perfume bottle. The vanity table was definitely out of fashion, replaced by the desk of the career oriented woman. It wasn't until the late 1970's and the 1980's that the trend started to reverse and once again a variety of beautiful bottles were available to the consumer.

Today perfume bottles are being made and exported to the U.S. from Czechoslovakia, East Germany, West Germany, Austria, France, Scotland, England, Italy, Japan, Taiwan, and India. American craftsmen are also producing excellent hand-made bottles in a multitude of designs. Collectors do need to be on the alert for bottles copied from older designs. Usually the experienced collectors can easily recognize the inferior workmanship of these newer bottles. Even they, though, can have difficulty in distinguishing the differences between the old and new bottles currently being made from the original glass moulds by companies in Japan and Europe. These bottles are showing up with increasing frequency in American stores as the demand for period designs such as Art Deco grows stronger.

5. Clear glass cologne bottle with triple ball stopper made by the Imperial Art Glass Co. for the Irving W. Rice Co. during World War II. This bottle has the original Irice U.S.A. paper label. Circa early 1940's. (4-1/2").

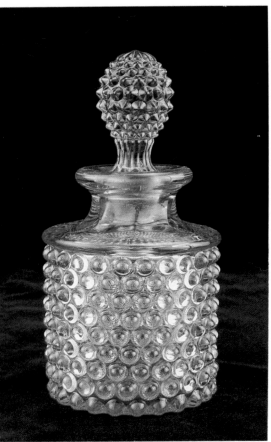

6. Made by the Imperial Art Glass Co. for the Irving W. Rice Co. this cologne bottle has a single bird on ball stopper. Circa early 1940's. (7-1/2").

7. This rose colored hobnail glass 8 oz. cologne bottle was made by Duncan and Miller. The style was sold for many years beginning in the 1930's. Circa 1940. (6-1/2").

8. Hand-made paperweight bottle with crescent moon stopper, probably made in the United States. Circa 1940's. (5").

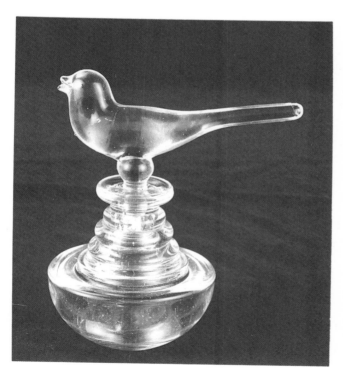

9. American made heavy paperweight bottle has a graceful bird on ball stopper. The same stopper was sold with a different bottle in a 1943 Sears catalog. (4-3/4").

10. Simple modern lines enhance this hand-made perfume bottle made by the Duncan & Miller Glass Co. of Washington, Pennsylvania. Circa 1943. (6-1/2").

11. Blue opalescent hobnail bottle with the original wood and cork stopper made by Fenton Art Glass exclusively for Wrisley to hold "Gardenia", "Carnation", or "Apple Blossom" cologne. The bottle also came in white opalescent glass. Circa 1939-1940. (6").

13. Beautiful hand-made blue overlay perfume bottle with clear glass ruffled collar and stopper made by the Fenton Art Glass Co. Circa early 1940's. (5-7/8").

15. White opalescent optic pattern bottle with white opalescent collar and stopper was made by Fenton Art Glass for the DeVilbiss Co. of Toledo, Ohio. Circa 1940's. (4-1/2").

12. Striking bottle with a feather design in white opalescent glass was hand-made by Fenton Art Glass for the DeVilbiss Co. Circa 1940's. (5-3/4").

14. Clear glass bottle with unusual cranberry optic pattern hand-made by the Fenton Art Glass Co. Circa early 1940's. (4-1/2").

16. White opalescent dots decorate this bottle made by Fenton Art Glass for the DeVilbiss Co. of Toledo, Ohio. Circa 1940's. (4-1/2").

17. Fenton's hobnail perfume bottle changed stoppers in the late 1940's and only came in blue, white, and cranberry opalescent glass. Circa 1948. (4-1/2'').

19. Crystal perfume bottle with ground to fit stopper hand-made at the Gundersen-Pairpoint Glass Works for the Irving W. Rice Co. (7-1/2'').

18. Crystal perfume bottle with ground to fit stopper hand-made at the Gundersen-Pairpoint Glass Works for the Irving W. Rice Co. (6'').

20. Crystal perfume bottle with ground to fit stopper hand-made at the Gundersen-Pairpoint Glass Works for the Irving W. Rice Co. (5-3/4'').

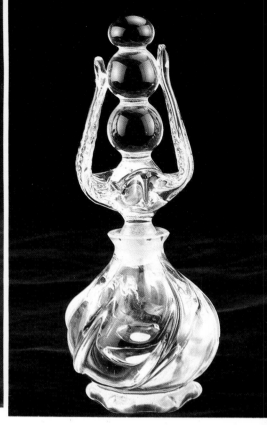

21. White opalescent hobnail combination powder box and perfume bottle was called a "Boxtle" by Fenton Art Glass. It was only made for one year. Circa 1953. (7-1/2").

22-27. Heavy, high lead content, crystal perfume bottles with ground to fit stoppers were hand-made at the Gundersen-Pairpoint Glass Works in New Bedford, Massachusetts for the Irving W. Rice Co. They were first marketed during World War II. Sets with matching tray, powder box, and perfume bottles were also made. Circa early 1940's-early 1950's.

23. 7"

25. 6-1/2"

22. 7-3/4"

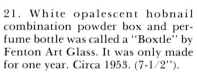

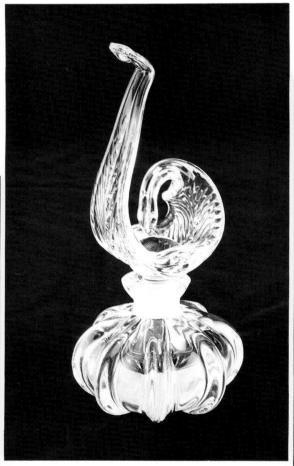

24. 6-3/4"

26. 4-1/2"

27. 10-1/2'' long

28-31. Pressed glass perfume bottles with 'Made in Occupied Japan' embossed on the bottoms. All items made in Japan for export between September 1945 until April 1952, when American troops occupied the country, were required to have this mark.

29. 3-3/4''

30. 3-3/4''

31. 4''

33. Pressed glass perfume bottle with 'Made in Japan' embossed on the bottom. (4'').

32. Pink pressed glass tray holds a pink and a blue perfume bottle. The tray has an embossed 'Made in Japan' mark. Circa 1950's. (4-1/4'').

34. Cut glass perfume bottle and atomizer with sterling silver tops were made in Birmingham, England in 1951. (4'', 4-1/2'').

35. Hand-blown, Latticino perfume bottle with pink flower shaped stopper was bought in Italy during the late 1970's. (5-1/2'').

37. Milk glass hobnail bottle was used by Wrisley to hold various scents of cologne. An advertisement in 1955 claimed the container was an authentic replica of an 18th century bottle. The price for the cologne and bottle in 1955 was $2.00. Circa 1950's. (6'').

39. Yellow, hand-blown, Venetian glass bottle has clear glass foot and feather shaped stopper. Circa late 40's and 50's. (5'').

36. Hand-blown, cut glass perfume bottle made in England about 1955. (5-7/8'').

38. Lightweight, hand-blown, art glass perfume bottle with red spiral pattern has the original Murano Italy paper tag. Circa late 1940's and 1950's. (6'').

40. Heavy, hand-blown, art glass bottle with polished bottom has a white glass inner layer and a clear glass outer layer decorated with gold mica and air bubbles flowing from top to bottom. The bottle still has the original paper tag that reads 'Made in Murano Italy Venetian glass'. Circa late 1940's and 1950's. (8-1/2'').

41. Small, round, clear pressed glass tray holds a pink, a blue, and a green bottle with clear stoppers. The set is marked "Japan". Circa 1950's. (4").

42. Milled brass purse perfume bottle is decorated with rhinestones. The container received U.S. patent 158,445 filed March 5, 1948 by William A. Cotter. (2-1/4").

43. Trapped air bubbles of uniform size decorate this two piece dresser set of hand-blown Venetian glass. The paper labels say 'Italy Mrano Cesare Toso Venezia'. Bottles with the original company labels are rare. Circa late 1940's and 1950's. (7-1/4", 8").

45. Sunburst yellow carnival glass perfume bottle was only produced for six months in 1982 by the Imperial Glass Co. (6-1/4'').

44. Hand-blown perfume bottle of pink satin glass cased over frosted white has an unusual flower shaped stopper. Circa 1960's. (5'').

46. Flashed red cherry pattern on clear glass atomizer was made by Stourbridge of England. The company closed in 1982. (4-3/4'').

50. Classic cut crystal dresser bottle with a paper tag that says "ATLANTIS - Full lead crystal hand blown and cut for Block Crisal Portugal". Circa 1984. (4-3/4").

47. Cobalt blue and clear glass paperweight perfume bottle with inserted glass canes hand-made by Perthsire in Cruff, Scotland. Circa 1984. (5-1/4").

51. French, hand-made, crystal atomizer by Alexandre de Paris. The paper label says 'Alexandre de Paris, Cristal Fait Main'. Circa 1984. (4-1/2").

52. Frosted glass, ribbon pattern perfume bottle hand made in England by Cowdy of Gloucestershire. Circa 1984. (4").

48. High quality cut crystal perfume bottle made by Waterford glassworks in Ireland. Waterford opened in 1951 to produce glass similar to that made in the 18th century. Circa 1980's. (4-1/2").

49. Cut crystal atomizer with sterling silver top made by Royal Brierley of England. The crystal has a high lead content not less than 30%. Circa 1984. (5-1/2").

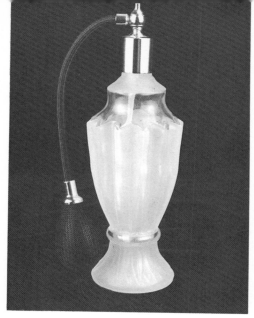

53. Tall, elegant atomizer in frosted and clear glass made in France by Novex Paris. Circa 1984. (8-1/4'').

56. Red "end-of-the-week" glass canes perfume bottle hand-made by Perthsire in Cruff, Scotland. Circa 1984. (5'').

54. Pressed frosted glass perfume bottle with sea shell stopper made in Taiwan for Sigma, a Towle company. Circa 1984. (4-3/4'').

55. Heavy, palest pink crystal perfume bottle with double flower stopper hand made by Cristallo Di Censo of Italy. Circa 1984. (5-1/4'').

57. Modern hand cut crystal perfume bottles came in every color of the rainbow including clear glass. Bottles made by glass houses in West Germany, East Germany, Austria, Japan, and Czechoslovakia can easily be found. Circa 1970's and 1980's. (5-1/4'').

58. Deco inspired, dark blue cased with frosted glass perfume bottle hand-made in 1984 by T. Bueikner. (5-1/2'').

59. Modern hand cut and polished crystal perfume bottle made in Japan for Tilso. Circa 1980's. (8").

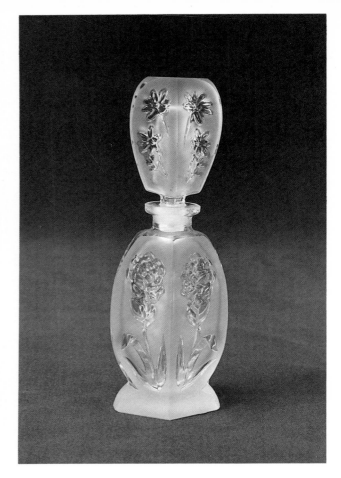

61. An example of a new Irice perfume bottle of pressed glass made for the company in Japan. Irice also imports lead crystal bottles from West Germany. Circa 1984. (6-1/8").

60. Crystal perfume bottle decorated with engraved flowers was made in Western Germany. The paper label on its says 'Kristallglas Handgeschliffen'. Circa 1980's. (4-1/2").

62. Opaline glass bottle with pretty butterfly stopper made in France by Waltersperger. Circa 1980's. (3-1/2").

63. Beautiful hand-made art glass perfume bottle made by Robert Eickholt of Ohio. Circa 1985. (4").

65. Clear and frosted glass atomizer decorated with frosted pinwheels made in France by Marcel Franck. Circa 1984. (4-1/2").

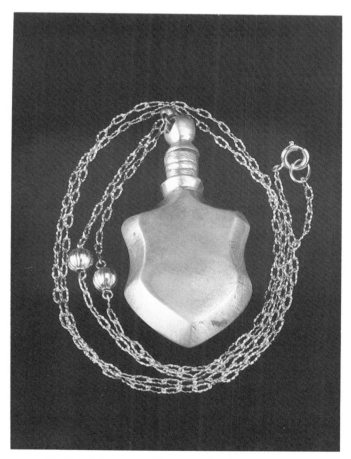

64. Perfume bottle with a blue iridescent finish similar to Tiffany or Steuben glass made by Dux. Circa 1980's. (5").

66. Solid brass, necklace, perfume bottle hand made in India. These can be found in many different shapes and sizes. Circa 1980's. (2-3/4").

67. Opaque black glass atomizer that comes in several different styles made for Willitts of California by Pompadour of Vienna, Austria. Circa 1985. (3-3/4'').

69. Frosted purple, pressed glass atomizer was made for Irice, to their design, in Japan. Circa 1984. (3-1/2'').

68. Opaque pink glass hand-made perfume bottle decorated wth applied blue glass trailing has a clear glass stopper. The bottle was made by Roger Roland of Idaho. Circa 1985. (4-3/4'').

Bottle Care and Tips

* Denatured alcohol is the best cleaning agent to use inside a perfume or cologne bottle to remove hardened perfume residue and stubborn stains. This can easily be found at hardware, art, and paint supply stores. The next best cleaning agents are toilet bowl cleaners, denture cleaners, isopropyl alcohol (rubbing alcohol), and warm water and soap.
* A small metal funnel, an ideal type is the kind made to transfer perfume into a purse bottle, should be used to fill a bottle with the cleaning agent when the original labels are still intact. Cleaning solutions can remove or damage the labels, so be careful!
* To remove stoppers that are stuck or frozen, run warm water around the neck of the bottle to soften the perfume resins, then gently apply pressure to the stopper.
* Do not scrub, especially with abrasive cleaners, perfume bottles decorated with enamelling or gilding as the ornamentation can be rubbed off or chipped easily.
* Perfume bottles decorated with hand staining or painting should be cleaned with care. Check that the decoration is color fast before you submerge the bottle in water or a cleaning solution.
* To remove stubborn dirt and grime in the crevices of cut or engraved glass bottles, use a very soft toothbrush applied with caution.
* To help prevent accidental chipping or breakage of bottles use a rubber or plastic mat in the sink when cleaning bottles.
* Use a lint free paper towel to dry your bottles after cleaning.
* After both the inner and outer surface of the bottle is thoroughly cleaned and the stopper replaced, I normally use a window or glass cleaner that dries with a streakless finish to keep the bottle sparkling.
* The misty bloom on the inner surface of a bottle can often be removed with liquid laundry bleach. Pour the bleach into the bottle and let stand for a few hours. The bloom can also be treated professionally with acid to repolish the interior. Do not attempt this method yourself.
* A bottle with an iridescent, whitish, or scaly surface or interior cannot be fixed. This condition is the result of underground burial or exposure to dampness for a long period of time which causes a permanent chemical change in the glass to occur.
* A bottle with minor chips in the glass or a broken dapper can be ground smooth by a glass grinder. The repair of a broken bottle, however, is a complicated art and should only be attempted by a knowledgeable person in the field.
* The commercial bottle collector should consider pouring out any remaining perfume and thoroughly cleaning the bottle before adding it to a collection. The often cloying or rancid fragrance of an old perfume is unpleasant, and if left standing in a bottle for a lengthy period of years can harm the surface, biting into it or leaving behind a scummy unsightly residue.
* Direct sunlight over a period of time can change the chemical composition of a clear glass bottle occasionally, causing the bottle to turn an amethyst, amber, or grey color. Lighted display cabinets are an excellent way to both protect and show off a perfume bottle collection.

* When choosing the place in your home to display your bottle collection avoid areas with fluctuating temperature extremes. A steady temperature and humidity is the best because a rapid change in air temperature can crack or shatter a bottle.
* When displaying perfume bottles with uneven bottoms, use a piece of double-sided tape or a putty like clay to secure them to the shelf.
* When storing or transporting perfume bottles it is better and safer to use several small boxes instead of a few large boxes. A large box can be extremely awkward and heavy to handle when fully packed. It is also a good idea to reinforce the bottom of the boxes with a heavy strapping tape. Wrap each bottle and stopper individually with bubble wrap, tissue paper, newspaper, or other protective material.
* Hunt for bottles to add to your collection at flea markets, antique shows, antique shops, auctions, estate sales, garage sales, bottle dumps, bottle club conventions and sales, rummage sales, and junk shops. Ads stating the specific type of perfume bottles you are looking for can also be placed in newspapers and magazines specializing in antiques, bottles, or glass.
* When searching for bottles carry a magnifying glass with you to check for imperfections, cracks, chips, repairs, and identifying marks. A damaged bottle is far less valuable than one in perfect condition.
* A large majority of the perfume and cologne bottles made were in clear glass, so the colored glass bottles are usually more valuable and harder to find.
* When buying signed art glass perfume bottles made, for example, by Moser, Stueben, Tiffany, Lalique, etc., expect to pay premium prices for them.
* When upgrading the quality of your collection, trade or sell less valuable bottles to help finance the acquisition of better pieces.
* Keep an inventory of your collection. It should include a photograph for each bottle with description, present condition, repairs made, current value, date and place purchased, and the amount paid. A duplicate copy should be kept in a separate place for safety.
* To find worn, faint, or faded acid-etched marks on the bottom of a bottle, try rubbing the bottom briskly on a bath towel or a piece of denim until warm to the touch. This will bring the acid to the surface for a few seconds. Breath immediately on the surface to frost the mark. You may have to try several times, holding the bottle at different angles to a strong light to find a mark.

1. First perfume atomizer designed by Thomas A. DeVilbiss which received a patent was filed August 23, 1909.

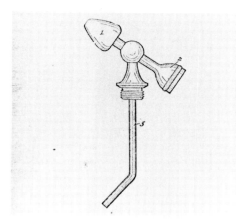

2. Patent 46,430 designed by Thomas A. DeVilbiss was filed July 2, 1914.

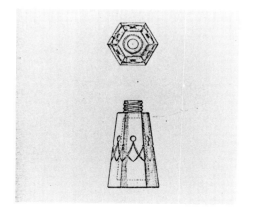

3. Patent 50,467 for an atomizer bottle designed by Thomas A. DeVilbiss was filed June 16, 1916.

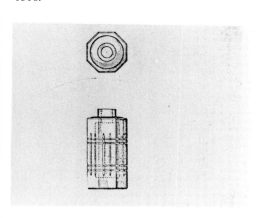

4. Patent 50,466 for an atomizer bottle designed by Thomas A. DeVilbiss was filed June 16, 1916.

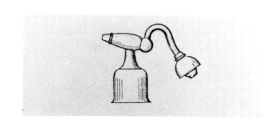

5. Patent 59,624 designed by Thomas A. DeVilbiss was filed February 12, 1920.

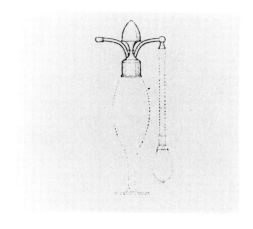

6. Patent 60,782 designed by Thomas A. DeVilbiss was filed June 4, 1921.

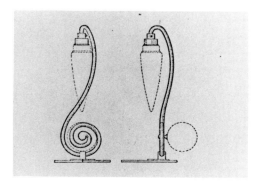

7. Patent 75,899 designed by Thomas A. DeVilbiss was filed April 7, 1928.

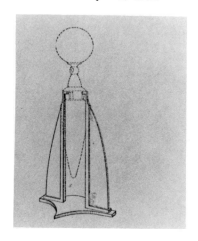

8. Patent 75,900 for an atomizer support designed by Thomas A. DeVilbiss was filed April 7, 1928.

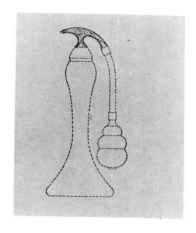

9. Patent 75,901 designed by Thomas A. DeVilbiss was filed April 7, 1928.

10. Patent 75,902 designed by Thomas A. DeVilbiss was filed April 7, 1928.

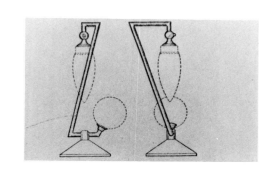

11. Patent 76,463 designed by Thomas A. DeVilbiss was filed April 7, 1928.

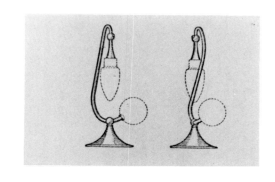

12. Patent 76,464 designed by Thomas A. DeVilbiss was filed April 7, 1928.

13. Patent 76,465 designed by Thomas A. DeVilbiss was filed April 7, 1928.

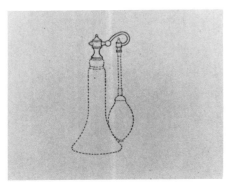

14. Patent 77,466 designed by Thomas A. DeVilbiss was filed October 10, 1928.

15. Patent 77,467 designed by Thomas A. DeVilbiss was filed October 10, 1928.

16. Patent 77,468 designed by Thomas A. DeVilbiss was filed October 10, 1928.

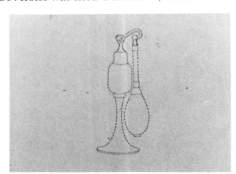

17. Patent 77,469 designed by Thomas A. DeVilbiss was filed October 10, 1928.

18. Patent 77,470 designed by Thomas A. DeVilbiss was filed October 10, 1928.

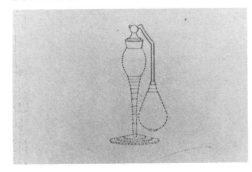

19. Patent 77,471 designed by Thomas A. DeVilbiss was filed October 10, 1928.

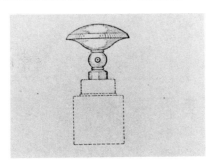

20. Patent 77,752 designed by Thomas A. DeVilbiss was filed April 7, 1928.

21. Patent 77,753 designed by Thomas A. DeVilbiss was filed April 7, 1928.

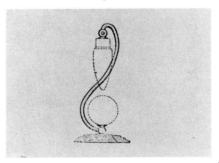

22. Patent 77,754 designed by Thomas A. DeVilbiss was filed April 7, 1928.

23. Patent 77,755 designed by Thomas A. DeVilbiss was filed April 7, 1928.

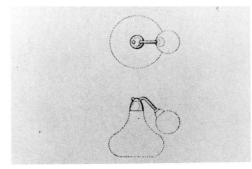

24. Patent 88,273 designed by Frederic A. Vuillemenot for the DeVilbiss Co. was filed May 25, 1932.

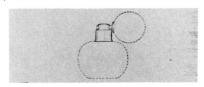

25. Patent 91,419 designed by Paul B. Brown for the DeVilbiss Co. was filed May 22, 1933.

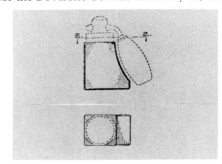

26. Patent 91,695 designed by Frederic A. Vuilemenot for the DeVilbiss Co. was filed December 20, 1933.

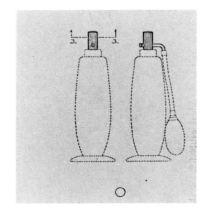

27. Patent 93,446 designed by Paul B. Brown for the DeVilbiss Co. was filed August 10, 1934.

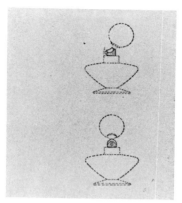

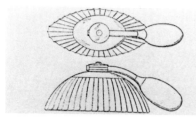

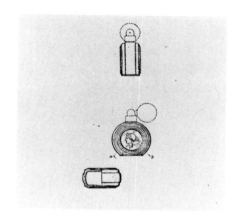

28. Patent 93,447 designed by Paul B. Brown for the DeVilbiss Co. was filed August 10. 1934.

32. Patent 101,656 designed by Frederic A. Vuillemenot for the DeVilbiss Co. was filed September 14, 1936.

37. Patent 102,012 designed by Frederic a. Vuillemenot for the DeVilbiss Co. was filed September 8, 1936.

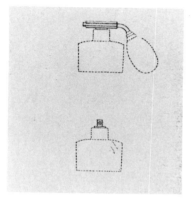

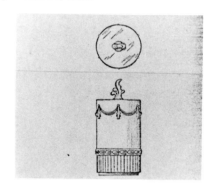

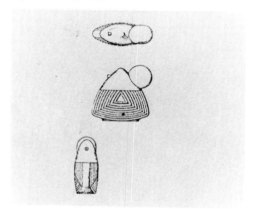

29. Patent 93,647 designed by Paul B. Brown for the DeVilbiss Co. was filed August 10, 1934.

33. Patent 101,901, filed September 2, 1936, was for an atomizer case sold by the DeVilbiss Co. made by Lenox.

38. Patent 102,013 designed by Frederic A. Vuillemenot for the DeVilbiss Co. was filed September 9, 1936.

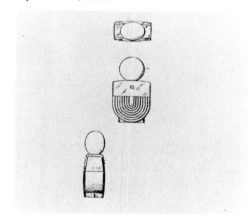

30. Patent 97,420 designed by Frederic A. Vuillemenot for the DeVilbiss Co. was filed February 23, 1935.

34. Patent 101,903 designed by Frederic A. Vuillemenot for the DeVilbiss Co. was filed September 8, 1936.

39. Patent 102,014 designed by Frederic A. Vuillemenot for the DeVilbiss Co. was filed September 9, 1936.

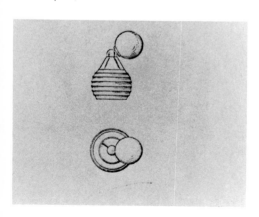

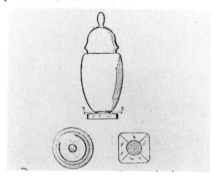

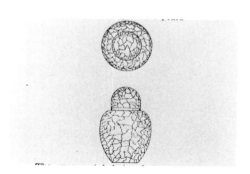

31. Patent 97,515 designed by Frederic A. Vuillemenot for the DeVilbiss Co. was filed February 23, 1935.

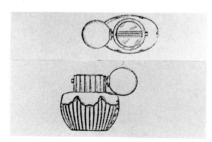

36. Patent 102,011 designed by Frederic A. Vuillemenot for the DeVilbiss Co. was filed September 2, 1936.

35. Patent 101,904, filed September 18, 1936, was for a glass hand-decorated atomizer case sold by DeVilbiss.

40. Patent 102,154, filed October 23, 1936, was for an atomizer case sold by DeVilbiss.

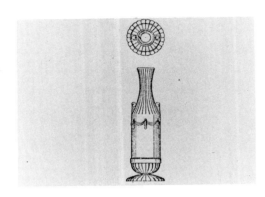

41. Patent 102,155, filed October 23, 1936,, was for an atomizer case sold by the DeVilbiss Co. made by Lenox.

42. Patent 102,156, filed October 23, 1936, was for an atomizer case sold by DeVilbiss.

43. Patent 102,198, filed October 23, 1936, was for a rabbit shaped atomizer case made by Lenox for the DeVilbiss Co.

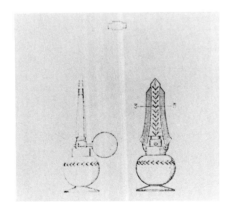

44. Patent 102,199 designed by Frederic A. Vuillemenot for the DeVilbiss Co. was filed October 23, 1936.

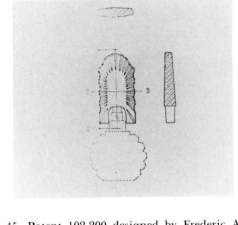

45. Patent 102,200 designed by Frederic A. Vuillemenot for the DeVilbiss Co. was filed October 23, 1936.

46. Patent 102,201 designed by Frederic A. Vuillemenot for the DeVilbiss Co. was filed October 23, 1936.

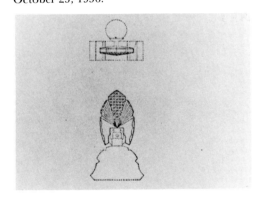

47. Patent 102,202 designed by Frederic A. Vuillemenot for the DeVilbiss Co. was filed October 23, 1936.

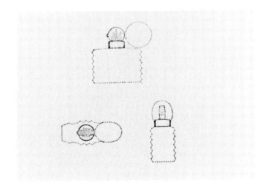

48. Patent 103,171 designed by Frederic A. Vuillemenot for the DeVilbiss Co. was filed January 2, 1937.

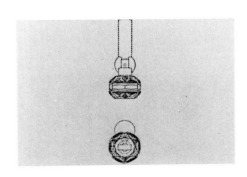

49. Patent 105,044 designed by Frederic A. Vuillemenot for the DeVilbiss Co. was filed May 12, 1937.

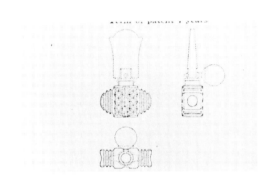

50. Patent 105,045 designed by Frederic A. Vuillemenot for the DeVilbiss Co. was filed May 12, 1937.

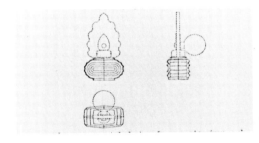

51. Patent 105,046 designed by Frederic A. Vuillemenot for the DeVilbiss Co. was filed May 12, 1937.

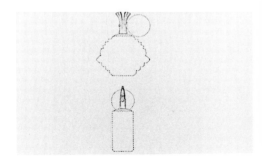

52. Patent 106,336 designed by Frederic A. Vuillemenot for the DeVilbiss Co. was filed August 26, 1937.

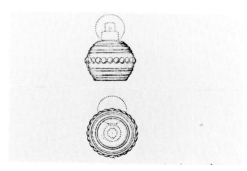

53. Patent 106,337 designed by Frederic A. Vuillemenot for the DeVilbiss Co. was filed August 26, 1937.

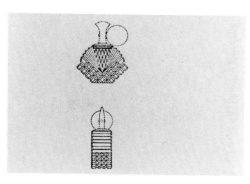

57. Patent 107,709 designed by Robert P. Vuillemenot for the DeVilbiss Co. was filed November 17, 1937.

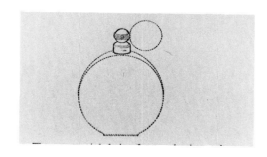

61. Patent 114,243 designed by Frederic A. Vuillemenot for the DeVilbiss Co. was filed February 9, 1939.

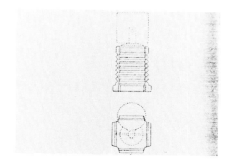

54. Patent 106,462 designed by Frederic A. Vuillemenot for the DeVilbiss Co. was filed August 26, 1937.

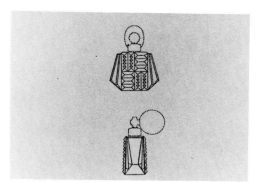

58. Patent 109,431 designed by Frederic A. Vuillemenot for the DeVilbiss Co. was filed March 1, 1938.

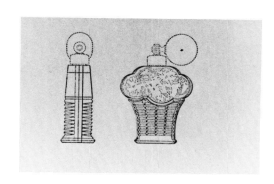

62. Patent 114,570 designed by Frederic A. Vuillemenot for the DeVilbiss Co. was filed March 9, 1939.

55. Patent 106,463 designed by Frederic A. Vuillemenot for the DeVilbiss Co. was filed August 26, 1937.

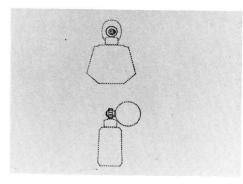

59. Patent 112,731 designed by Frederic A. Vuillemenot for the DeVilbiss Co. was filed March 1,, 1938.

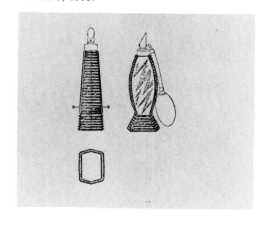

63. Patent 114,571 designed by Frederic A. Vuillemenot for the DeVilbiss Co. was filed March 9, 1939.

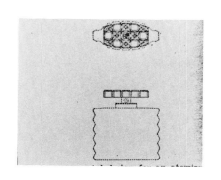

56. Patent 107,566 designed by Frederic A. Vuillemenot for the DeVilbiss Co. was filed November 15, 1937.

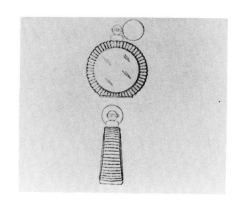

60. Patent 114,242 designed by Frederic A. Vuillemenot for the DeVilbiss Co. was filed February 9, 1939.

64. Patent 115,137 designed by Frederic A. Vuillemenot for the DeVilbiss Co. was filed February 24, 1939.

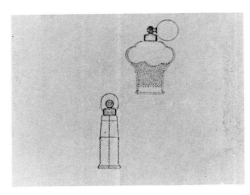

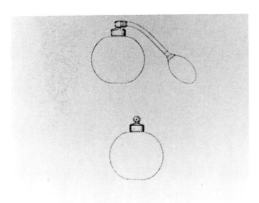

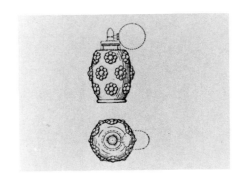

65. Patent 115,138 designed by Frederic A. Vuillemenot for the DeVilbiss Co. was filed March 9, 1939.

69. Patent 118,922 designed by Frederic A. Vuillemenot for the DeVilbiss Co. was filed December 18, 1939.

73. Patent 124,086 designed by Frederic A. Vuillemenot was filed October 28, 1940. The glass was made by Fenton.

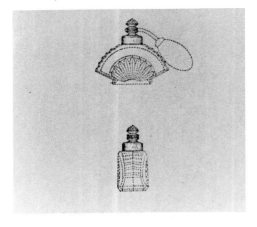

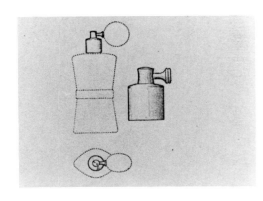

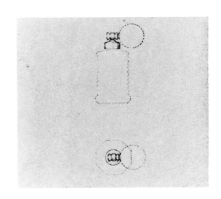

66. Patent 115,243 designed by Frederic A. Vuillemenot for the DeVilbiss Co. was filed March 11, 1939.

70. Patent 120,763 designed by Joy B. Schmitt for the DeVilbiss Co. was filed February 19, 1940.

74. Patent 124,216 designed by Frederic A. Vuillemenot for the DeVilbiss Co. was filed November 16, 1940.

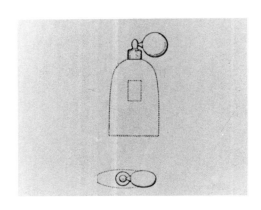

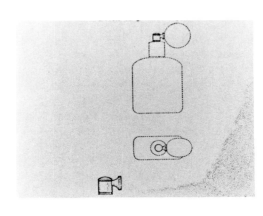

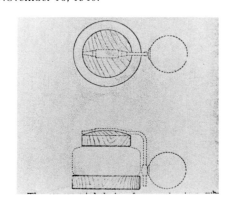

67. Patent 118,228 designed by Frederic A. Vuillemenot for the DeVilbiss Co. was filed November 2, 1939.

71. Patent 121,404 designed by Frederic A. Vuillemenot for the DeVilbiss Co. was filed February 19, 1940.

75. Patent 129,297 designed by Carl W. Sundberg for the DeVilbiss Co. was filed July 5, 1941.

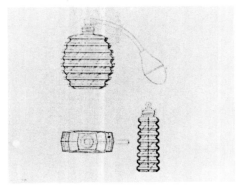

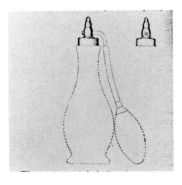

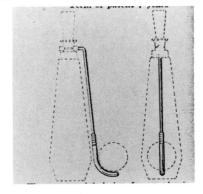

68. Patent 118,921 designed by Frederic A. Vuillemenot for the DeVilbiss Co. was filed December 18, 1939.

72. Patent 121,909 designed by Frederic A. Vuillemenot for the DeVilbiss Co. was filed June 25, 1940. The glass was made by Fenton.

76. Patent 129,661 designed by Frederic A. Vuillemenot for the DeVilbiss Co. was filed June 27, 1941.

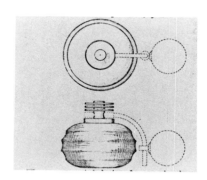

77. Patent 129,662 designed by Frederic A. Vuillemenot for the DeVilbiss Co. was filed July 2, 1941.

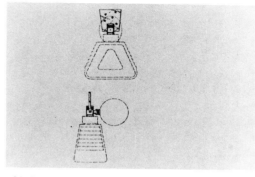

81. Patent 168,003 designed by Carl W. Sundberg for the DeVilbiss Co. was filed June 28, 1952.

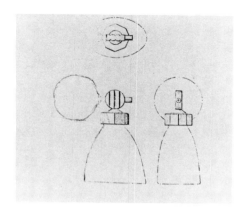

85. Patent 107,431 designed by F.W. Lohse for the T.J. Holmes Co. was filed April 13, 1937.

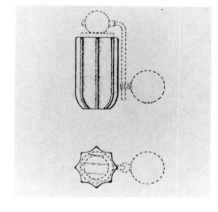

78. Patent 129,736 designed by Frederic A. Vuillemenot for the DeVilbiss Co. was filed July 2, 1941.

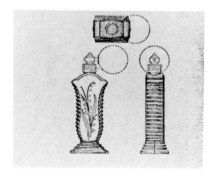

82. Lily of the valley bottle designed by Frederick R. Hoch for T.J. Holmes Co. Inc. was patented in 1939. (6-1/2").

86. Patent 107,432 designed by F.W. Lohse for the T.J. Holmes Co. was filed April 13, 1937.

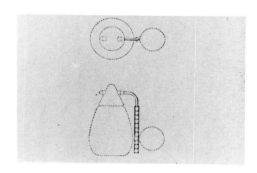

79. Patent 130,511 designed by Carl W. Sundberg for the DeVilbiss Co. was filed July 5,

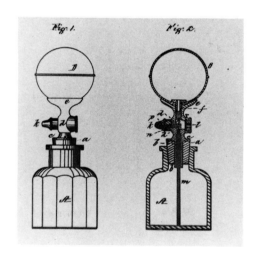

83. Patented in 1876 this atomizer was designed by Thomas J. Holmes for both medicine and perfume.

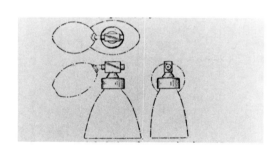

87. Patent 107,690 designed by F.W. Lohse for the T.J. Holmes Co. was filed April 13, 1937.

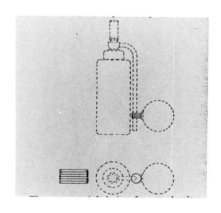

80. Patent 130,653 designed by Frederic A. Vuillemenot for the DeVilbiss Co. was filed June 27, 1941.

84. Patent 107,024 designed by F.W. Lohse for the T.J. Holmes Co. was filed April 13, 1937.

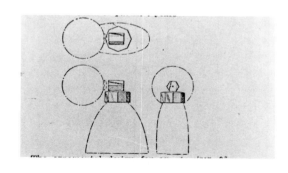

88. Patent 107,691 designed by F.W. Lohse for the T.J. Holmes Co. was filed April 13, 1937.

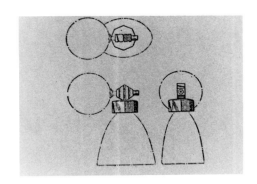

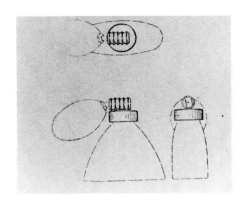

89. Patent 107,692 designed by F.W. Lohse for the T.J. Holmes Co. was filed April 13, 1937.

93. Patent 113,364 designed by F.W. Lohse for the T.J. Holmes Co. was filed April 13, 1937.

97. Patent 115,792 designed by F.R. Hoch for the T.J. Holmes Co. was filed November 15, 1938.

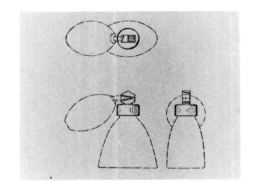

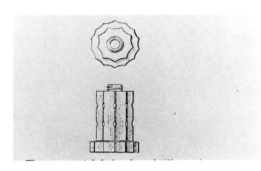

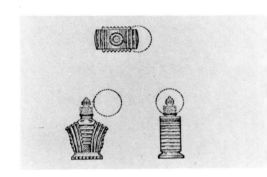

90. Patent 107,693 designed by F.W. Lohse for the T.J. Holmes Co. was filed April 13, 1937.

94. Patent 115,554 designed by F.R. Hoch for the T.J. Holmes Co. was filed November 15, 1938.

98. Patent 116,710 designed by F.R. Hoch for the T.J. Holmes Co. was filed June 23, 1939.

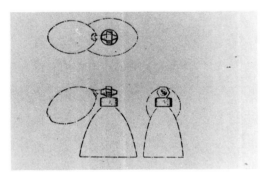

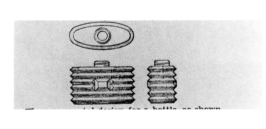

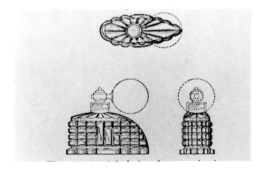

91. Patent 107,694 designed by F.W. Lohse for the T.J. Holmes Co. was filed April 13, 1937.

95. Patent 115,790 designed by F.R. Hoch for the T.J. Holmes Co. was filed November 15, 1938.

99. Patent 116,741 designed by F.R. Hoch for the T.J. Holmes Co. was filed June 23, 1939.

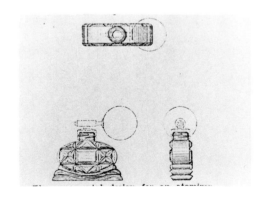

92. Patent 110,873 designed by F.W. Lohse for the T.J. Holmes Co. was filed January 10, 1938.

96. Patent 115,791 designed by F.R. Hoch for the T.J. Holmes Co. was filed November 15, 1938.

100. Patent 118,778 designed by F.R. Hoch for the T.J. Holmes Co. was filed September 6, 1939.

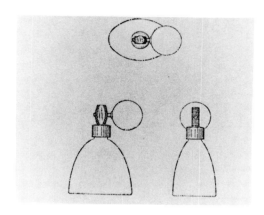

101. Patent 118,782 designed by F.W. Lohse for the T.J. Holmes Co. was filed September 6, 1939.

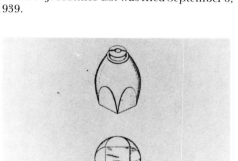

102. Patent 128,491 designed by F.R. Hoch for the T.J. Holmes Co. was filed March 5, 1941.

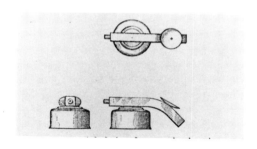

103. Patent 130,938 designed by F.R. Hoch for the T.J. Holmes Co. was filed August 26, 1941.

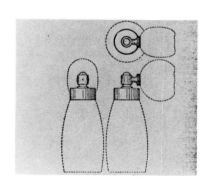

104. Patent 140,598 designed by Fred R. High for the T.J. Holmes Co. was filed December 30, 1944.

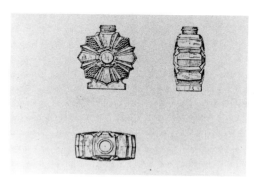

105. Patent 152,969 designed by Fred R. High for the T.J. Holmes Co. was filed April 2, 1948.

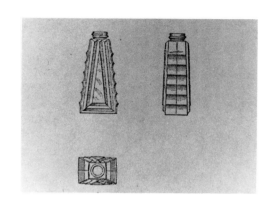

106. Patent 154,477 designed by Fred R. High for the T.J. Holmes Co. was filed April 22, 1948.

107. Patent 154,478 designed by Fred R. High for the T.J. Holmes Co. was filed April 22, 1948.

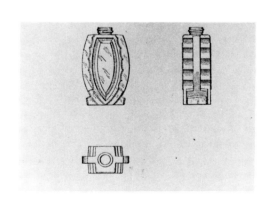

108. Patent 154,479 designed by Fred R. High for the T.J. Holmes Co. was filed April 22, 1948.

109. Patent 154,480 designed by Fred R. High for the T.J. Holmes Co. was filed April 22, 1948.

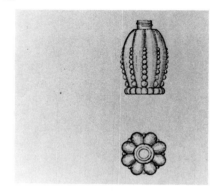

110. Patent 154,481 designed by Fred R. High for the T.J. Holmes Co. was filed April 22, 1948.

111. Patent 155,803 designed by Fred R. High for the T.J. Holmes Co. was filed August 28, 1948.

112. Patent 165,122 designed by Fred R. High for the T.J. Holmes Co. was filed January 9, 1951.

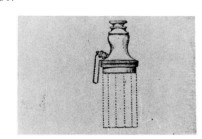

113. Patent 71,861 designed by Martha Bruells of Bois Colombes, France was filed July 20, 1926.

1. Street lamp perfume bottle given patent 21,973 filed September 24, 1892 was assigned to Herman Tappan of New York.

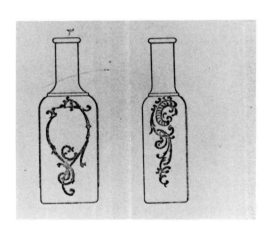

2. Bottle and holder shaped like a man riding a bicycle received patent 21,925 filed September 24, 1892 and was assigned to Herman Tappan of New York.

3. Patent 35,894 filed on March 31, 1902 by Richard Hudnut for an unknown scent.

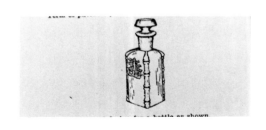

4. Filed on June 28, 1907 patent 38,710 was for a bottle used by Vantine & Co. New York.

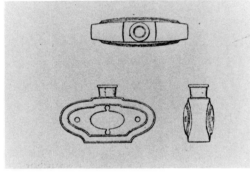

5. Victor Vivaudou of New York filed for patent 49,236 on April 12, 1916 on this bottle.

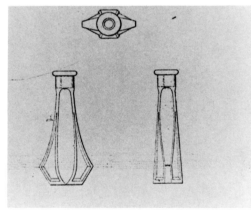

6. Patent 49,289 filed on April 17, 1916 was for a bottle used by Victor Vivaudou of New York.

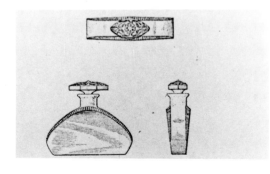

7. Bottle with patent 49,406 filed on May 24, 1916 used by Victor Vivaudou.

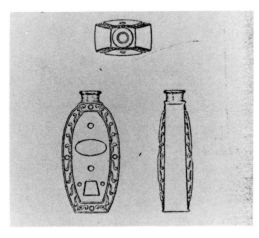

8. Patent 62,995 filed on February 3, 1923 was for a bottle used by "4711" Mulhens Co.

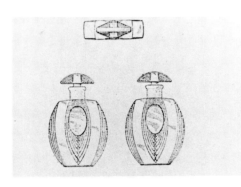

9. Filed on February 3, 1923, patent 62,996 was for a bottle used by "4711" Mulhens Co.

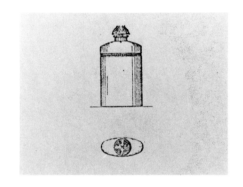

10. Bottle used by Coty granted patent 63,351 filed on May 3, 1923.

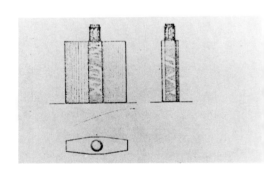

11. Bottle granted patent 63,352 filed on May 3, 1923 was used for "Emeraude" by Coty. The bottle was designed by Edouard P. Benois.

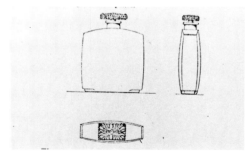

12. Bottle designed by Edouard P. Benois for "Muguet des Bois" by Coty was granted patent 63,354 filed May 3, 1923.

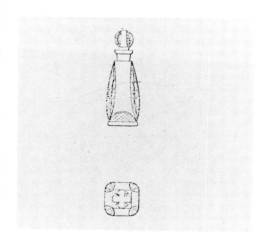

13. Patent 63,433 filed June 2, 1923 is for an unknown Louis Phillippe perfume.

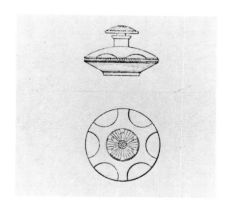

14. Bottle used for "Je Pense A Vous" by Louis Phillippe was granted patent 63,434 filed on June 27, 1923.

15. Baccarat made this bottle for "Ming Toy" by Forest of Paris. The bottle designed by Leon Cohn was granted patent 64,297 filed on September 26, 1923.

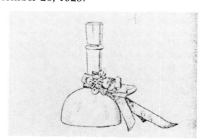

16. Boué Soeurs, Inc. of New York was assigned patent 64,417 filed April 26, 1923 for this bottle used for many scents.

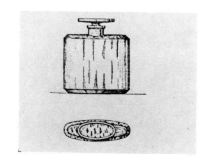

17. Patent 64,659 filed January 14, 1924 was given to the bottle used by Caron for "Tabac Blond" introduced in 1919.

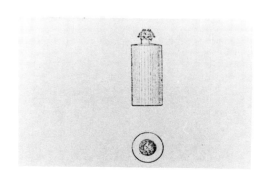

18. Bottle used by Coty for an unknown scent was granted patent 65,157 filed May 3, 1923.

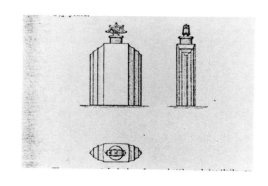

19. Forest Perfumes of Paris was assigned patent 66,071 filed September 27, 1924 for this bottle used for "Lucky Scents" perfume.

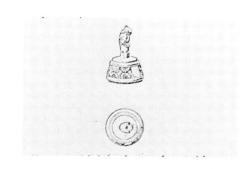

20. Hand-painted parrot stoppered bottle designed by Joseph Fields for "Bouquet" by Jovoy of Paris was granted patent 66,532 filed July 22, 1924. The bottle was made by Verreries Brosse.

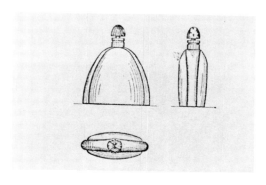

21. Bottle designed by George Dumoulin received patent 66,619 filed December 10, 1924. It was assigned to the Lenthéric Company.

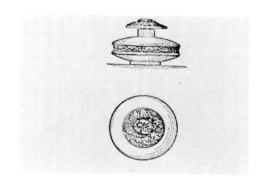

22. Embossed crystal bottle for "Lotus d'Or" by Lenthéric, designed by Georges Dumoulin, was granted patent 66,620 filed December 10, 1924.

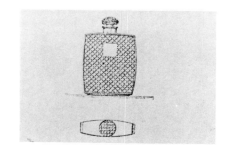

23. Patent 67,949 filed April 15, 1925 was given to the bottle designed by Fernaud Javal for "En Visite" by Houbigant.

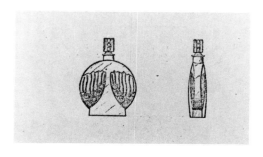

24. "Toujours Moi" by Corday bottle, covered with gold leaf, was given patent 68,340 filed June 30, 1925. The bottle was designed by Charles J. Oppenheim, Jr.

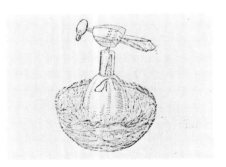

25. "Toodleoo" by Corday bottle, sold in a feather nest, was granted patent 68,820 filed December 12, 1924. The bird stoppered bottle was designed by Charles L. Marcus.

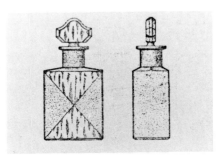

29. Louis Becker of Paris, France received patent 70,310 filed April 2, 1926 for this perfume bottle.

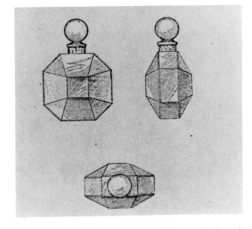

33. Opaque black glass D'Orsay "Dandy" bottle was by Sue et Mare received patent 71,782 filed August 30, 1926. The bottle was designed by Paul C. Delaize.

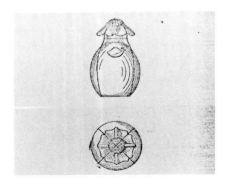

26. Ciro was assigned patent 68,841 filed September 29, 1925 for this bottle used to hold "Bouquet Antique", designed by Guy T. Gibson.

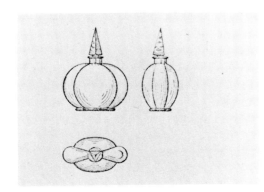

30. Introduced to the U.S. in 1925, "Tais-toi mon Coeur" by Drecoll was granted patent 70,361 filed February 25, 1926 for its bottle designed by Pierre de Wagner.

34. Budda bottle made for the A.A. Vantine Co. of New York was granted patent 73,267 filed March 25, 1927.

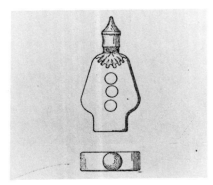

27. Patent 69,177 filed September 29, 1925 was for Ciro's "Parfum Maskee" bottle, designed by Guy T. Gibson.

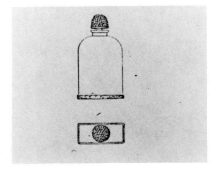

31. The "Cypria" by Grenoville of Paris bottle received patent 70,957 filed May 20, 1926. The bottle was designed by Georges Guerin.

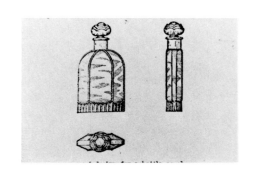

35. Patent 73,428 filed June 1, 1927 was assigned to Cheramy for its "Biarritz" bottle.

28. Dog figural bottle used by Jovoy of Paris was granted patent 69,976 filed on December 12, 1924.

32. Louis Becker of Paris, France was granted patent 71,125 filed April 2, 1926 for this perfume bottle.

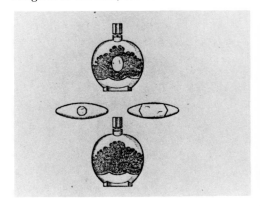

36. "Le Fleuve Bleu" by Lionceau bottle received patent 74,320 filed November 8, 1927.

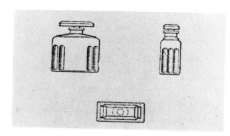

37. "Djedi" perfume made its debut to commemorate Guerlain's 100th Anniversary. The bottle received patent 74,418 filed June 30, 1927.

38. Introduced to the U.S. in 1925, Lucien Lelong's "Tout le Long" bottle received patent 75,852 on July 24, 1928.

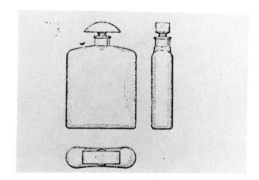

39. Candle bottle, granted patent 76,116 filed June 16, 1928, was assigned to Spencer Perfume Co. Inc. of South Bend, Indiana.

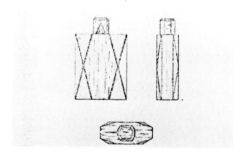

40. Filed June 1, 1928 patent 76,138 was for the "Au Matin" by Houbigant bottle.

41. Ganna Walska Co. of Pantin, France was granted patent 76,142 filed October 3, 1927 for this "Divorcons" bottle.

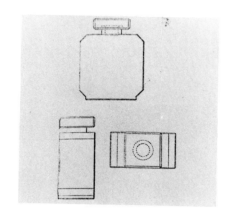

42. Coty introduced the perfume "L'Aimant" to the U.S. in 1927. The bottle received patent 76,180 filed May 11, 1928.

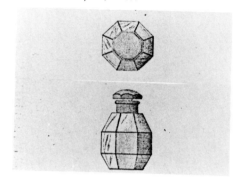

43. André Lavault of Paris, France designed this bottle for "Jodelle" granted patent 76,405 filed November 25, 1927. The name "Jodelle" was trademarked in 1927 by the Associated Merchandising Corp., New Jersey.

44. Patent 77,826 filed June 5, 1928 was for Ciro's "Gardenia Sauvage" bottle.

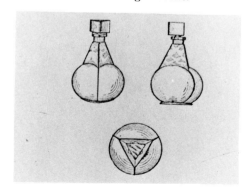

45. The clear crystal bottle introduced in 1928 that held "Asphodèle" by Lenthéric received patent 78,616 filed January 12, 1929.

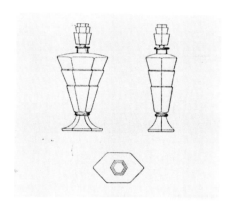

46. Bottle designed by Abraham Levy granted patent 78,826 filed April 3, 1929 was assigned to YBRY Inc.

47. Perfume bottle granted patent 78,844 filed April 9, 1929 was assigned to the George W. Button Corp. New York.

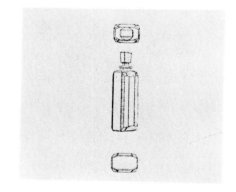

48. Bottle for "Acaciosa" by Caron was granted patent 78,878 filed February 4, 1929. The perfume "Acaciosa" was introduced in 1924.

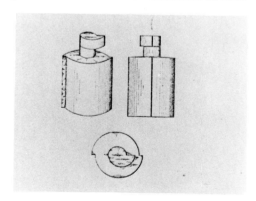

49. The "Mimosa" by Isabey of Paris bottle in opaque yellow glass was granted patent 79,760 filed August 20, 1929.

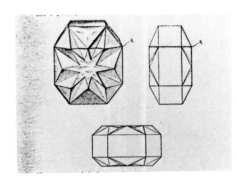

50. Louise Peszynska of Paris, France received patent 79,935 filed June 28, 1929 for this perfume bottle.

51. This bottle granted patent 80,572 filed October 15, 1929 was assigned to Marcel Guerlain, Inc. of Paris.

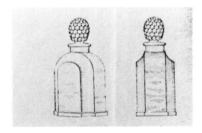

52. The bottle for "Amour-Amour" introduced in 1925 by Jean Patou was granted U.S. patent 80,729 filed April 16, 1929. The bottle was designed by Georges Huret and made by Verreries Brosse.

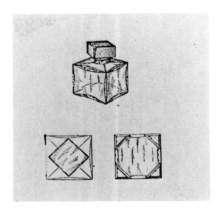

53. "Le Pirate" by Lenthéric was introduced to the U.S. in 1928. The bottle was granted patent 81,633 filed March 21, 1930.

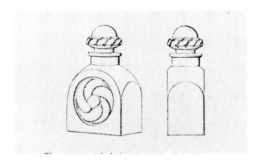

54. Patent 82,652 filed October 11, 1930 designed by Raymond Barbas was for the bottle to hold both "Cocktail Dry" and "Cocktail Sweet" by Jean Patou.

55. Raymond Barbas of Paris, France designed the bottle granted patent 82,716 filed October 11, 1930 and assigned to Jean Patou Inc.

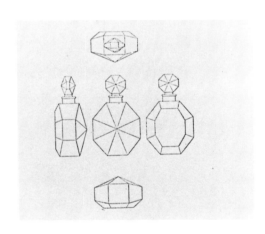

56. "Surrender" by Ciro bottle of jewel-faceted crystal was designed by Guy T. Gibson and granted U.S. patent 86,566 filed January 8, 1932.

57. Caron's "Fleurs de Rocaille" introduced to the U.S. in 1933 received bottle patent 88,067 filed August 13, 1932.

58. Patent 90,093 filed December 9, 1932 was for the bottle "La Fougeraie Au Crepuscule" by Coty. The bottle designed by F.R. Tourtois had a frosted glass stopper.

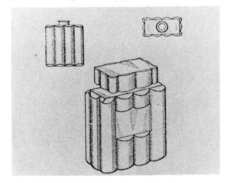

59. The Lucien Lelong perfume "Murmure" was introduced in the U.S. as "Whisper" in 1932. The bottle was granted patent 90,196 filed January 7, 1933.

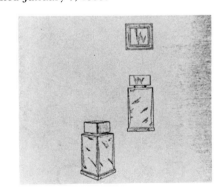

60. Crystal bottle with metal stopper cover designed by Rene Tricard received patent 90,558 filed May 12, 1933. The bottle was used by Lenthéric for "Numèro 12".

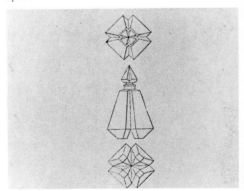

61. Clear crystal faceted bottle designed by Guy T. Gibson for "Reflexions" by Ciro was granted patent 91,169 filed October 11, 1933.

62. Interesting bottle for "Vol de Nuit" by Guerlain was granted patent 92,078 filed March 12, 1934.

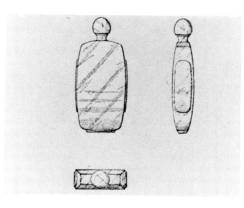

66. Mary Chess Inc. New York used this bottle patent 95,547 filed February 26, 1935 for many flower perfumes. The star shaped bottle was designed by Walter S. Nuckols.

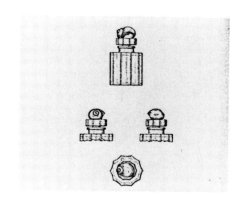

70. "Tempest" by Sherick of Paris, France bottle designed by M.R. De Mascolo received patent 98,455 filed July 19, 1935.

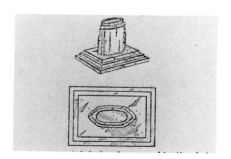

63. Bottle and stand for "Zibeline" by Weil was patented 93,341 filed February 1, 1934. The bottle was designed by Paul H. Ganz.

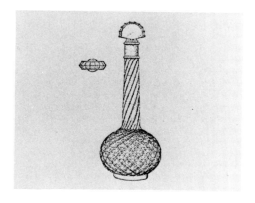

67. This long-stemmed, crested bottle designed by Joseph S. Stein was copied from a graceful antique scent bottle and used for "French Lavender" by Lucien Lelong. The bottle received patent 95,873 filed February 25, 1938.

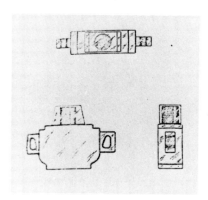

71. Patent 98,577 filed December 18, 1935 for the bottle designed by Rene Durand to hold "Gardenia de Tahiti" by Lenthéric.

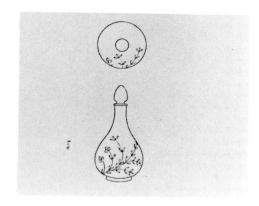

64. Hand-etched crystal presentation decanter used for Lenthéric perfumes received patent 95,325 on December 22, 1933. The bottle was designed by C.S. Gage and W.D. Canaday.

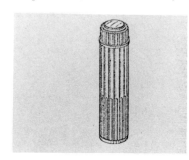

68. Bottle designed by Arthur R. Botham of New York granted patent 96,089 filed April 15, 1935 was assigned to Coty.

72. Frosted glass handles and stopper cover on clear glass Oriental inspired bottle designed by Frank McIntosh held "Shanghai" by Lenthéric. The bottle received patent 100,435 filed May 27, 1936.

65. A bottle designed by Paul H. Ganz suggests a Chinese pagoda was used for "Bamboo" by Weil. The bottle was granted patent 95,326 filed November 15, 1934.

69. A crystal Roman column bottle granted patent 98,427 filed December 5, 1935 was used for "Cassandra" by Weil. The bottle was designed by Paul H. Ganz.

73. Patent 100,929 filed April 20, 1936 was for a travel size bottle shaped like a lady's purse used by Lucien Lelong for different scents.

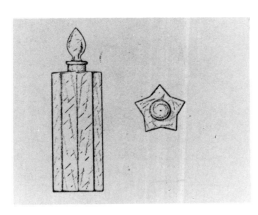

74. Mary Chess Inc. of New York bottle, patent 102,303 filed May 2, 1936, used for many different perfumes.

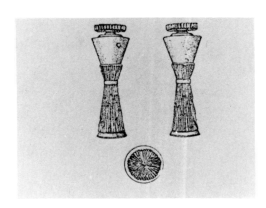

75. Sunburst flacon of frosted and clear glass held the perfume "Impromptu" by Lucien Lelong. The bottle was granted patent 104,414 on May 4, 1937.

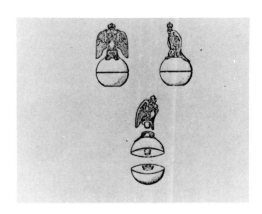

76. Inspired by the helmet of an officer in the Chevalier Garde, crowned with a double eagle, this bottle held Chevalier Garde perfumes "Fleur de Perse", "Roi de Rome", and "H.R.H.". Patent 105,299 was granted the bottle on July 13, 1937, designed by Basil Sabaneeff.

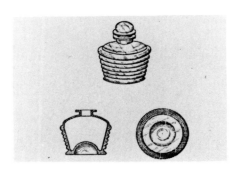

77. Named for a constellation, the perfume "Vega" by Guerlain received bottle patent 105,378 on July 27, 1937. The bottle was made by Baccarat.

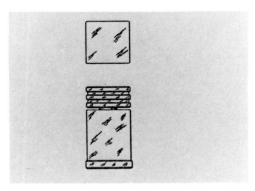

78. Patent 105,379 filed June 12, 1937 was for a bottle to hold "L'Heure Blue" by Guerlain introduced in 1913.

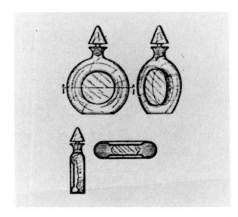

79. Square glass bottle for "Numero 12" by Lenthéric received patent 105,396 filed June 11, 1937. The bottle was designed by Frank McIntosh.

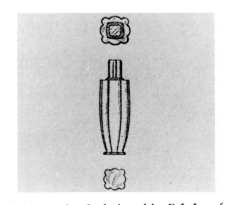

80. Cologne bottle designed by E.J. Lux for Harriet Hubbard Ayer, Inc. was granted patent 106,601 on October 19, 1937.

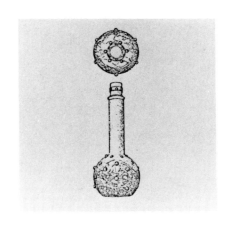

81. The crackled hobnail glass cologne bottle for "Indiscrete" by Lucien Lelong received patent 106,647 filed August 25, 1937.

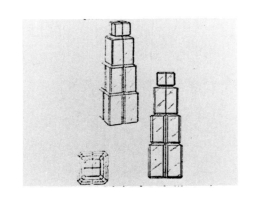

82. Skyscraper bottle held Helena Rubinstein's perfume "715" which took its name from the Rubinstein salon at 715 Fifth Ave., New York in 1937. The bottle designed by Walter Nuckols was granted patent 106,900 filed September 11, 1937.

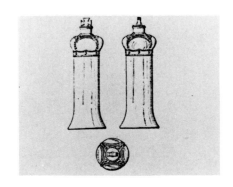

83. Glass crown on cylinder bottle, granted patent 107,035 filed May 11, 1937, was used by Prince Matchabelli for cologne and talc. The bottle was designed by Eula M. Stone.

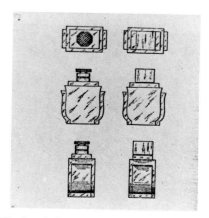

84. The bottle for "Anticipation" by Lenthéric was of clear glass with metal stopper cover. The bottle designed by Frank McIntosh was granted patent 107,360 filed November 2, 1937.

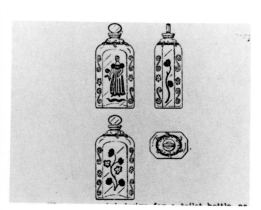

85. Black opaque glass stopper shaped like Napolean's hat topped this bottle of "1811" by Molinard. The bottle designed by R. Honnorat was granted patent 107,426 on December 14, 1937.

86. Double eagle bottle granted patent 110,793 filed May 14, 1938 was designed by Vladimir Bobri for Chevalier Garde.

87. The designs in colored enamels for "Early American Old Spice" by Shulton bottles were inspired by 'brides' boxes' in the Metropolitan Museum of Art. The bottle designed by W.L. Schultz was granted patent 110,881 filed June 17, 1938.

88. Patent 113,422 filed December 2, 1938 was for a new bottle designed by Philippe Hiolle to replace the pyramid shaped "Opening Night" by Lucien Lelong bottle.

89. Patent 114,653 filed September 19, 1938 was for a perfume bottle holder with three miniature feather shaped bottles of clear crystal with round brass lids. The sets designed by John D. Buckingham was called "Les Plumes" and contained three Lucien Lelong perfumes.

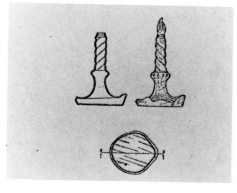

90. Charming Baccarat crystal candlestick bottle with red glass, flame stopper received patent 116,055 filed June 21, 1939. It was designed by Elsa Schiaparelli for her "Sleeping" perfume.

91. Gold bottle and stopper granted patent 116,214 filed June 20, 1939 held the perfume "Adastra" by Caron.

92. White and gold sunrise bottle, patent 116,756 filed June 30, 1939, held the Caron perfume "Alpona".

93. Frosted glass bow-tie bottle was granted patent 117,718 filed September 1, 1939. The bottle was used for "Jabot" perfume by Lucien Lelong.

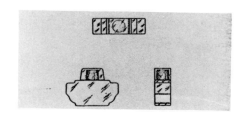

94. Patent 118,381 filed March 16, 1939 was for a bottle used by Lenthéric for "Shanghai" perfume.

95. Six-sided bottle with rosebud stopper designed by Laurence J. Colwell held the perfume "Moss Rose" by Charles of the Ritz. It was granted patent 124,016 filed October 1, 1940.

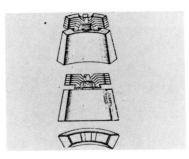

99. Beautiful Art Deco inspired eagle bottle designed by A.R. Tobia held the perfume "New Horizons" by Ciro. The bottle received patent 129,194 filed March 15, 1941.

103. Twisted rope shape glass bottle introduced in 1942 held the perfume "Sirôcco" by Lucien Lelong. Patent 135,569 was awarded the designer John D. Buckingham on April 27, 1943.

96. A porcelain-type cameo flacon in rose, blue, ivory, and green held different L'Orle of New York scents. The bottle designed by Abraham Levy received patent 124,636 filed November 5, 1940.

100. Patent 129,968 filed June 17, 1941 was for a chess piece bottle designed by Grace Chess Robinson for Mary Chess, Inc. New York.

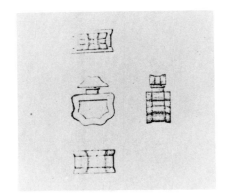

104. Bottle granted patent 137,711 filed July 13, 1943 was used during World War II by the Caron Corp. in New York without the knowledge or consent of the main office in Paris.

97. Patent 124,724 filed September 28, 1940 was for the presentation flacon of "Pink Party" by Lenthéric. Products in the "Pink Party" line were specially marketed to appeal to teenagers.

101. Parasol bottle with a wooden handle stopper was designed by Fred Bettiol and granted patent 130,820 filed November 3, 1941. It held "Spring Rain" cologne by Charles of the Ritz.

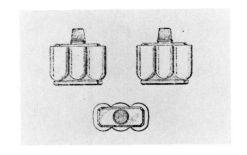

105. This bottle designed by Javier Serra held the perfume "Emir" by Dana. It was granted patent 140,755 on April 3, 1945.

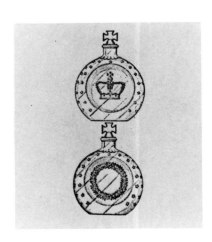

98. Prince Matchabelli presented "Christmas Rose" cologne in this crown and star decorated bottle and later used it for other colognes. The bottle designed by Paul H. Ganz was granted patent 124,856 filed April 12, 1940.

102. "Balalaika" by Lucien Lelong introduced in 1941 had a gold swirled clear glass bottle with matching stopper cover. It was granted patent 131,830 filed January 5, 1942.

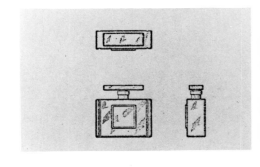

106. "Taglio" by Lucien Lelong was introduced in 1945 and received patent 141,775 filed April 2, 1945 on the bottle.

107. Renoir perfumes of Paris, France used this flask, patent 146,098 filed July 14, 1945, for many of its scents. It was designed by Amedee d'Anselme.

111. Patent 149,593 filed January 17, 1947 was for a figural bottle designed by Adele Simpson and assigned to Renoir Parfums, Ltd. New York.

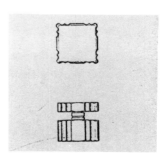

115. Square shaped bottle designed by Josephine Von Miklos for Dermetics, Inc. New York was granted patent 157,451 filed February 24, 1949.

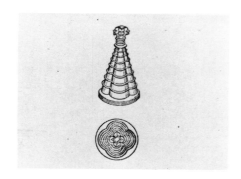

108. Temple shaped bottle with three elephants forming the stopper held the perfumes "Pagoda" and "Pagan" by Ravel introduced in 1945. The bottle designed by Elvira B. Barrios was granted patent 147,313 on August 19, 1947.

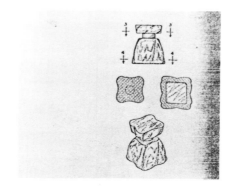

112. Designed by Josephine Von Miklos for Jacqueline Cochran Inc., this bottle received patent 151,862 on November 23, 1948.

116. Pleated glass bottle held the perfume "Fleur de Feu" by Guerlain. The patent 158,071 filed January 24, 1949 was given to Jean Pierre Guerlain for the bottle.

109. Lucien Lelong presented "Orgueil" in a gold bottle granted patent 148,078 on December 9, 1947.

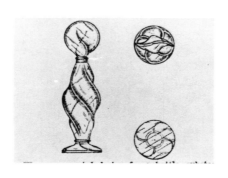

113. Bottle of twisted glass designed by Jacques Guerin held the perfume "Divine" by D'Orsay. Patent 152,962 filed January 23, 1948 was granted the bottle.

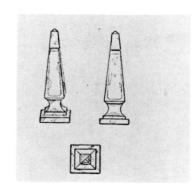

117. Beautiful crystal pedestal bottle made by Baccarat for Christian Dior was designed by Serge Heftler-Louiche and was granted patent 158,381 filed December 10, 1948.

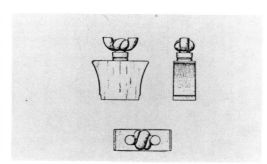

110. Clear bottle with frosted stopper held the perfume "Dark Brilliance" by Lenthéric introduced in 1947. The bottle designed by Frank McIntosh was granted patent 149,507 on May 4, 1948.

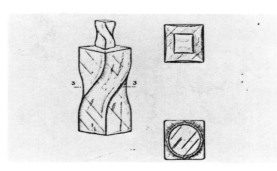

114. Square twisted glass bottle designed by Jacob S. Wiedhopf for Ciro was granted patent 153,194 filed January 13, 1948.

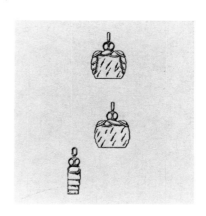

118. Designed by Eric de Kolb for Gourielli, Inc. New York, this bottle received patent 158,557 filed January 24, 1949.

119. Patent 160,408 filed November 16, 1949 was for the bottle to hold "Repartee" cologne by Lenthéric. A similar cylinder shaped bottle was also patented for the perfume.

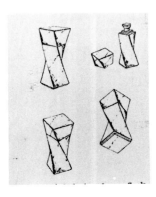

120. Patent 168,932 filed April 28, 1951 was designed by Sophie Frydlender for Lancôme of Paris, France.

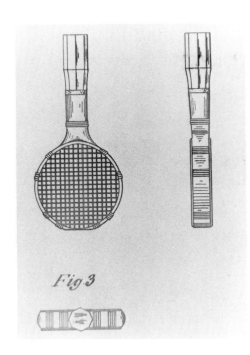

Fig 3

1. The lines of gut are embossed on this tennis racquet perfume bottle patented by the Karoff Co. of New York in 1941.

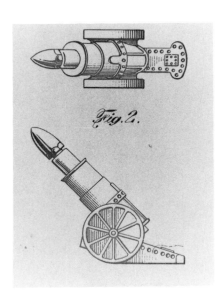

Fig.2.

2. Karoff of New York patented this unusual cannon perfume bottle in 1943 during World War II.

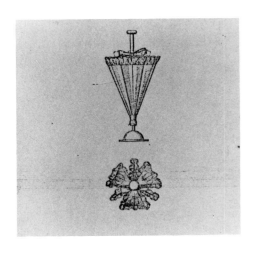

3. Patent 141,240 filed November 23, 1944 was for a combined umbrella shaped display container and bottles for the Karoff Co. of New York.

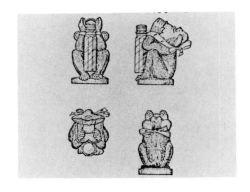

4. Design for a combined perfume bottle and holder in the form of a monkey holding a bottle was granted patent 126,737 filed March 17, 1941. It was designed by Jean Vivaudou for De Marsay Inc.

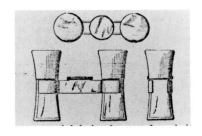

5. Perfume bottle in the shape of a pair of binoculars was granted patent 164,449 filed October 31, 1950. It was designed by Paul Roehrich for the Richford Corp. of New York.

Manufacturers

ADRIAN: "Saint", Advertisement 1945; "Sinner", Advertisement 1945.

JEAN D'ALBERT, Paris, France: "Ecusson", U.S. introduction 1953 "Casaque", U.S. introduction 1957.

LUCRETIA ALLEN, New York: "Gardenia", Advertisement 1934; "Wild Rose", Advertisement 1934; "Bouquet", Advertisement 1934; "Violet", Advertisement 1934; "Bluebonnet", Advertisement 1936.

ANJOU, New York: "Apropos", Article 1949; "Devastating", Article 1950 "Side Glance", New 1952.

ANTOINE, Paris, France: "Rue Cambon", U.S. introduction 1939.

ELIZABETH ARDEN, New York: "La Joie d'Elizabeth", New 1928; "Lélan d'Elizabeth", Article 1930; "L'Amour d'Elizabeth", Advertisement 1930; "Tuberose", New 1933; "Blue Grass", New 1934; "Gone with the Wind", New 1937; "Cyclamen", New 1938; "It's You", New 1939; "Mille Fleurs", New 1942; "On Dit", New 1946; "My Love", New 1949; "Mémoire Chérie", New 1956.

ARLY, Paris, France: "La Bohème", U.S. introduction 1915.

ARYS, Paris, France: "Un Jardin La Nuit", U.S. introduction 1922; "Secret d'Arys", U.S. introduction 1922; "Musky", U.S. introduction 1922; "L'Amour Dans Le Coeur", U.S. introduction 1922; "Fox Trot", Advertisement 1922; "Un Jour Viendra", Advertisement 1922; "Diamant Impérial", U.S. introduction 1927.

ATKINSON'S, London, England: "Columbine", U.S. introduction 1924.

HARRIET HUBBARD AYER, New York, Paris, France: "Muguet", U.S. introduction 1932; "Harriet Hubbard Ayer", U.S. introduction 1937; "Yu", U.S. introduction 1938; "Pink Clover", Catalog 1943; "Honeysuckle", Catalog 1943; "Golden Hour", Advertisement 1945; "Golden Chance", Article 1951; "Sweet William", Article 1951.

AZZARO, Paris, France: "Azzaro", U.S. introduction 1970; "Azzaro 9", U.S. introduction 1984;

BABANI, Paris, France: "Ligeia", U.S. introduction 1920; "Ambre De Delhi", U.S. introduction 1921; "Ming", U.S. introduction 1922; "Daimo", U.S. introduction 1922; "Rose Gullistan", U.S. introduction 1922; "Afghani", U.S. introduction 1922; "Saigon", U.S. introduction 1922; "Fleurs D'Annam", U.S. introduction 1922; "Yasmak", U.S. introduction 1922; "Oeillet", U.S. introduction 1922; "Abdullah", U.S. introduction 1927; "Jasmin de Corée", U.S. introduction 1927; "Just a Dash", U.S. introduction 1928.

BALENCIAGA, Paris, France: "Le Dix", U.S. introduction 1947; "La Fuite des Heures", U.S. introduction 1952; "Quadrille", Article 1956; "Prélude", U.S. introduction 1982.

BALMAIN, Paris France: "Vent Vert", U.S. introduction 1947; "Jolie Madame", U.S. introduction 1954; "Miss Balmain", U.S. introduction 1967; "Ivoire", U.S. introduction 1981.

BECHOFF, Paris, France: "21", Article 1925.

HENRI BENDEL: "10 West", U.S. introduction 1951.

BERTAE: "Narcissus", Catalog 1928.

BIENAIME, France: "Eveil", U.S. introduction 1935; "Fleurs D'Ete", U.S. introduction 1935; "Parfum Vermeil", U.S. introduction 1935; "La Vie en Fleurs", U.S. introduction 1935; "Les Carnations", U.S. introduction 1943.

BLANCHARD, New York: "Jealousy", Advertisement 1951; "Evening Star", Advertisement 1951; "Conflict", Advertisement 1951.

BLUE KAMEL: "Lilac", Catalog 1933; "Sweet Pea", Catalog 1933; "Lily of the Valley", Catalog 1933.

BOUE SOEURS, Paris, France: "Boué Soeurs", Article 1923.

PRINCE DE BOURBON: "Flame d'Amour", Article 1943.

BOURGET, France: "Sweet Pea", Catalog 1931; "Gardenia", Catalog 1931; "Rose", Catalog 1931; "Jasmine", Catalog 1931.

BOURJOIS, Paris, France (est. 1849): "Mandarine", U.S. introduction 1924; "Ashes of Roses", New 1909; "Mon Parfum", New 1914; "Evening in Paris", U.S. introduction 1929; "Springtime in Paris", New 1931; "Kobako", U.S. introduction 1936; "Mais Oui", U.S. introduction 1938; "Courage", U.S. introduction 1942; "Beau Belle", U.S. introduction 1949; "Endearing", U.S. introduction 1951; "Roman Holiday", U.S. introduction 1955.

BRAJAN: "Secret de Minuit", U.S. introduction 1927; "Matin Clair", Article 1926; "Loukita", Article 1927.

BROCARD OF MOSCOW: "Milaja", Advertisement 1913.

JEAN-CHARLES BROSSEAU, Paris, France: "Ombre Rose", U.S. introduction 1982.

CADOLLE: "Amour en Cage", U.S. introduction 1927; "Le Bois Sauvage", U.S. introduction 1927.

CALLOT, Paris, France: "La Fille du Roi de Chine", Article 1925; "Il Pleut des Baisers", Article 1925; "Chichicallot", Article 1925; "Le Louis d'Or", Article 1925.

PIERRE CARDIN, Paris, France: "Cardin", U.S. introduction 1976; "Paradoxe", U.S. introduction 1983.

HATTIE CARNEGIE, New York: "Hattie Carnegie", Advertisement 1928; "49", New 1944; "Carnegie Blue", Advertisement 1946; "Hypnotic", Advertisement 1946; "7", Advertisement 1946; "11", Advertisement 1946.

CARON, Paris, France (est.1903): "Royal Emilia", U.S. introduction 1904; "Royal Caron", U.S. introduction 1904; "Radiant", U.S. introduction 1904; "Modernis", U.S. introduction 1906; "Ravissement", U.S. introduction 1906; "Chantecler", U.S. introduction 1906; "Affolant", U.S. introduction 1908; "Isador", U.S. introduction 1910; "Rose Précieuse", U.S. introduction 1910; "Narcisse Noir", U.S. introduction 1911; "Jacinthe Précieuse", U.S. introduction 1911; "Elegancia", U.S. introduction 1911; "L'Infini", U.S. introduction 1912; "N'Aimez Que Moi",

U.S. introduction 1916; "Mimosa", U.S. introduction 1917; "Bell Amour", U.S. introduction 1917; "London-Paris", U.S. introduction 1917; "Tabac Blond", U.S. introduction 1919; "Nuit de Noel", U.S. introduction 1922; "Narcisse Blanc", U.S. introduction 1923; "Acaciosa", U.S. introduction 1924; "Bellodgia", U.S. introduction 1927; "Pois de Senteur de Chez Moi", U.S. introduction 1927; "En Avion", U.S. introduction 1930; "Fleurs de Rocaille", U.S. introduction 1933; "Pour un Homme", U.S. introduction 1934; "Cancan", U.S. introduction 1936; "La Fête Des Roses", U.S. introduction 1936; "Voeu de Noël", U.S. introduction 1939; "Alpona", U.S. introduction 1939; "Adastra", U.S. introduction 1939; "Royal Bain de Champagne", U.S. introduction 1941; "Pour Une Femme", U.S. introduction 1942; "Farnesiana", U.S. introduction 1947; "Or et Noir", U.S. introduction 1949; "Rose", U.S. introduction 1949; "With Pleasure", U.S. introduction 1949; "Muguet Du Bonheur", U.S. introduction 1952; "Poivre", U.S. introduction 1954; "Coup de Fouet", U.S. introduction 1954; "Infini", U.S. introduction 1970; "Nocturnes", U.S. introduction 1981.

CARVEN, Paris, France: "Ma Griffe", U.S. introduction 1946; "Robe d'un Soir", Article 1956; "Madame de Carven", U.S. introduction 1979.

CHANEL, Paris, France: "5", U.S. introduction 1921; "1", Article 1925; "11", Article 1925; "14", Article 1925; "21", Article 1925; "27", Article 1925; "Une Idée de Chanel", U.S. introduction 1930; "Ivoire", U.S. introduction 1932; "Glamour", U.S. introduction 1933; "Coco", U.S. Introduction 1985.

CHARBERT: "de toi je chante", U.S. introduction 1933; "Mechante", U.S. introduction 1933; "Gardenia", Advertisement 1936; "Yours Sincerely", U.S. introduction 1936; "Drumbeat", U.S. introduction 1936; "21 W 52", U.S. introduction 1937; "Grand Prix", U.S. introduction 1938; "Fabulous", U.S. introduction 1941; "Breathless", U.S. introduction 1942; "The French Touch", U.S. introduction 1947.

CHARLES OF THE RITZ, New York: "Spur", New 1938; "Moss Rose", New 1940; "Love Potion", New 1941; "Spring Rain", New 1942; "Little Women", New 1945; "Directoire", New 1951; "Ishah", New 1954.

CHERAMY, Paris, France New York: "Cappi", U.S. introduction 1922; "Nuée D'Or", U.S. introduction 1923; "April Showers", U.S. introduction 1927; "Cordon Bleu", U.S. introduction 1935; "Frolic", Article 1947.

MARY CHESS, New York: "Tapestry", New 1934; "Yram", New 1934; "Floral Odeurs", New 1935; "Carnation", New 1939; "Elizabethan", New 1941; "Strategy", New 1942; "Souvenir D'un Soir", New 1956.

CHEVALIER GARDE: "Fleur de Perse", U.S. introduction 1937; "Roi de Rome", U.S. introduction 1937; "H. R. H.", U.S. introduction 1937.

NICKY CHINI: "Mon Ami", Article 1957.

CIRO, Paris, France: "Chevalier De La Nuit", U.S. introduction 1925; "Parfum Maskee", U.S. introduction 1925; "Bouquet Antiqua", U.S. introduction 1925; "Doux Jasmin", U.S. introduction 1925; "Gardenia Sauvage", U.S. introduction 1928; "Surrender", U.S. introduction 1932; "Reflexions", U.S. introduction 1933; "Camelia du Maroc", Article 1936; "Trois Notes de Ciro", U.S. introduction 1937; "Danger", U.S. introduction 1938; "New Horizons", U.S. introduction 1941; "Acclaim", U.S. introduction 1950.

CLAMY: "A Tire d'Ailés", U.S. introduction 1927; "Femmes Ailees", U.S. introduction 1927.

FRANCES CLYNE, New York Paris, France: "F", U.S. introduction 1927; "C", U.S. introduction 1927; "FC", U.S. introduction 1927.

JACQUELINE COCHRAN; "Shining Hour", U.S. introduction 1953.

COLGATE, New York Jersey City, New Jersey (est.1806): "Speciosa", New 1886; "Wedding March", New 1879; "Fleurette", New 1890; "Myself", New 1920; "Dawn", New 1920; "Florient Perfume", Advertisement 1921; "Claire de Lune", New 1921; "Piquant", New 1921; "Princess Harran", New 1921; "San DaLay", New 1921; "Hope", New 1921; "Cashmere Bouquet", New 1907; "Seventeen", New 1928.

CORDAY, Paris, France: "Toodleoo", U.S. introduction 1925; "Toujours Moi", U.S. introduction 1925; "Orchidee Bleue", U.S. introduction 1925; "Femme du jour", New 1926; "L'Ardente Nuit", U.S. introduction 1930; "Quand?", U.S. introduction 1930;"L'heure Romantique", U.S. introduction 1930; "La Promesse", Article 1933; "Voyage A Paris", New 1933; "Tzigane", U.S. introduction 1938; "Possession", U.S. introduction 1939; "Jet", U.S. introduction 1940; "Frenzy", Advertisement 1945; "Fame", U.S. introduction 1947; "Zigane", U.S. introduction 1949; "Toujours Toi", U.S. introduction 1951.

COTY, Paris, France (est. 1904): "Rose de Jacqueminot", U.S. introduction 1904; "Ambreine", U.S. introduction 1906; "La Violette Pourpre", U.S. introduction 1906; "Le Vertige", U.S. introduction 1906; "L'Origan", U.S. introduction 1909; "L'Effleurt", U.S. introduction 1909; "Styx", U.S. introduction 1912; "L'Or", U.S. introduction 1912; "Ambre Antique", U.S. introduction 1913; "Chypre", U.S. introduction 1917; "Emeraude", U.S. introduction 1918; "Eau de Coty", U.S. introduction 1920; "Jasmin De Corse", Before 1921; "Paris", U.S. introduction 1922; "Muguet des Bois", U.S. introduction 1923; "L'Aimant", U.S. introduction 1927; "La Fougeraie Au Crepuscule", New 1932; "A Suma", U.S. introduction 1934; "La Jacée", U.S. introduction 1941; "Muse", U.S. introduction 1945; "Le Soulier de Ballerine", U.S. introduction 1946; "Coquillage", U.S. introduction 1946; "Meteor", U.S. introduction 1951; "Imprévu", U.S. introduction 1965; "Complice", U.S. introduction 1973.

COURREGES, Paris, France: "Empreinte", U.S. introduction 1971; "Amérique", U.S. introduction 1974; "Courrèges in Blue", U.S. introduction 1983.

COUTURIERS: "Tricot", U.S. introduction 1941.

LILLY DACHE, New York: "Dashing", New 1941; "Drifting", New 1941; "Just Because", New 1945.

DANA, Spain Paris, France New York: "Tabu", U.S. introduction 1931; "20 Carats", U.S. introduction 1933; "Emir", U.S. introduction 1936; "Platine", U.S. introduction 1939; "Voodoo", U.S. introduction 1932, "Ambush", U.S. introduction 1955.

DEGAS, Paris, France: "Danseuse Etoile", Advertisement 1947; "Estampe", Advertisement 1947.

ELLYN DELEITH, New York: "Pampa", Advertisement 1946; "Spindrift", Advertisement 1946.

DELETTREZ: "Inalda", Article 1935.

DELTAH: "Midnight Hour", Catalog 1934; "Ecstasy", Catalog 1934; "Mon Bijou", Catalog 1934; "Une Sentour", Catalog 1934.

FRANCES DENNEY: "Snow Blossom", Article 1951; "Hope", U.S. introduction 1952.

DERMAY: "Fete de Coeur", Catalog 1928.

DERMETICS, New York: "Goddess of Crete", Advertisement 1952; "Bouquet", Advertisement 1952.

JEAN DESPREZ, Paris, France: "Grande Dame", U.S. introduction 1939; "Etourdissant", U.S. introduction 1939; "Votre Main", U.S. introduction 1939; "Bal à Versailles", U.S. introduction 1962; "Jardanel", U.S. introduced 1972.

JEAN DESSES, Paris, France: "Diffusion", U.S. introduction 1949.

JEAN D'HENNERY, Paris, France: "Kim", Advertisement 1946.

DIMITRY: "Credo", U.S. introduction 1933.

CHRISTIAN DIOR, Paris, France: "Miss Dior", U.S. introduction 1947; "Diorama", U.S. introduction 1948; "Diorissimo", U.S. introduction 1957; "Eau Sauvage", U.S. introduction 1967; "Diorella", U.S. introduction 1972; "Dioressence", U.S. introduction 1979.

D'ORSAY, Paris, France: "Toujours Fidèle", New 1915; "Dandy", U.S. introduction 1926; "Duo D'Orsay", U.S. introduction 1929; "Ganika", New 1923; "Trophée", U.S. introduction 1936; "Milord", U.S. introduction 1933; "Bell de Jour", U.S. introduction 1938; "Intoxication", U.S. introduction 1942; "Divine", U.S. introduction 1948; "Fantastique", U.S. introduction 1953.

DRALLE, Paris, France: "Illusions", New 1909.

DRECOLL, Paris, France: "Tai-toi mon Coeur", U.S. introduction 1925.

DU BARRY, New York Paris, France: "Seven Winds", U.S. introduction 1957.

MARY DUNHILL, London, England: "Frou Frou du Gardenia", U.S. introduction 1934; "Flowers of Devonshire", U.S. introduction 1936; "Amulet", U.S. introduction 1938; "Bewitching", Advertisement 1941; "White Hyacinth", Catalog 1942; "Escape", U.S. introduction 1943.

SHERRY DUNN, Hollywood, California: "Macabre", New 1946.

EASTMAN, New York: "Aloha", 1885; "Snow Lily", 1890.

EDOUARDO: "Egyptian", U.S.introduction 1927; "Lotus", U.S. introduction 1927.

EISENBERG, Chicago, Illinois: "847", New 1938.

ELMO: "Going My Way", Article 1947.

EMEF, Rome, Italy: "Argento", U.S. introduction 1939; "Scherzo", U.S. introduction 1939; "Arabeske", U.S. introduction 1939; "Roma Antica", U.S. introduction 1939.

GI. VI. EMME, Italy: "Insidia U.S. introduction 1948

ESME OF PARIS, New York: "Green Eyes", Advertisement 1946.

EVYAN: "White Shoulders", U.S. introduction 1945; "Gay Diversion", Advertisement 1947; "Golden Shadows", Article 1950; "Menace", Article 1943; "Most Precious", U.S. introduction 1947.

FABERGE: "Aphrodisia", U.S. introduction 1938; "Tigress", U.S. introduction 1939; "Woodhue", Article 1949; "Act IV", U.S. introduction 1950; "Flambeau", U.S. introduction 1956.

MAX FACTOR, United States: "Electrique", New 1954.

FAITOUTE MUNN: Floral scents, Article 1923.

FAY: "Absolute Essence of Gardenia", Article 1936.

FIORET, Paris, France New York: "Jouir", Advertisement 1924; "Le Dernier Roman", Advertisement 1924; "Prevert", Advertisement 1924; "La Muse", Advertisement 1924.

FLORIS, London, England (est. 1730): "English Bluebells", U.S. introduction 1938; "Lily of the Valley", U.S. introduction 1938.

FONTANIS, Paris, France: "Fleurs de Bagdad", U.S. introduction 1924; "Quel Delice", U.S. introduction 1924; "Sous la Charmille", U.S. introduction 1924.

FOREST PERFUME, Paris, France: "Ming Toy", U.S. introduction 1923; "Lucky Scents", U.S. introduction 1924; "Beaucaire", U.S. introduction 1925; "Mon Ceau", U.S. introduction 1926.

FRACY, France: "Charmeuse", Advertisement 1924; "Jasmin", Advertisement 1924; "Passionata", Advertisement 1924; "Rose-Joli", Advertisement 1924; "Silhouette", Advertisement 1924.

JOHN FREDERIC, United States: "Golden Arrow", New 1935.

GABILLA, Paris, France: "Mon Cheri", U.S. introduction 1910; "La Vierge Folle", U.S. introduction 1910; "Xantho", U.S. introduction 1911; "Minne", U.S. introduction 1912; "Musardises", U.S. introduction 1912; "Longchamp", U.S. introduction 1921; "Fleur du Jour", Advertisement 1924; "Moda", U.S. introduction 1920; "Mon Talisman", U.S. introduction 1928; "Bijou d'Amour", U.S. introduction 1928; "Hossegor", U.S.introduction 1929; "Rêve a deux", U.S. introduction 1936; "Sinful Soul", Advertisement 1934; "Foolish Virgin", Advertisement 1940; "Dream for Two", Advertisement 1940.

PRINCE GAGARIN: "Bouquet", U.S. introduction 1935; "Special", U.S. introduction 1935; "Lilac", U.S. introduction 1935.

GAL, HOUSE OF, Spain: "Pravia Hay", Advertisement 1924; "Alma", Advertisement 1924; "Talavera Flowers", Advertisement 1924.

LE GALION: "Sortilège", Article 1949.

PRINCE GEORGE OF RUSSIA: "Tiara", Article 1938.

ANNE GERARDE: "Mistral", U.S. introduction 1927.

GIVENCHY, Paris, France: "L'Interdict", U.S. introduction 1957; "Ysatis", U.S. introduction 1984.

GOLNAY, Paris, France: "Yapana", Advertisement 1922.

BARBARA GOULD, New York: "Skylark", New 1941; "Moon Struck", New 1947; "Garden Fragrance", Catalog 1950; "Nocturne", New 1952.

GOURIELLI: "Something Blue", U.S. introduction 1943; "Tipsy", U.S. introduction 1947; "Five O'Clock", U.S. introduction 1947; "Fourth Dimension", U.S. introduction 1953.

GRASSE, France: "Christmas Bells", U.S. introduction 1927.

DOROTHY GRAY: "Elation", Article 1936; "Lady in the Dark", U.S. introduction 1941; "Savoir Faire", Article 1948; "Nosegay", Advertisement 1949; "Wedgewood", U.S. introduction 1953; "Aureate", Article 1957.

GRENOVILLE, Paris, France (est. 1879): "Revêrie", U.S. introduction 1910; "Ambre Hindou", U.S. introduction 1910; "Muguet D'Orly", U.S. introduction 1910; "Cypria", U.S. introduction 1926; "Chaine d'Or", U.S. introduction 1926; "Bluet", U.S. introduction 1926; "Byzance", U.S. introduction 1926; "Avant l'été", New 1931; "Casanova", New 1929; "Eillet Fane", Article 1934; "Piège", U.S. introduction 1939; "Envoi de France", U.S. introduction 1945.

GRES, Paris, France: "A", U.S. introduction 1947; "Cabochard", U.S. introduction 1958; "Alix", U.S. introduction 1982.

JACQUES GRIFFE, Paris, France: "Mistigri", U.S. introduction 1954.

J. GROSSMITH & SON, London: "Shem-el-Nessim", U.S. introduction 1924.

NICOLE GROULT, Paris, France: "Le Bleau", U.S. introduction 1928; "Le Rose", U.S. introduction 1928.

GUCCI, Italy: "Parfum 1", U.S. introduction 1972; "No. 3", U.S. introduction 1985.

GUELDY, Paris, France: "Le Triomphe de Gueldy", Advertisement 1922; "Vasthi", Advertisement 1922; "L'Empyrée", Advertisement 1922; "La Rose de Gueldy", Advertisement 1922; "Le Bois Sacré", Advertisement 1922; "Loki", Advertisement 1922; "Lelys Rouge", Advertisement 1924; "Le Prestige", Advertisement 1924; "Le Jasmin", Advertisement 1924.

GUERLAIN, Paris, France (est. 1828): "Eau Impériale", U.S. introduction 1853; "Muguet", U.S. introduction 1873; "Jicky", U.S. introduction 1889; "Hegemonienne", Article 1890; "Cuir de Russie", U.S. introduction 1890; "Le Jardin de Mon Curé", U.S. introduction 1895; "Mouchoir de Monsieur", U.S. introduction 1904; "ChampsElysées", U.S. introduction 1904; "Secret de Bonne Femme", U.S. introduction 1906; "Après L'Ondee", U.S. introduction 1906; "Sillage", U.S. introduction 1908; "Super Dulci", U.S. introduction 1912; "L'Heure Bleue", U.S. introduction 1913; "Mi-Mai", U.S. introduction 1914; "Poudre Aux Ballons", U.S. introduction 1920; "Guerlinade", U.S. introduction 1922; "Mitsouko", U.S. introduction 1922; "Rue de la Paix", Advertisement 1922; "Bouquet de Faunes", U.S. introduction 1923; "Candide Effleuve", U.S. introduction 1924; "Shalimar", U.S. introduction 1926; "DJEDI", U.S. introduction 1927; "A Travers Champs", Article 1927; "Liu", U.S. introduction 1928; "Guerlilas", U.S. introduction 1930; "Guerlarose", U.S. introduction 1930; "Vol de Nuit", New 1932; "Sous Le Vent", U.S. introduction 1934; "Verveine", U.S. introduction 1936; "Vega", U.S. introduction 1937; "Coque D'Or", U.S. introduction 1938; "Fleur de Feu", U.S. introduction 1949; "Ode", U.S. introduction 1956; "Chant d' Arômes", U.S. introduction 1962; "Chamade", U.S. introduction 1969; "Parure", U.S. introduction 1975; "Jardins de Bagatelle", U.S. introduction 1983.

MARCEL GUERLAIN, Paris, France (est.1923): "Masque Rouge", New 1925; "Contes Choisis", Article 1927; "Caravelle", New 1924.

HARTNELL: "Menace", Advertisement 1943.

ANN HAVILAND, United States: "Daphne", Article 1935; "Céleste", New 1939; "Perhaps", New 1941; "Jasmin of the Night", New 1948.

HERMES, Paris, France: "Doblis", U.S. introduction 1956; "Calèche", U.S. introduction 1962; "Amazone", U.S. introduction 1974; "Parfume d'Hermès", U.S. introduction 1984.

HOUBIGANT, Paris, France (est. 1775): "Fougère Royale", U.S. introduction 1882; "Coeur de Jeannnette", U.S. introduction 1899; "Eau d'Houbigant", U.S. introduction 1899; "Ideal", U.S. introduction 1900; "Premier Mai", U.S. introduction 1908; "Parfum Inconnu", U.S. introduction 1910; "La Rose France", U.S. introduction 1911; "Quelques Fleurs", U.S. introduction 1912; "Quelques Violettes", U.S. introduction 1914; "Evette", Advertisement 1918; "Mon Boudoir", U.S. introduction 1919; "Mes Delices", U.S. introduction 1920; "Un Peu d'Ambre", U.S. introduction 1920; "D'Argeville", Advertisement 1922; "Le Temps des Lilas", Advertisement 1922; "Jasmin Floral", Advertisement 1922; "Violette Houbigant", Advertisement 1922; "Subtilite", U.S. introduction 1924; "En Visite", U.S. introduction 1925; "Heureuse Surprise, U.S. introduction 1926; "La Ball Saison", U.S. introduction 1926; "Au Matin", U.S. introduction 1928; "Essence Rare", U.S. introduction 1929; "Fleur Bienaimée", New 1927; "Festival", U.S. introduction 1931; "Etude", U.S. introduction 1931; "Subterfuge", U.S. introduction 1931; "Bois Dormant", Advertisement 1933; "Présence", New 1933; "Country Club", U.S. introduction 1936; "Demi Jour", New 1929; "Chantilly", U.S. introduction 1941; "Transparence", Advertisement 1947; "Flatterie", U.S. introduction 1954; "Ciao", U.S. introduction 1980; "Raffinée", U.S. introduction 1982.

PEGGY HOYT, New York Paris, France: "Flowers", Advertisement 1923.

RICHARD HUDNUT, New York Paris, France (est. 1895): "Violet Sec", U.S. introduction 1896; "Du Barry", U.S. introduction 1900; "Aimée",

U.S. introduction 1902; "Cardinal", U.S. introduction 1902; "Le Rêve", U.S. introduction 1904; "Chrysis", U.S. introduction 1904; "Vanity", U.S. introduction 1910; "Vogue", Advertisement 1910; "Three Flowers", U.S. introduction 1915; "Tout Mon Jardin", Advertisement 1916; "Watteau", U.S. introduction 1919; "Serenade", U.S. introduction 1923; "Silhouette", U.S. introduction 1923; "Deauville", U.S. introduction 1923; "Les Cascades", U.S. introduction 1927; "Le Debut", U.S. introduction 1927; "Narcisse", Catalog 1929; "Rose", Catalog 1929; "Lilac", Catalog 1929; "Jasmine", Catalog 1929; "Gemey", U.S. introduction 1931; "Teak", U.S. introduction 1937; "R.S.V.P.", U.S. introduction 1937; "Yanky Clover", Catalog 1944; "Prediction", U.S. introduction 1946; "Angel Choir", U.S. introduction 1946.

ISABEY, Paris, France: "Bleu de Chine", U.S. introduction 1926; "Sourire Fleuri", U.S. introduction 1926; "Gardenia", U.S. introduction 1927; "Rayon Vert", U.S. introduction 1927; "Jasmin", U.S. introduction 1927; "Mon Seul Ami", U.S. introduction 1928; "Mimosa", U.S. introduction 1928; "Lilas", U.S. introduction 1928; "Violette", U.S. introduction 1928; "Grand Slam", U.S. introduction 1935.

IVEL: "Mon Désir", Article 1956.

RICHARD JAECKEL, Paris, France: "Are Jay", U.S. introduction 1938.

JAQUET: "Fire Magic", Advertisement 1945.

JARDIN, Paris, France Boston, Massachusetts: "Jardin de Rose Extract", Advertisement 1920; "Jardin de Lilas Extract", Advertisement 1920.

JARNAC, Paris, France: "Shamly", U.S. introduction 1951.

JAY-THORPE, New York: "Jaytho", New 1927; "Hearts and Flowers", New 1940.

GEORG JENSEN: "Fire Orchid", Article 1947.

JEURELLE: "Libretto de Jeurelle", Advertisement 1936; "Lisette", U.S. introduction 1941.

JOUBERT CIE, New York: "Blue Garden", New 1927; "Blue Waltz", New 1927.

JOVOY, Paris, France: "Bouquet", U.S. introduction 1924.

HARRY KAYE, New York: "Modouka", New 1924.

KERKOFF, Paris, France: "Djer-Kiss", Advertisement 1913.

KISLAV, Paris, France: "Kislav", U.S. introduction 1955; "6I", U.S. introduction 1956.

KONDAZIAN, Paris, France: "Fibi", New 1926.

LA DORE, Paris, France: "White Rose", Catalog 1923; "Narcissus", Catalog 1923; "Lily of the Valley", Catalog 1923; "Trailing Arbutus", Catalog 1923.

LAGERFELD, Paris, France: "Chloé", U.S. introduction 1975; "K.L.", U.S. introduction 1982.

LANCHERE: "Blue Rose", Advertisement 1926.

LANCOME, Paris, France: "Bocages", U.S. introduction 1935; "Conquête", U.S. introduction 1935; "Nutrix", U.S. introduction 1935; "Marrakech", U.S. introduction 1942; "Lait Des Hesperides", U.S. introduction 1942; "Galateis", U.S. introduction 1942; "La Vallee Bleue", U.S. introduction 1943; "Limpidis", U.S. introduction 1945; "Qui Sait", U.S. introduction 1946; "Tropiques", U.S. introduction 1946; "Cuir de Lancôme", U.S. introduction 1947; "Magie", U.S. introduction 1952; "Trésor", U.S. introduction 1953; "Envol", U.S. introduction 1957; "Flèches D'Or", U.S. introduction 1957.

LANCRY, Paris, France: "Tango", Advertisement 1946; "Guess", Advertisement 1946; "Baachanale", Advertisement 1946; "Nous Deux", Advertisement 1946.

LANIER: "Folie de Minuit", U.S. introduction 1955.

LANVIN, Paris, France: "My Sin", New 1923; "Arpège", U.S. introduction 1928; "Scandal", U.S. introduction 1931; "Rumeur", U.S. introduction 1935; "Prétexte", U.S. introduction

1937.

GUY LAROCHE: "Fidji", U.S. introduction 1966; "J'ai Osé", U.S. introduction 1977.

ESTEE LAUDER, United States: "Youth Dew", New 1953; "Aramis", New 1964; "Private Collection", New 1972; "Cinnabar", New 1978; "White Linen", New 1978; "Beautiful", New 1985.

LEGRAND, Paris, France: "Violettes Du Czar", U.S. introduction 1862; "Marions-Nous", U.S. introduction 1928; "Camélia du Nile", U.S. introduction 1929; "Soleil de Minuit", U.S. introduction 1932.

LEIGH, New York (est.1890): "Risqué", New 1926; "Poetic Dream", New 1930; "Heartbeat", Advertisement 1943; "Dulcinea", New 1919; "Desert Flower", New 1947.

LUCIEN LELONG, Paris, France: "Tout le Long", Article 1925; "A", U.S. introduction 1928; "B", U.S. introduction 1928; "C", U.S. introduction 1928; "N", U.S. introduction 1928; "J", U.S. introduction 1928; "Murmure", U.S. introduction 1932; "Mon Image", U.S. introduction 1933; "Cooling Cologne", U.S. introduction 1933; "Opening Night", U.S. introduction 1934; "French Lavender", U.S. introduction 1935; "Indiscret", U.S. introduction 1936; "Ingenue", U.S. introduction 1936; "Impromptu", U.S. introduction 1937; "Tailspin", U.S. introduction 1939; "Jabot", U.S. introduction 1939; "Balalaika", U.S. introduction 1941; "Sirôcco", U.S. introduction 1942; "Taglio", U.S. introduction 1945; "Orgueil", U.S. introduction 1947; "Cachet", U.S. introduction 1949; "Passionement", U.S. introduction 1951; "Edition Limiteé", U.S. introduction 1951.

LENEL, New York: "Trifling", Advertisement 1944; "Bellezza", Advertisement 1956; "Caressant", Advertisement 1956; "Private Affair", New 1950.

LENGYEL: "Parfum Impérial", U.S. introduction 1936.

LENIEF, Paris, France: "Devine?", Article 1925.

LENTHERIC, Paris, France (est. 1879): "Lotus d'Or", U.S. introduction 1924; "Ambre Mousse", U.S. introduction 1924; "Coeur de Paris", U.S. introduction 1924; "Miracle", U.S. introduction 1925; "Le Matin Au Bois", U.S. introduction 1925; "Asphodéle", U.S. introduction 1928; "Le Pirate", U.S. introduction 1928; "Numéro 12", U.S. introduction 1933; "Tweed", U.S. introduction 1935; "Gardenia de Tahiti", Advertisement 1936; "Shanghai", U.S. introduction 1936; "Bal Masque", U.S. introduction 1936; "Anticipation" U.S. introduction 1937; "A Bientôt", New 1930; "Pink Party", U.S. introduction 1940; "Confetti", U.S. introduction 1940; "Tanbark", U.S. introduction 1941; "Bandbox", U.S. introduction 1941; "Tombola", U.S. introduction 1942; "Dark Brilliance", U.S. introduction 1947; "Repartee", U.S. introduction 1949; "Adam's Rib", U.S. introduction 1957.

LEONARD, Paris, France (est.1969): "Fashion", U.S. introduction 1970; "Eau Fraiche", U.S. introduction 1974; "Tamango", U.S. introduction 1977.

LERYS: "Parfum Orbruni", Advertisement 1926; "Le Presentoir", Advertisement 1926; "Pour Blonde", Article 1927; "Pour Brune", Article 1927.

LEONID DE LESCINSKIS, Paris, France: "Eau de Fleurs", U.S.introduction 1949.

LIONCEAU, Paris, France: "Place de l'Opera", U.S. introduction 1927; "Le Fleuve Bleu", Advertisement 1927; "Poème Arabe", U.S. introduction 1928.

L'ORLE, New York: "Wine, Women, and Song", New 1940; "Fiesta", New 1940; "Scenario", New 1940; "Argentina", New 1940; "Landscape", New 1946.

LOURNAY, Paris, France New York: "Qui Sait", U.S. introduction 1920; "Fleur Vivant", U.S. introduction 1920; "Fleur de Mignon", U.S.

introduction 1920; "L'Ile d'Amour", Advertisement 1921; "Vivante", U.S. introduction 1923.

LUBIN, Paris, France (est.1793): "Bouquet de Papillons", Advertisement 1921; "Epidor", Advertisement 1921; "Chypre", Advertisement 1921; "Douce France", Advertisement 1921; "Amaryllis", U.S. introduction 1926; "L'Ocean Bleu", U.S. introduction 1928; "Monjoly", U.S. introduction 1928; "Ferveur", U.S. introduction 1928; "Nuit de long-champ", U.S. introduction 1956.

LUYNA, France: "Chanson d'Eté", U.S. introduction 1922; "Fleur Ardente", U.S. introduction 1922; "Maya", Advertisement 1923; "La Violette", Advertisement 1923; "Le Jasmin", Advertisement 1923.

LYDES, Paris, France: "L'Ambre des Pagodes", Advertisement 1924; "Diamant Noir", U.S. introduction 1927; "Bibelot", U.S. introduction 1927.

LYNETTE, New York: "Apple Blossom", Catalog 1944; "Spice Bouquet", Catalog 1944; "Conspiracy", New 1945.

M.G.: "Kadour", U.S. introduction 1927; "Kesako", U.S. introduction 1927.

MARCEAU, Paris, France: "Baiser de Colombine", Advertisement 1925; "Diables Bleus", Advertisement 1925; "Narcisses de Nikylla", Advertisement 1925; "Madouka", Advertisement 1925; "Ambre Noir", Advertisement 1925; "Lilas", Advertisement 1925.

ALEXANDRA DE MARKOFF: "Tiara", U.S. introduction 1955.

MARQUAY, Paris, France: "Prince Douka", U.S. introduction 1951.

MARTIAL et ARMAND, Paris, France: "Un Rien", U.S. introduction 1926; "Place Vendome", U.S. introduction 1926.

MASSENET: "Rhapsodie de Massenet", Advertisement 1946; "Altesse", Advertisement 1946; "Mandalay", Advertisement 1946.

PRINCE MATCHABELLI, Paris, France: "Princess Nina", U.S. introduction 1927; "Ambre Royal", U.S. introduction 1927; "Imperial Violet", U.S. introduction 1927; "Princess Marie", U.S. introduction 1933; "Grace Moore", U.S. introduction 1934; "Ave Maria", New 1926; "Duchess of York", Advertisement 1934; "Honeysuckle", Advertisement 1935; "Lilac", Advertisement 1935; "Carnation", Advertisement 1935; "Muguet", Advertisement 1935; "Infanta", U.S. introduction 1937; "Abano", U.S. introduction 1938; "Princess of Wales", U.S. introduction 1939; "Christmas Rose", U.S. introduction 1940; "Crown Jewel", U.S. introduction 1946; "Beloved", U.S. introduction 1950; "Stradivari", Advertisement 1950; "Wind Song", U.S. introduction 1953; "Added Attraction", U.S. introduction 1956.

MELBA, Chicago, Illinois: "Lov'me", New 1913.

MIAHATI, New York: "Blue Fox", Advertisement 1955; "Audacious", Advertisement 1955; "Jaunty", Advertisement 1955; "My Fancy", Advertisement 1955.

MILLOT, Paris, France (est.1839): "Crêpe de Chine", New 1929; "Recital", U.S. introduction 1938; "Revelry", Advertisement 1949.

MOLINARD, Paris, France (est. 1849): "Le Mimosa", U.S. introduction 1923; "Xmas Bells", New 1926; "Calendal", U.S. introduction 1936; "Violette du Roi", U.S. introduction 1936; "Iscles d'Or", U.S. introduction 1936; "Jasmin", U.S. introduction 1936; "Fleurettes", U.S. introduction 1936; "Madrigal", Advertisement 1937; "1811", U.S. introduction 1937; "Nirmala", U.S. introduction 1955; "Molinard", U.S. introduction 1980.

MOLINELLE, London, England: "English Roses", Advertisement 1930; "No. 29", Advertisement 1930; "Beau Geste", Advertisement 1930; "Lilac", U.S. introduction 1933; "Venez Voir", U.S. introduction 1936.

MOLYNEUX, Paris, France: "3", U.S. introduction 1925; "5", U.S. introduction 1925; "14", U.S.

introduction 1925; "Charme", U.S. introduction 1929; "Fete", New 1927; "Le Chic de Molyneux", U.S. introduction 1930; "Le Parfum Connu", Advertisement 1930; "Vivre", U.S. introduction 1971; "Quartz", U.S. introduction 1977; "Gauloise", U.S. introduction 1981.

GERMAINE MONTEIL: "Laughter", U.S. introduction 1941; "Nostalgia", Article 1947; "Gigolo", U.S. introduction 1951; "Rigolade", Advertisement 1952.

"4711" FRED MUHLENS, Germany: "L'Offrande", U.S. introduction 1922; "Tosca", U.S. introduction 1930; "Karat", U.S. introduction 1935; "Troika", U.S. introduction 1935; "Rhinegold", Article 1938.

MURY, Paris, France: "Siva", U.S. introduction 1922; "Notturno", U.S. introduction 1926; "Patricia", U.S. introduction 1926; "Le Narcisse Bleu", U.S. introduction 1927; "Amadis", Article 1927.

DE MUSSET, Paris, France: "Poeme", U.S. introduction 1928; "Royal Gardenia", U.S. introduction 1928; "Royal Pois de Senteur", U.S. introduction 1928.

MYON, Paris, France: "Coeur de Femme", U.S. introduction 1933; "3 Passions", U.S. introduction 1933; "1000 Joies", U.S. introduction 1933; "Exaltation", U.S. introduction 1934.

MYRURGIA, Spain: "Orgia", U.S. introduction 1922; "Flores del Mal", U.S. introduction 1922; "Flor de Blason", U.S. introduction 1926; "Clavel de España", Article 1938; "Joya", U.S. introduction 1956.

NEMEEIA, Paris, France: "Nemesis", U.S. introduction 1910.

OLD SOUTH, United States: "Plantation Garden", New 1940.

ORLIK, New York: "Sans Nom", Advertisement 1938.

ORLOFF, New York: "Nikki", New 1939; "American Blossoms", Advertisement 1941; "Indies Spice", Advertisement 1941; "Carnation Imperiale", Advertisement 1941; "Attar of Petals", Catalog 1945.

OUTDOOR GIRL: "Dawn", Catalog 1935; "Noon", Catalog 1935; "Night", Catalog 1935.

CECIL PAGE, New York: "Persian Lilac", New 1940; "English Garden", New 1940.

PERCY E. PAGE, New York: "Rose", Advertisement 1918; "Violet", Advertisement 1918; "Corylopsis", Advertisement 1918; "Wistaria", Advertisement 1918; "Floral Bloom", New 1923.

SOLON PALMER, New York (est. 1847): "Dress Parade", New 1939.

MICHEL PASQUIER, New York: "Tobruk", Article 1952.

JEAN PATOU, Paris, France: "Que sais-je?", U.S. introduction 1925; "Amour-Amour", U.S. introduction 1925; "Adieu Sagesse", U.S. introduction 1925; "Huile de Chaldée", U.S. introduction 1927; "Cocktail Sweet", U.S. introduction 1930; "Cocktail Dry", U.S. introduction 1930; "L'Amour est Roi", U.S. introduction 1930; "Joy", U.S. introduction 1931; "Invitation", U.S. introduction 1932; "Moment Suprême", U.S. introduction 1931; "Vacances", U.S. introduction 1934; "Normandie", U.S. introduction 1935; "Colony", U.S. introduction 1937.

PERUGIA, Paris, France: "Matin", Article 1929; "Après-midi", Article 1929; "Soir", Article 1929; "Atmosphere", U.S. introduction 1938.

PIERRE: "Number X", Article 1928.

PINAUD, (est. 1810): "Lis de France", U.S. introduction 1894; "Royal Lavender", U.S. introduction 1900; "Flirt", U.S. introduction 1910; "Preface", U.S. introduction 1944; "Lilianelle", Advertisement 1945.

ROBERT PIQUET, Paris, France: "Visa", U.S. introduction 1945; "Fracas", U.S. introduction 1948; "Brigand", U.S. introduction 1954. Advertisement 1945.

L.T. PIVER, Paris, France (est.1774): "Le Trèfle Incarnat", U.S. introduction 1898; "Azurea", U.S. introduction 1907; "Ilka", U.S. introduction

1912; "Fétiche", U.S. introduction 1925; "Pompeia", U.S. introduction 1926; "Floramye", U.S. introduction 1926; "Rocroy", U.S. introduction 1927; "Astris", New 1908; "Misti", New 1923; "Mascarade", U.S. introduction 1928; "Carminade", U.S. introduction 1928; "Rêve d'Or", U.S. introduction 1930.

PLASSARD: "De Fleur en Fleur", U.S. introduction 1927.

PLEVILLE, Paris, France: "Flamme de Gloire", U.S. introduction 1925; "Triomphe de Pleville", New 1923; "Le Secret de la Perle", U.S. introduction 1926; "Plaisdir d'Orient", U.S. introduction 1927; "Jardin d'Or", U.S. introduction 1927.

PREMET, Paris, France: "Etrange Inconnu", Article 1925.

LUCE PRINTAMP: "Rive Gauche", U.S. introduction 1930; "Rive Droite", U.S. introduction 1930.

EMILIO PUCCI, Paris, France: "Vivara", U.S. introduction 1967; "Zadig", U.S. introduction 1972.

PURITAN: "Jasmine", Catalog 1935; "Gardenia", Catalog 1935.

QUEEN, Chicago, Illinois: "Crabapple", Advertisement 1905; "Lily of the Valley", Advertisement 1905.

KATHLEEN QUINLAN: "Rhythm", Advertisement 1936.

QUI SAIT: "Garden Fragrance", Article 1937.

RACARMA: "Reine de Fleurs", Advertisement 1916; "Excentrique Perfume", Advertisement 1916; "L'Esprit de Rose", Advertisement 1916.

RAFFY: "Tour Eiffel", U.S. introduction 1926.

RAFIN: "Elle et Lui", U.S. introduction 1927.

RALLET, "Confession", U.S. introduction 1935; Rallet's Number 1", Advertisement 1955.

RAMSES, Cairo, Egypt: "Secret du Sphinx", U.S. introduction 1919.

RAPHAEL, Paris, France: "Réplique", U.S. introduction 1946.

RAQUEL, New York: "Olor de la Noche", U.S. introduction 1925; "Orange Blossom Fragrancia", Advertisement 1927; "L'Endeley", Advertisement 1927.

RAVEL: "Pagoda", U.S. introduction 1945; "Pagan", U.S. introduction 1945; "Adagio", U.S. introduction 1945.

DE RAYMOND: "Mimzy", New 1925; "Demain", Article 1935; "Mon Gardenia", New 1928; "Pinx", Article 1936; "Deviltry", U.S. introduction 1936.

REBOUX, Paris, France: "Green", Article 1929; "Red", Article 1929; "Yellow", Article 1929; "Black", Article 1929.

RENAUD, Paris, France (est.1817): "Jardins Célestes", U.S. introduction 1920; "Sur Deux Notes", U.S. introduction 1940; "Glissade", U.S. introduction 1943.

RENOIR, Paris, France New York: "Impetuous", U.S. introduction 1941; "Chichi", U.S. introduction 1942; "My Alibi", Catalog 1945; "Futur", U.S. introduction 1945; "Messager", U.S. introduction 1951; "Grande Epoque", U.S. introduction 1953; "Doña Sol", U.S. introduction 1955.

MAURICE RENTNER: "Twenty One", U.S. introduction 1945; "Eight Thirty", U.S. introduction 1947.

REVILLON, Paris, France: "Carnet de Bal", U.S. introduction 1938; "Cantilene", U.S. introduction 1950; "Detchema", U.S. introduction 1953; "Turbulences", U.S. introduction 1981.

REVLON, United States: "Intimate", New 1956; "Norell", New 1968; "Charlie", New 1973; "Jontue", New 1975.

NINA RICCI, Paris, France: "Coeur-Joie", U.S. introduction 1951; "L'Air du Temps", U.S. introduction 1946; "Fille d'Eve", U.S. introduction 1952; "Capricci", U.S. introduction 1960; "Farouche", U.S. introduction 1974; "Fleurs de Fleurs", U.S. introduction 1982.

RICHELIEU: "Gardenia", Catalog 1933; "Or

Leay", Catalog 1933; "Humoresque", Catalog 1933; "Cardinal", Catalog 1933; "Tete-A-Tete", Catalog 1933.

THEO RICKSECKER, New York (est. 1881): "Golden Gate", New 1884; "Lily of the Valley", New 1884; "Subroga", New 1884; "Mizpah", New 1884.

PAUL RIEGER: "Flower-Drops", Advertisement 1910; "Violet", Advertisement 1910; "Rose", Advertisement 1910; "Lily of the Valley", Advertisement 1910.

RIGAUD, Paris, France (est.1875): "Mi Nena", U.S. introduction 1909; "Mary Garden", Advertisement 1913; "Geraldine Farrar Perfume", Advertisement 1913; "Lilas de Rigaud", Advertisement 1916; "Un Air Embaumé", Advertisement 1920; "Azur Nuit", U.S. introduction 1925; "Souviens-Toi", U.S. introduction 1925; "Igora", U.,S. introduction 1931; "Typhon", U.S. introduction 1938; "Outre Mer", U.S. introduction 1938; "Près de Vous", U.S. introduction 1945; "Ombrages", U.S. introduction 1946; "Cantate", U.S. introduction 1946; "Tumultes", U.S. introduction 1946; "Violettes de Toulouse", U.S. introduction 1957.

RIMMELL, France: "Golden Fern", U.S. introduction 1911.

ROCCA, Paris, France: "Divin Muguet", U.S. introduction 1926.

MARCEL ROCHAS, Paris, France: "Air Jeune", U.S. introduction 1936; "Audace", U.S. introduction 1936; "Avenue Matignon", U.S. introduction 1936; "Femme", U.S. introduction 1947; "Mouche", U.S. introduction 1948; "Mousseline", Article 1952; "Madame Rochas", U.S. introduction 1960; "Mystere", U.S. introduction 1978; "Lumière", U.S. introduction 1984.

ROGER & GALLET, Paris, France New York: "Vera-Violetta", U.S. introduction 1892; "Fleurs d'Amour", U.S. introduction 1902; "Le Jade", U.S. introduction 1924; "Ausonia", U.S. introduction 1926; "Pavots d'Argent", U.S. introduction 1926; "Feu-Follet", U.S. introduction 1931; "Frivolités", U.S. introduction 1934; "Fugue", U.S. introduction 1937; "Prestige", U.S. introduction 1943; "Night of Delight", Catalog 1943; "Oeillet Bleu", Catalog 1943; "Innuendo", Advertisement 1946.

NETTIE ROSENSTEIN, New York: "After Hours", New 1946; "Odalisque", New 1946; "Tianne", New 1948.

ROSINE, Paris, France: "Coeur en Folie", New 1924; "Connais-tule-Pays", Article 1925; "Avenue de Bois", U.S. introduction 1926; "Maharadjah", Advertisement 1928; "Hahna", Advertisement 1928; "Le Coupe D'Or", Advertisement 1928; "Borgia", Advertisement 1928; "Arlequinade", Advertisement 1928; "Toute Le Foret", Advertisement 1928; "Qui-es-tu?", New 1926; "Nuit de Chine", New 1913.

HELENA RUBINSTEIN, New York: "Mahatma", Advertisement 1928; "Water Lily", New 1934; "Enchante", Article 1934; "Town", New 1936; "Country", New 1936; "715", New 1937; "Slumber Song", Article 1938; "Orchid", New 1939; "Gala Performance", New 1940; "Heaven Sent", New 1941; "White Flame", New 1943; "Command Performance", New 1947; "Noa Noa", New 1954.

YVES SAINT LAURENT, Paris, France: "Y", U.S. introduction 1964; "Rive Gauche", U.S. introduction 1971; "Opium", U.S. introduction 1977; "Paris", U.S. introduction 1983.

SARDEAU: "Suspicion", U.S. introduction 1951.

SCHERICK, Paris, France: "Nabu", U.S. introduction 1935; "Tempest", U.S. introduction 1935.

SCHERK, Berlin, Germany: "Renaissance", Advertisement 1943; "Mysticum", U.S. introduction 1926; "Arabian Nights", Catalog 1946.

SCHIAPARELLI, Paris, France: "Salut", U.S. introduction 1934; "Soucis", U.S. introduction 1934; "Schiap", U.S. introduction 1934; "Shocking", U.S. introduction 1936; "Sleeping",

U.S. introduction 1939; "Snuff", U.S. introduction 1939; "Roi Soleil", U.S. introduction 1946; "Zut", U.S. introduction 1949; "Succes Fou", U.S. introduction 1953; "Si", U.S. introduction 1957.

P.J. SCHUMACHER CO., New York: "La Musa", New 1920.

SHULTON, United States: "Early American Old Spice", New 1937; "Friendship's Garden", New 1940.

SIMONETTA, Rome, Italy "Incanto", U.S. introduction 1955.

SUZANNE: "Secret de Suzanne", New 1924; "Tout de Suite", U.S. introduction 1941; "Permettez Moi", U.S. introduction 1946.

SUZY, Paris, France: "Ecarlate de Suzy", U.S. introduction 1940; "Golden Laughter", U.S. introduction 1942; "Madrigal", U.S. introduction 1946.

J. SUZANNE TALBOT, Paris, France: "J", Article 1925; "S", Article 1925; "T", Article 1925.

TAPPAN, New York (est. 1881): "Sweet Bye and Bye", New 1881; "Little Casino", Catalog 1920; "Dime", Catalog 1920.

TERRI, New York: "Erotique", New 1927.

TILFORD, United States: "Vain", Advertisement 1957; "High Heels", Advertisement 1957; "Woody Glen", Advertisement 1957; "My Desire", Advertisement 1957; "No. 3", Advertisement 1957; "Adventure 1957.

TRE-JUR, New York: "Tre-Jur", New 1925; "Non Chalant", New 1936; "Gardenia", Catalog 1936; "Carnation", Catalog 1936; "Lilac", Catalog 1936; "Varva", New 1938.

TUSSY, Paris, France: "Terpsichore", Article 1947; "Optimiste", U.S. introduction 1949; "Midnight", Catalog 1950; "Charme Rose", Article 1951.

TUVACHE, New York: "Highlander", New 1938; "Ze Zan", New 1945; "Tuvara", New 1946.

UNGARD, Paris, France: "Diva", U.S. introduction 1983.

VANAE CIE: "Narcisse", Catalog 1928.

GLORIA VANDERBILT: "Diamant Bleu", Advertisement 1946.

A.A. VANTINE, New York (est. 1894): "Hi Yang", New 1908; "Ka Sai", New 1908.

VARVA: "Suivez-Moi", Article 1940; "Follow Me", Advertisement 1943.

VIGNY, Paris, France: "Le Golliwogg", U.S. introduction 1922; "La Fleur Celeste", U.S. introduction 1923; "Le Chick-Chick", U.S. introduction 1923; "Lionette", U.S. introduction 1923; "L'Infidele", Advertisement 1924; "Jamerose", Advertisement 1924; "Heure Intime", U.S. introduction 1933; Guili-Guili", Advertisement 1934; "Echo Troublant", U.S. introduction 1936; "Beau Catcher", Catalog 1942.

VIOLET, Paris, France: "Kassya", Advertisement 1913; "Parfum Les Sylvies", Advertisement 1923; "Chypre", Advertisement 1924; "Pour Rêver", New 1926.

V. VIVAUDOU, New York: "Mavis", New 1915; "Fleur de France", New 1915; "Fortuna", New 1915; "Lady Mary", New 1915; "Myrtis", New 1920; "Parfumez-Vous", New 1920; "Nuit Folle", New 1934.

VOLNAY: "Rosée des Bois", Article 1927; "Tres Francais", U.S. introduction 1937.

GANNA WALSKA, France: "Divorcons", U.S. introduction 1927.

WEIL, Paris, France: "Chinchilla", Article 1928; "Zibeline", New 1927; "Bamboo", U.S. introduction 1934; "Cassandra", U.S. introduction 1935; "Violette Victorienne", U.S. introduction 1936; "Noir", U.S. introduction 1937; "Cobra", U.S. introduction 1941; "Antilope", New 1935.

WOODWORTH, New York Paris, France (est.1854): "Karess", Advertisement 1928; "Fiancee", Catalog 1929.

WORTH, Paris, France: "Dans la Nuit", U.S. introduction 1924; "Sans Adieu", U.S. introduction 1929; "Honeysuckle", Article 1931; "Je

Reviens", U.S. introduction 1932; "Vers Toi", Article 1933; "Projects", U.S. introduction 1936; "Imprudence", U.S. introduction 1938; "Requête", U.S. introduction 1946; "Miss Worth", U.S. introduction 1977.

WRISLEY, United States: "San Toy" Advertisement 1915; "Gardenia", Article 1940; "Carnation", Article 1940; "Apple Blossom", Article 1940; "Blue Fern", New 1947.

YARDLEY, London, England (est.1770): "Old English Lavender", U.S. introduction 1894; "Vanity Fair", U.S. introduction 1918; "Bond Street", Advertisement 1924; "Red Rose", Catalog 1930; "Orchis", Advertisement 1931; "Scintilla", U.S. introduction 1934; "Fragrance", U.S. introduction 1934; "April Violets", U.S. introduction 1938; "Lotus", U.S. introduction 1949; "Flair", U.S. introduction 1952; "Lavenesque", U.S. introduction 1952.

YBRY, Paris, France: "Femme de Paris", U.S. introduction 1925; "Mon Ame", U.S. introduction 1925; "Dèsir du Coeur", U.S. introduction 1925; "Devinez", U.S. introduction 1927; "Les Fleurs d'Ybry", U.S. introduction 1929; "L'Amour toujours", U.S. introduction 1932; "Joie de Vivre", U.S. introduction 1935; "Old Fashioned Garden", U.S. introduction 1939.

Bibliography

Arwas, Victor. *Lalique*. New York: Rizzoli, 1980.

Bestetti, Carlo. *Murano*. Milan, Italy: Mariacher, 1969.

Bloch-Dermant, Janine. *The Art of French Glass*. New York: Vendome Press, 1974.

Boggess, Bill and Louise. *Identifying American Brilliant Cut Glass*. New York: Crown Publishers, 1984.

Brooks, John A. *Glass*. London, England: BPCC, 1984.

Charon, Mural K. *Ludwig (Ludvik) Moser King of Glass*. Hillsdale, Michigan: Charon/Ferguson, 1984.

Crompton, Sidney. *English Glass*. New York: Hawthorn, 1968.

Czechoslovakian Glass 1350-1980. New York: Dover Publications, Inc., 1981.

Davis, Derek C. *English Bottles & Decanters 1650-1900*. New York: The World Publishing Co., 1972.

Davis, Frank. *Antique Glass and Glass Collecting*. Feltham, England: Hamlyn, 1973.

Drahotova, Olga. *European Glass*. New York: Excalibur, 1983.

Duncan, Alastair and George de Bartha. *Glass by Gallé*. New York: Harry N. Abrams, Inc., 1984.

Faÿ-Hallé, Antoinette and Barbara Mundt. *Porcelain of the Nineteenth Century*. New York: Rizzoli, 1983.

Florence, Gene. *The Collector's Encyclopedia of Depression Glass*. Paducah, Kentucky: Collector Books, 1986.

Forsythe, Ruth. *Made in Czechoslovakia*. Marietta, Ohio: Richardson Printing Corp., 1982.

Foster, Kate. *Scent Bottles*. London, England: The Connoisseur, 1966.

Gardner, Paul V. *The Glass of Frederick Carder*. New York: Crown Publishers, Inc., 1971.

Grover, Ray and Lee. *Carved & Decorated European Art Glass*. Rutland, Vermont: Charles E. Tuttle Co., 1970.

Grow, Lawrence. *Pressed Glass*. New York: Warner Books, 1982.

Heacock, William. *Collecting Glass Volume 1 & 2*. Marietta, Ohio: Richardson Printing Corp., 1985.

_____, *Fenton Glass The First Twenty-Five Years*. Marietta, Ohio: O-Val Advertising Corp., 1978.

_____, *Fenton Glass The Second Twenty-Five Years*. Marietta, Ohio: O-Val Advertising Corp., 1980.

Hillier, Bevis. *The Connoisseur Complete Encyclopedia of Antiques*. New York: Excalibur, 1962.

James, Margaret. *Black Glass*. Paducah, Kentucky: Collector Books, 1981.

Ketchum, William. *A Treasury of American Bottles*. New York: The Ridge Press Inc., 1975.

Klein, Dan. *All Color Book of Art Deco*. New York: Crown, 1974.

Launert, Edmund. *Perfüm und Flakons*. Germany: Callwey, 1985.

Lee, Ruth Webb. *Nineteenth-Century Art Glass*. New York: M. Barrows & Co., 1952.

McClinton, Katharine Morrison. *Introduction to Lalique Glass*. Des Moines, Iowa: Wallace-Homestead, 1978.

McKearin, George S. and Helen. *American Glass*. New York: Crown Publishers, 1941.

Mackay, James. *An Encyclopedia of Small Antiques*. London, England: Bracken Book, 1975.

Manley, C.C. *British Glass*. Des Moines, Iowa: Wallace-Homestead, 1968.

Mehlman, Felice. *Phaidon Guide to Glass*. New Jersey: Prentice-Hall, 1982.

Middlemas, Keith. *Antique Glass in Color*. New York: Doubleday, 1971.

Morris, Edwin T. *Fragrance*. New York: Charles Scribner's Sons, 1984.

National Cambridge Collectors, Inc. *Colors in Cambridge Glass*. Paducah, Kentucky: Collector Books, 1984.

Padgett, Leonard E. *Pairpoint Glass*. Des Moines, Iowa: Wallace-Homestead, 1979.

Percy, Christopher Vane. *The Glass of Lalique*. New York: Charles Scribner's Sons, 1977.

Revi, Albert Christian. *American Pressed Glass and Figure Bottles*. New York: Thomas Nelson & Sons, 1964.

————, *Nineteenth Century Glass*. New York: Galahad Books, 1959.

Röntgen, Robert E. *Marks on German, Bohemian, and Austrian Porcelain*. Exton, Pennsylvania: Schiffer Publishing Ltd., 1981.

Savage, George. *Glass & Glassware*. London, England: Octopus, 1973.

Schwartz, Marvin D. *American Glass*. New York: Weathervane Books, 1972.

Snyder, Bob. *Bottles in Miniature*. Amarillo, Texas: 1972.

Weatherman, Hazel Marie. *Colored Glassware of the Depression Era 2*. Ozark, Missouri: Weatherman Glassbooks, 1974.

Weiss, Gustav. *The Book of Glass*. New York: Praeger Publishers, 1966.

Yeakley, Virginia and Loren. *Heisey Glass in Color*. Marietta, Ohio: Richardson Printing Corp., 1978.

Zweck, Dina. *The Woman's Day Dictionary of Glass*. Secaucus, New Jersey: Citadel Press, 1983.

Index

Price Guide

LEGEND FOR *PRICE GUIDE*

r. - rare   p. - pressed glass
d. - damaged   p.b. - pressed glass bottom
ea. - each   d.s. - double stopper
pr. - pair   -- no price available

/ - indicates the difference in price for the same bottle in clear and colored crystal, respectively.

* prices for Chapter 1 not available.

Front Cover Photo $125

CHAPTER 2

1. 150	27. 150	53. 950	79. 275	105. 700
2. 130	28. 35-45	54. 375	80. 325	106. 250
3. 300	29. 75 each	55. 1500	81. 300	107. 425
4. 60	30. 135	56. 850	82. 300	108. 425
5. 65	31. 165	57. 750	83. 300	109. —
6. 200	32. 85	58. 750	84. 125	110. 250
7. 250	33. 250	59. 1350	85. 125	111. 250
8. 180	34. 175	60. 350	86. 125	112. 700
9. 275	35. 800 pair	61. 450	87. 350	113. 175
10. 60	36. 275	62. 175	88. 300	114. 250
11. 125	37. 250	63. 350	89. 325	115. 300
12. 185	38. 275	64. 135	90. 300	116. 275
13. 150	39. 225	65. 300	91. 300	117. 325
14. 275	40. 400	66. 250	92. 425	118. 475
15. 150	41. 800	67. 125	93. 175	119. 600
16. 750	42. 85	68. 145	94. 200	120. 225
17. 375	43. 250	69. 225	95. 250	121. 450
18. 650	44. 275	70. 165	96. 350	122. 350
19. 575	45. 300	71. 215	97. 225 each	123. 150
20. 575	46. 1000	72. 225	98. 250	124. 150
21. 375	47. 550	73. 375	99. 300	125. 130
22. 600	48. 1500	74. 375	100. —	126. 60 each
23. 250	49. 650	75. 375	101. 375	127. 325
24. 125	50. 825	76. 225	102. 300	128. 150
25. 300	51. 425	77. 800	103. 950	129. 150
26. 260	52. 850	78. 375	104. 175	130. 150

CHAPTER 3

1. 100	12. 5000	23. -	34. 3500	45. 125
2. 1500	13. 8000	24. -	35. 750	46. 275
3. 7500	14. 1250	25. -	36. 450	47. 35
4. 10,000	15. 2500	26. 2000	37. 1000	48. -
5. 2500	16. 1250	27. -	38. 2500	49. 2200
6. 400	17. 10,000	28. 450	39. 10,000	50. 50
7. 650	18. 450	29. 8500	40. 2000	51. 3500
8. 2500	19. 1250	30. 4000	41. 15,000	52. 125
9. 1200	20. 4000	31. 1500	42. 375	53. -
10. -	21. 400	32. 850	43. 275	54. -
11. 850	22. 7500	33. 4000	44. 75	55. -

CHAPTER 4

1. 40	25. 45	49. 95 set	73. 850	97. 170
2. 40	26. 50	50. 175 set	74. 40	98. 60
3. 60	27. 125 set	51. 85	75. 150	99. 85
4. 45	28. 35 each	52. 145 set	76. 40 each	100. 135
5. 40	29. 30 each	53. 60 each	77. 60	101. 150
6. 45	30. 60	54. 60	78. 40	102. 150
7. 10 (d)	31. 135 set	55. 90	79. 30	103. 350 set
8. 55	32. 50	56. 35	80. 35	104. 50
9. 75	33. 30	57. 35	81. 35	105. 40
10. 150 set	34. 50	58. 30	82. 45	106. 90
11. 55	35. 45	59. 30	83. 60	107. 80
12. 135	36. 40	60. 250	84. 100 set	108. 60
13. 60	37. 30	61. 275	85. 50	109. 95
14. 50	38. 40	62. 300	86. 100 each	110. 40
15. —	39. 40 each	63. 150	87. 40	111. 75
16. —	40. 100	64. 150	88. 65	112. 45 each
17. —	41. 35	65. 300	89. 80	113. 25
18. —	42. 45	66. 250	90. 175	114. 50
19. 35 (d)	43. 125 set	67. 275	91. 250	115. 90
20. 80	44. 75	68. 550	92. 25	116. 55
21. 85	45. 125	69. 525	93. 35	117. 65
22. 45	46. 125	70. 275	94. 75	118. 50
23. 250 set	47. 85	71. 175	95. 135	119. 85
24. 65	48. 40	72. 130	96. 200	120. 85

CHAPTER 5

1. 50	11. 25	21. 60	31. 85	41. 35
2. 45	12. 25	22. 60	32. 40	42. 40
3. 45	13. 25	23. 65	33. 40	43. 25
4. 35	14. 125 set	24. 35	34. 30	44. 15
5. 60	15. 30	25. 55	35. 35	45. 20
6. 45	16. 35	26. 65	36. 45	46. 125
7. 40	17. 35	27. 30	37. 45	47. 125
8. 30	18. 35	28. 35	38. 40	48. 125
9. 30	19. 35	29. 20	39. 45	
10. 25	20. 25	30. 20	40. 50	

CHAPTER 6

1. 1200
2. 475
3. 475
4. 135
5. 200
6. 75
7. 70
8. 65
9. 65
10. 100
11. 60
12. 125
13. 435
14. 350
15. 55
16. 45
17. 55
18. 425 set
19. 400
20. 110
21. 95
22. 475 set
23. 100
24. 125
25. 145 set
26. —
27. —
28. —
29. 85
30. 95
31. —
32. —
33. 45
34. 65
35. 75
36. 25
37. 100
38. 75
39. 65
40. 55
41. 85
42. 15
43. 25
44. 25 each
45. 45
46. 25
47. 20
48. 80 set
49. 25
50. —
51. —
52. 125
53. 100
54. 125
55. 75
56. 50
57. 160
58. 75
59. 65
60. 125
61. 125
62. 250
63. 150
64. 90
65. 200
66. 85
67. 65
68. 85
69. 200
70. 85
71. 150
72. 55
73. 45
74. 40
75. 25
76. 100
77. 125
78. 125
79. 125
80. 85
81. 95
82. 15
83. 15
84. 25
85. 85

CHAPTER 7

1. 375
2. 35
3. 35
4. 50
5. 75
6. 150
7. 45
8. 65
9. 125
10. 65
11. 65
12. 65
13. 95
14. 75
15. 45
16. 45
17. 45
18. 45
19. 45
20. 95
21. 45
22. 65
23. 65
24. 85
25. 60
26. 85
27. 75
28. 75
29. 65 each
30. 40 each
31. 90
32. 50
33. 120
34. 95 each
35. 85 each
36. 175 set
37. 95 each
38. 95 each
39. 95 each
40. 135
41. 145
42. 155
43. 155
44. 145
45. 155
46. 125
47. 155
48. 165
49. 155
50. 145
51. 450
52. 140
53. 140
54. 140
55. 140
56. 140
57. 85
58. 145
59. 135
60. 250
61. 135
62. 145
63. 185
64. 85
65. 135
66. 135
67. 165
68. 135
69. 135
70. 155
71. 145
72. 145
73. 165
74. 185
75. 165
76. 85
77. 120
78. 145
79. 300
80. 155
81. 350
82. 155
83. 265
84. 265
85. 195
86. 135 (p.b.)
87. 375
88. 165
89. 450
90. 275
91. 185
92. 145
93. 165
94. 165
95. 145
96. 165
97. 165
98. 150
99. 165
100. 175
101. 200
102. 125
103. 175
104. 175
105. 145
106. 185
107. 175
108. 175 (p.b.) (d.s.)
109. 250 (d.s.)
110. 125
111. 125 (p.b.)
112. 155
113. 125
114. 375
115. 145
116. 150
117. 40 new
118. 150
119. 275
120. 195
121. 125
122. 135
123. 125
124. 100 (p.b.)
125. 125
126. 135
127. 135
128. 135
129. 165
130. 135
131. 85 (p.b.)
132. 100 (p.b.)
133. 135
134. 185
135. 135
136. 135
137. 135
138. 135
139. 145
140. 135
141. 135
142. 135
143. 175
144. 135
145. 185
146. 115
147. 25 (p.) new
148. 115
149. 115
150. 135
151. 135
152. 135
153. 135
154. 135
155. 135

CHAPTER 8

1. 25
2. 75
3. 50
4. 125
5. 85
6. 15, 25, 35
7. 45
8. 20
9. 90
10. 30
11. 60
12. 40
13. 45
14. 100 with box
15. 80
16. 175
17. 125
18. 40
19. 40
20. 45
21. 250
22. 450
23. 60
24. 30 each
25. 55 with box
26. 80
27. 75
28. 125
29. 250
30. 125
31. 70, 80, 150
32. 150
33. 130
34. 100
35. —
36. —

37. —
38. —
39. —
40. 90
41. —
42. 375
43. 45
44. 35
45. 125
46. 200
47. 50
48. 250 with box
49. 45, 85
50. 55
51. 85 with box
52. 75
53. 30
54. 100
55. 25
56. 10
57. 40
58. 85
59. 35
60. 35 with box
61. 600
62. 45
63. 350
64. 85, 60, 85
65. 25
66. 15
67. 75
68. 45
69. 70
70. 35
71. 145
72. 30

73. 70
74. 75
75. 75
76. 30
77. 200
78. 25
79. 25
80. 135
81. 40
82. 100
83. 135
84. 100
85. 85
86. 75
87. 20
88. 85
89. 85 with box
90. 55
91. 55
92. 135
93. 40
94. 45 with box
95. 35 with box
96. 20
97. 15
98. 35
99. 150, 100
100. 80
101. 250
102. 300
103. 25
104. 50
105. 20
106. 100
107. 20
108. 20

109. 150
110. 20
111. 375 with box
112. 25
113. —
114. 300
115. 20
116. 20
117. 35
118. 85
119. 100
120. 35
121. 8
122. 10
123. 15
124. 10
125. —
126. 30
127. 85
128. 10
129. 50
130. —
131. 20, 30
132. 40 each
133. 160
134. 10
135. 45
136. 45
137. 30
138. 45
139. 25
140. 75
141. 45
142. 60
143. 100
144. 85

145. 5
146. 35
147. 45
148. 35
149. 25
150. 40 with box
151. —
152. 10
153. 100
154. 10
155. 15
156. 300
157. 50
158. 10
159. 125 with box
160. —
161. 60
162. 35
163. 20
164. 10
165. 35 with box
166. 40
167. 20
168. 90
169. 85
170. 30, 40
171. 65
172. 100
173. 30
174. —
175. 45
176. 25 each
177. 30

CHAPTER 9

1. 80
2. 55
3. 20-60 each
4. 75 with box
5. 35
6. 50
7. 20
8. 40
9. 75 with box
10. 35
11. 20
12. 65 with box

13. 20
14. 20
15. 10
16. 30
17. 25
18. 25 each
19. 12
20. 25
21. 25
22. 6
23. 10-20 each
24. 6

25. 15
26. 10
27. 60
28. 50
29. 35
30. 30
31. 25
32. 25
33. 15-25 each
34. 15-25 each
35. 12-20 each
36. 25

37. 20
38. 6
39. 30
40. 40
41. 35
42. 35
43. 6
44. 32
45. 35
46. 50
47. 20
48. 20

49. 20
50. 12
51. 15
52. 35
53. 15
54. 10
55. 30
56. 20
57. 18
58. 10 each
59. 20

CHAPTER 10

1. 125
2. 110
3. 60
4. 75
5. 135 set
6. 150
7. —
8. 125 set
9. 125 set
10. 75
11. 65
12. 65
13. 65
14. 65
15. 65
16. 55
17. 50
18. 65
19. 65
20. 70
21. 45
22. 45
23. 150 pair
24. 150 set
25. 80
26. 75
27. 75
28. 75
29. 60
30. 75
31. 125
32. 75
33. 55
34. 55
35. 50
36. 75
37. 65
38. 125
39. 115 each
40. 40
41. 55
42. 40
43. 40 each
44. 35
45. 45
46. 45
47. 45
48. 45
49. 35
50. 45
51. 45
52. 100
53. 85
54. 45 each
55. 35 each
56. 75
57. 35
58. 75
59. 25
60. 45
61. 45
62. 45
63. 45
64. 45
65. 45
66. 45
67. 45
68. 75
69. 45 each
70. 45
71. 55
72. 10
73. 35
74. 75
75. 35
76. 40
77. 30
78. 30
79. 35
80. 45
81. 50
82. 40
83. 45
84. 40
85. 45
86. 45
87. 45
88. 40
89. 50
90. 65
91. 45
92. 30
93. 50
94. 65
95. 65
96. 50
97. 30
98. 50 each
99. 45
100. 65
101. 60
102. 50
103. 40
104. 35
105. 40
106. 35
107. 35
108. 65
109. 65
110. 35
111. 35
112. 35
113. 40
114. 40
115. 45
116. 45
117. 35
118. 50
119. 45
120. 45
121. 50
122. 50
123. 65
124. 50
125. 45
126. 50
127. 75
128. 60
129. 65
130. 40
131. 35
132. 40
133. 80
134. 35
135. 35
136. 40
137. 45
138. 40
139. 40
140. 40
141. 45

CHAPTER 11

1. 95
2. 95 set
3. 30
4. 25
5. 20
6. 25
7. 15
8. 35
9. 35
10. 40
11. 42
12. 45
13. 30
14. 40
15. 35
16. 35
17. 25
18. 165
19. 185
20. 125
21. 100
22. 125
23. 65
24. 85
25. 135
26. 65
27. 135
28. 40 set
29. 15
30. 15
31. 15
32. 25 set
33. 15
34. 90 set
35. 55
36. 35
37. 15
38. 40
39. 55
40. 75
41. 35 set
42. 25
43. 125 set
44. 55
45. 37
46. 180
47. 350
48. 65
49. 125
50. 60
51. 75
52. 60
53. 50
54. 10
55. 150
56. 60
57. —
58. —
59. —
60. —
61. —
62. 20
63. 60
64. 58
65. 85
66. 25
67. —
68. 90
69. —

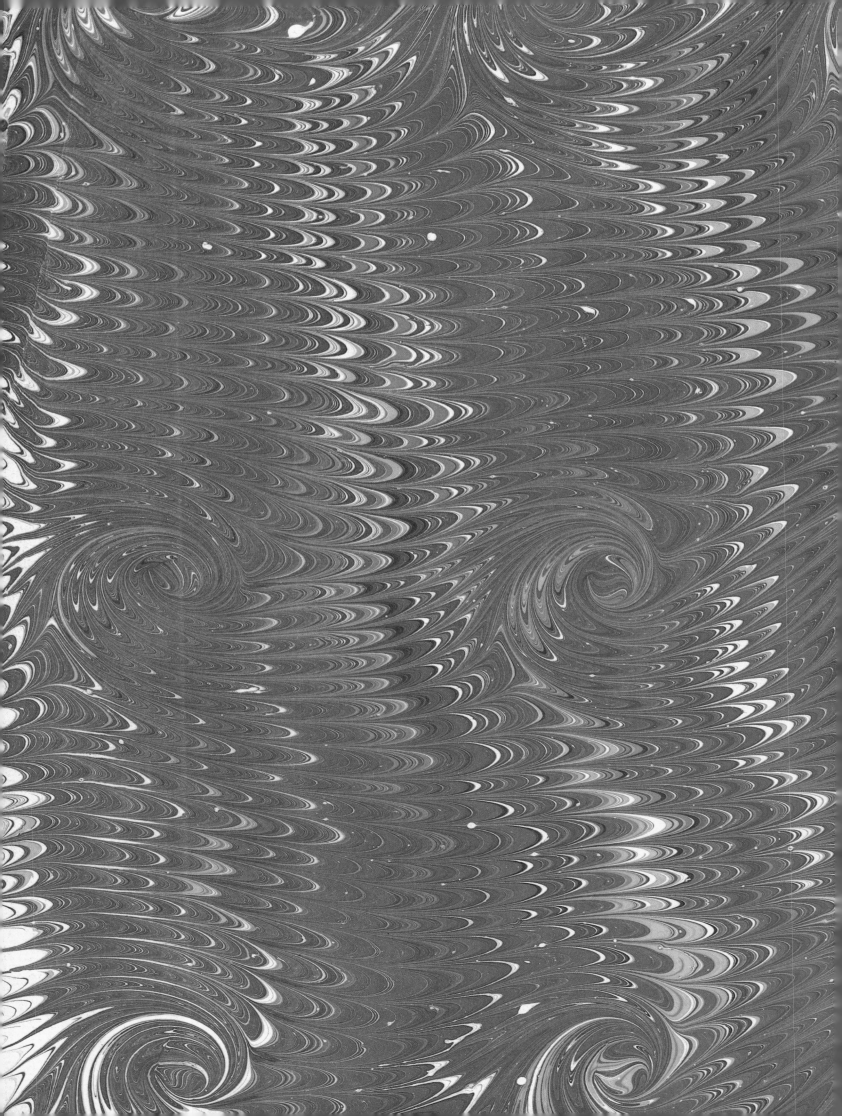